FOLKLORE OF SCOTTISH LOCHS

AND SPRINGS.

Also published by Llanerch:

Symbolism of the Celtic Cross
by Derek Bryce.

The Life of St Columba
by Adamnan.

Two Celtic Saints:
The Lives of Ninian and Kentigern,
by Joceline and Ailred.

The Chronicle of John of Fordun,
edited by W. F. Skene.

The Drolls, Traditions and Superstitions
of Old Cornwall, by Robert Hunt.

For a complete list, write to Llanerch Publishers,
Felinfach, Lampeter, Dyfed, SA48 8PJ.

FOLKLORE OF SCOTTISH LOCHS AND SPRINGS.

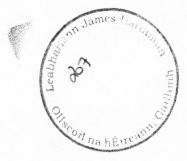

BY

JAMES M. MACKINLAY, M.A., F.S.A.Scot.

Facsimile reprint 1993 by
LLANERCH PUBLISHERS,
Felinfach, Wales.
ISBN 1 897853 23 8

GLASGOW: WILLIAM HODGE & Co.

1893.

PREFATORY NOTE.

No work giving a comprehensive account of Well-worship in Scotland has yet appeared. Mr. R. C. Hope's recent volume, "*Holy Wells: Their Legends and Traditions*," discusses the subject in its relation to England. In the following pages an attempt has been made to illustrate the more outstanding facts associated with the cult north of the Tweed. Various holy wells are referred to by name; but the list makes no claim to be exhaustive.

J. M. M.

4 WESTBOURNE GARDENS,
GLASGOW, *December, 1893.*

CONTENTS.

AMONG the works consulted are the following, the titles being given in alphabetical order:—

A Description of the Western Islands of Scotland. By John MacCulloch, M.D. 1819.

A Description of the Western Islands. By M. Martin. *Circa* 1695.

A Handbook of Weather Folklore. By the Rev. C. Swainson, M.A.

A Historical Account of the belief in Witchcraft in Scotland. By Charles Kirkpatrick Sharpe.

A Journey through the Western Counties of Scotland. By Robert Heron. 1799.

Ancient Legends: Mystic Charms and Superstitions of Ireland. By Lady Wilde.

An Etymological Dictionary of the Scottish Language. By John Jamieson, D.D.

Annals of Dunfermline and Vicinity. By Ebenezer Henderson, LL.D.

Antiquities and Scenery of the North of Scotland. By Rev. Charles Cordiner. 1780.

Archæological Sketches in Scotland: Districts of Kintyre and Knapdale. By Captain T. P. White.

A Tour in Scotland and Voyage to the Hebrides, MDCCLXXII. By Thomas Pennant.

A Tour in Scotland, MDCCLXIX. By Thomas Pennant.

Britannia; or, A Chorographical Description of the Flourishing Kingdoms of England, Scotland, and Ireland, and the Islands adjacent, from the Earliest Antiquity. By William Camden. Translated from the edition published by the Author in MDCVII. Enlarged by the latest discoveries by Richard Gough. The second edition in four volumes. 1806.

Celtic Heathendom. By Professor John Rhys.

Celtic Scotland: A History of Ancient Alban. By William Forbes Skene.

Churchlore Gleanings. By T. F. Thiselton Dyer.

LIST OF WORKS CONSULTED.

Daemonologie in Forme of a Dialogve. Written by the High and Mightie Prince James, by the Grace of God King of England, Scotland, France, and Ireland; Defender of the Faith. 1603.

Descriptive Notices of some of the Ancient Parochial and Collegiate Churches of Scotland. By T. S. Muir.

Domestic Annals of Scotland from the Reformation to the Revolution. By Robert Chambers, LL.D.

Ecclesiological Notes on some of the Islands of Scotland. By T. S. Muir.

English Folklore. By the Rev. T. F. Thiselton Dyer, M.A.

Essays in the Study of Folk Songs. By the Countess Evelyn Martinengo-Cesaresco.

Ethnology in Folklore. By G. L. Gomme.

Folklore.

Folklore Journal.

Folklore of East Yorkshire. By John Nicholson.

Folklore of Shakespeare. By Rev. T. F. Thiselton Dyer, M.A. Oxon.

Folklore; or, Superstitious Beliefs in the West of Scotland within this Century. By James Napier, F.R.S.E.

Gairloch in North-west Ross-shire: Its Records, Traditions, Inhabitants, and Natural History. By John H. Dixon.

Historical and Statistical Account of Dunfermline. By Rev. Peter Chalmers, A.M.

Kalendars of Scottish Saints. By the late Alexander Penrose Forbes, Bishop of Brechin.

Letters from a Gentleman in the North of Scotland to his Friend in London. Burt's Letters. 1754.

List of Markets and Fairs now and formerly held in Scotland. By Sir James David Marwick, LL.D.

Memorabilia Domestica; or, Parish Life in the North of Scotland. By the late Rev. Donald Sage, A.M., Minister of Resolis.

New Statistical Account of Scotland. *Circa* 1845.

Notes and Queries.

Notes on the Folklore of the North-east of Scotland. By the Rev. Walter Gregor.

LIST OF WORKS CONSULTED.

Notes on the Folklore of the Northern Counties of England and the Borders. By William Henderson.

Observations on Popular Antiquities, including the whole of Mr. Bourne's Antiquitates Vulgares. By John Brand, A.M.

Old Glasgow: The Place and the People. By Andrew MacGeorge.

Old Scottish Customs, Local and General. By E. J. Guthrie.

Ordnance Gazetteer of Scotland. Edited by Francis H. Groome.

Peasant Life in Sweden. By L. Lloyd.

Popular Antiquities of Great Britain. By John Brand, M.A.

Popular Romances of the West of England. By Robert Hunt, F.R.S.

Popular Tales of the West Highlands. By J. F. Campbell.

Pre-historic Annals of Scotland. By Daniel Wilson, LL.D.

Pre-historic Man. By Daniel Wilson, LL.D.

Primitive Culture, By Edward B. Tylor, D.C.L.

Proceedings of the Society of Antiquaries of Scotland. Old Series, 1851-1878; New Series, 1878-1891.

Rambles in the Far North. By R. Menzies Fergusson.

Scenes and Legends of the North of Scotland; or, The Traditional History of Cromarty. By Hugh Miller.

Scotland in Early Christian Times. By Joseph Anderson, LL.D.

Scotland in Pagan Times: The Bronze and Iron Ages. By Joseph Anderson, LL.D.

Scotland in the Middle Ages. By Professor Cosmo Innes.

Social Life in Scotland. By Charles Rogers, LL.D.

Statistical Account of Scotland. By Sir John Sinclair. *Circa* 1798.

The Antiquary.

The Archæological Journal. Published under the direction of The Council of the Royal Archæological Institute of Great Britain and Ireland.

The Book of Days: A Miscellany of Popular Antiquities in connection with the Calendar. Edited by R. Chambers.

The Darker Superstitions of Scotland. By John Graham Dalyell. 1834.

The Early Scottish Church: Ecclesiastical History of Scotland from the First to the Twelfth Centuries. By the Rev. Thomas M'Lauchlan.

LIST OF WORKS CONSULTED.

The Every-Day Book. By William Hone.

The Folklore of Plants. By T. F. Thiselton Dyer.

The Gentleman's Magazine Library—Manners and Customs. Edited by G. L. Gomme, F.S.A.

The Gentleman's Magazine Library—Popular Superstitions. Edited by G. L. Gomme, F.S.A.

The Golden Bough: A Study in Comparative Religion. By J. G. Frazer, M.A.

The History of St. Cuthbert. By Charles, Archbishop of Glasgow.

The History of St. Kilda. By the Rev. Kenneth Macaulay, minister of Ardnamurchan. 1769.

The Legendary Lore of the Holy Wells of England, including Rivers, Lakes, Fountains, and Springs. By R. C. Hope, F.S.A.

The Origin of Civilisation. By Sir J. Lubbock, Bart.

The Past in the Present. By Arthur Mitchell, M.D., LL.D.

The Popular Rhymes of Scotland. By Robert Chambers. 1826.

The Popular Superstitions and Festive Amusements of the Highlanders of Scotland. By William Grant Stewart.

The Surnames and Placenames of the Isle of Man. By A. W. Moore, M.A.

Traditions, Superstitions, and Folklore (chiefly Lancashire and the North of England). By Charles Hardwick.

Tree and Serpent Worship. By James Fergusson, D.C.L., F.R.S.

'Twixt Ben Nevis and Glencoe: The Natural History, Legends, and Folklore of the West Highlands. By the Rev. Alexander Stewart, LL.D.

Unique Traditions, chiefly of the West and South of Scotland. By John Gordon Barbour.

Wayfaring in France. By E. H. Barker.

Weather-lore: A Collection of Proverbs, Sayings, and Rules concerning the Weather. By R. Inwards, F.R.A.S.

Witch, Warlock, and Magician. By W. H. Davenport Adams.

FOLKLORE OF SCOTTISH LOCHS AND SPRINGS.

CHAPTER I.

WORSHIP OF WATER.

Archaic Nature-worship — Deification of Water Metaphors— Divination by Water — Persistence of Paganism — Shony— Superstitions of Sailors and Fishermen—Sea Serpent—Mer-folk —Sea Charms—Taking Animals into the Sea—Rescuing from Drowning—Ancient Beliefs about Rivers—Dead and Living Ford—Clay Image—Dunskey—Lakes—Dow Loch—St. Vigeans —St. Tredwell's Loch—Wells of Spey and Drachaldy—Survival of Well-worship—Disappearance of Springs—St. Margaret's Well—Anthropomorphism of Springs—Celtic Influence—Cream of the Well.

IN glancing at the superstitions connected with Scottish lochs and springs, we are called upon to scan a chapter of our social history not yet closed. A somewhat scanty amount of information is available to explain the origin and growth of such superstitions, but enough can be had to connect them with archaic nature-worship. In the dark dawn of our annals

B

much confusion existed among our ancestors concerning the outer world, which so strongly appealed to their senses. They had very vague notions regarding the difference between what we now call the Natural and the Supernatural. Indeed all nature was to them supernatural. They looked on sun, moon, and star, on mountain and forest, on river, lake, and sea as the abodes of divinities, or even as divinities themselves. These divinities, they thought, could either help or hurt man, and ought therefore to be propitiated. Hence sprang certain customs which have survived to our own time. Men knocked at the gate of Nature, but were not admitted within. From the unknown recesses there came to them only tones of mystery.

In ancient times water was deified even by such civilised nations as the Greeks and Romans, and to-day it is revered as a god by untutored savages. Sir John Lubbock, in his "*Origin of Civilisation*," shows, by reference to the works of travellers, what a hold this cult still has in regions where the natives have not yet risen above the polytheistic stage of religious development. Dr. E. B. Tylor forcibly remarks, in his "*Primitive Culture*," "What ethnography has to teach of that great element of the religion of mankind, the worship of well and lake, brook and river, is simply this—that what is poetry to us was philosophy to early man; that to his mind water acted not by laws of force, but by life and will; that the water-spirits of primæval mythology are as souls which cause the water's rush and rest, its kindness and its cruelty; that, lastly, man finds in the beings which, with such power, can work him weal and woe, deities with a wider influence over his life, deities to be feared and loved, to be prayed to and praised, and propitiated with sacrificial gifts."

In speaking of inanimate objects, we often ascribe life to them; but our words are metaphors, and nothing more. At an earlier time such phrases expressed real beliefs, and were not simply the outcome of a poetic imagination. Keats, in one of his Sonnets, speaks of

"The moving waters at their priest-like task
Of pure ablution round Earth's human shore."

Here he gives us the poetical and not the actual interpretation of a natural phenomenon.

We may, if we choose, talk of the worship of water as a creed outworn, but it is still with us, though under various disguises. Under the form of rites of divination practised as an amusement by young persons, such survivals often conceal their real origin. The history of superstition teaches us with what persistence pagan beliefs hold their ground in the midst of a Christian civilisation. Martin, who visited the Western Islands at the close of the seventeenth century, found how true this was in many details of daily life. A custom connected with ancient sea-worship had been popular

among the inhabitants of Lewis till about thirty
years before his visit, but had been suppressed
by the Protestant clergy on account of its pagan
character. This was an annual sacrifice at Hallow-
tide to a sea god called Shony. Martin gives the
following account of the ceremony:—"The inhabitants round the island came to the church of St.
Mulvay, having each man his provision along with
him; every family furnished a peck of malt, and
this was brewed into ale; one of their number was
picked out to wade into the sea up to the middle,
and, carrying a cup of ale in his hand, standing
still in that posture, cried out with a loud voice,
saying, 'Shony, I give you this cup of ale, hoping
that you'll be so kind as to send us plenty of sea-
ware for enriching our ground the ensuing year,'
and so threw the cup of ale into the sea. This was
performed in the night-time."

Sailors and fishermen still cherish superstitions of
their own. Majesty is not the only feature of the
changeful ocean that strikes them. They are keenly
alive to its mystery and to the possibilities of life
within its depths. Strange creatures have their
home there, the mighty sea serpent and the less
formidable mermen and mermaidens. Among the
Shetland islands mer-folk were recognised denizens
of the sea, and were known by the name of Sea-trows.

These singular beings dwelt in the caves of ocean,
and came up to disport themselves on the shores of
the islands. A favourite haunt of theirs was the

Ve Skerries, about seven miles north-west of Papa-
Stour. They usually rose through the water in the
shape of seals, and when they reached the beach
they slipped off their skins and appeared like
ordinary mortals, the females being of exceeding
beauty. If the skins could be snatched away on
these occasions, their owners were powerless to
escape into the sea again. Sometimes these creatures
were entangled in the nets of fishermen or were
caught by hooks. If they were shot when in seal
form, a tempest arose as soon as their blood was
mingled with the water of the sea. A family living
within recent times was believed to be descended
from a human father and a mermaid mother, the man
having captured his bride by stealing her seal's skin.
After some years spent on land this sea lady recovered
her skin, and at once returned to her native element.
The members of the family were said to have hands
bearing some resemblance to the forefeet of a seal.

"Of all the old mythological existences of Scotland," remarks Hugh Miller, in his "*Scenes and
Legends of the North of Scotland*," "there was none
with whom the people of Cromarty were better
acquainted than with the mermaid. Thirty years
have not yet gone by since she has been seen by
moonlight sitting on a stone in the sea, a little to
the east of the town; and scarcely a winter passed,
forty years earlier, in which she was not heard
singing among the rocks or seen braiding up her
long yellow tresses on the shore."

The magical power ascribed to the sea is shown in an Orcadian witch charm used in the seventeenth century. The charm had to do with the churning of butter. Whoever wished to take advantage of it watched on the beach till nine waves rolled in. At the reflux of the last the charmer took three handfuls of water from the sea and carried them home in a pail. If this water was put into the churn there would be a plentiful supply of butter. Sea water was also used for curative purposes, the patient being dipped after sunset. This charm was thought to savour strongly of the black art. Allusion has been made above to the rising of a storm in connection with the wounding of a sea-trow in Shetland. According to an Orcadian superstition, the sea began to swell whenever anyone with a piece of iron about him stept upon a certain rock at the Noup Head of Westray. Not till the offending metal was thrown into the water did the sea become calm again. Wallace, a minister at Kirkwall towards the end of the seventeenth century, mentions this belief in his "*Description of the Isles of Orkney,*" and says that he offered a man a shilling to try the experiment, but the offer was refused. It does not seem to have occurred to him to make the experiment himself.

Among the ancient Romans the bull was sacred to Neptune, the sea god, and was sacrificed in his honour. In our own country we find a suggestion of the same rite, though in a modified form, in the custom prevailing at one time of leading animals into the sea on certain festivals. In the parish of Clonmany in Ireland it was formerly customary on St. Columba's Day, the ninth of June, to drive cattle to the beach and swim them in the sea near to where the water from the Saint's well flowed in. In Scotland horses seem at one time to have undergone a similar treatment at Lammas-tide. Dalyell, in his "*Darker Superstitions of Scotland*," mentions that "in July, 1647, the kirk-session of St. Cuthbert's Church, Edinburgh, resolved on intimating publicly 'that non goe to Leith on Lambmes-day, nor tak their horses to be washed that day in the sea.'"

A belief at one time existed that it was unlucky to rescue a drowning man from the grasp of the sea. This superstition is referred to by Sir Walter Scott in "*The Pirate*," in the scene where Bryce the pedlar warns Mordaunt against saving a shipwrecked sailor. "Are you mad," said the pedlar, "you that have lived sae lang in Zetland, to risk the saving of a drowning man? Wot ye not, if you bring him to life again, he will be sure to do you some capital injury?" We discover the key to this strange superstition in the idea entertained by savages that the person falling into the water becomes the prey of the monster or demon inhabiting that element; and, as Dr. Tylor aptly remarks, "to save a sinking man is to snatch a victim from the very clutches of the water-spirit—a rash defiance of deity which would hardly pass unavenged."

Folklore thus brings us face to face with beliefs which owe their origin to the primitive worship of the sea. It also allows us to catch a glimpse of rivers, lakes, and springs as these were regarded by our distant ancestors. When we remember that, according to a barbaric notion, the current of a stream flows down along one bank and up along the other, we need not be surprised that very crude fancies concerning water at one time flourished in our land.

Even to us, with nineteenth-century science within reach, how mysterious a river seems, as, in the quiet gloaming or in the grey dawn, it glides along beneath overhanging treees, and how full of life it is when, swollen by rain, it rushes forward in a resistless flood! How much more awe-inspiring it must have been to men ignorant of the commonest laws of Nature! Well might its channel be regarded as the home of a spirit eager to waylay and destroy the too-venturesome passer-by. Rivers, however, were not always reckoned the enemies of man, for experience showed that they were helpful, as well as hurtful, to him. The Tiber, for instance, was regarded with reverence by the ancient inhabitants of Rome. Who does not remember the scene in one of Macaulay's Lays, where, after the bridge has been hewn down to block the passage of Lars Porsena and his host, the valiant Horatius exclaims—

> "O Tiber! father Tiber!
> To whom the Romans pray;
> A Roman's life, a Roman's arms,
> Take thou in charge this day?"

Then with his harness on his back he plunges head-long into the flood, and reaches the other side in safety.

In Christian art pagan symbolism continued long to flourish. Proof of this bearing on the present subject is to be found in a mosaic at Ravenna, of the sixth century, representing the baptism of Christ. The water flows from an inverted urn, held by a venerable figure typifying the river god of the Jordan, with reeds growing beside his head, and snakes coiling around it.

In our own country healing virtue was attributed to water taken from what was called a dead and living ford, i.e., a ford where the dead were carried and the living walked across. The same belief was entertained with regard to the water of a south-running stream. The patient had to go to the spot and drink the water and wash himself in it. Some-times his shirt was taken by another, and, after being dipped in the south-running stream, was brought back and put wet upon him. A wet shirt was also used as a Hallowe'en charm to foretell its owner's matrimonial future. The left sleeve of the shirt was to be dipped in a river where "three lairds' lands met." It was then to be hung up over-night before the fire. If certain rules were attended to, the figure of the future spouse would appear and turn the sleeve in order to dry the other side. In the Highlands the water of a stream was used for purposes of sorcery till quite lately. When any one wished evil to another he made a clay image of the person to be injured, and placed it in a stream with the head of the image against the current. It was believed that, as the clay was dissolved by the water, the health of the person represented would decline. The spell, however, would be broken if the image was discovered and removed from the stream. In the counties of Sutherland and Ross the practice survived till within the last few years. Near Dunskey, in the parish of Portpatrick, Wigtownshire, is a stream which, at the end of last century, was much resorted to by the credulous for its health-giving properties. Visits were usually paid to it at the change of the moon. It was deemed specially efficacious in the case of rickety children, whose malady was then ascribed to witchcraft. The patients were washed in the stream, and then taken to an adjoining cave, where they were dried.

In modern poetry a river is frequently alluded to under the name of its presiding spirit. Thus, in "*Comus*," Milton introduces Sabrina, a gentle nymph,

"That with moist curb sways the smooth Severn stream,"

and tells us that

"The shepherds at their festivals
Carol her goodness loud in rustic lays,
And throw sweet garland wreaths into her stream
Of pansies, pinks, and gaudy daffodils."

Lakes have always held an important place in legendary lore. Lord Tennyson has made us familiar with the part played by the Lady of the Lake in

Arthurian romance. Readers of the Idylls will recollect it was she who gave to the king the jewelled sword Excalibur, and who, on the eve of his passing, received it again. The wounded Arthur thus addresses Sir Bedivere:—

> "Thou rememberest how,
> In those old days, one summer morn, an arm
> Rose up from out the bosom of the lake
> Clothed in white samite, mystic, wonderful,
> Holding the sword—and how I row'd across
> And took it, and have worn it, like a king."

Scottish lochs form a striking feature in the landscape, and must have been still more fitted to arrest attention in ancient times when our land was more densely wooded than it is now. Dr. Hugh Macmillan, in his "*Holidays on High Lands*," alludes to the differences in the appearance of our lochs. "There are moorland tarns," he says, "sullen and motionless as lakes of the dead, lying deep in sunless rifts, where the very ravens build no nests, and where no trace of life or vegetation is seen— associated with many a wild tradition, accidents of straying feet, the suicide of love, guilt, despair. And there are lochs beautiful in themselves and gathering around them a world of beauty; their shores fringed with the tasselled larch; their shallows tesselated with the broad green leaves and alabaster chalices of the water-lily, and their placid depths mirroring the crimson gleam of the heather hills and the golden clouds overhead."

Near the top of Mealfourvounie, in Inverness-shire, is a small lake at one time believed to be unfathomable. How this notion arose it is difficult to say, for when soundings were taken the depth was found to be inconsiderable. In the parish of Penpont, Dumfriesshire, about a mile to the south of Drumlanrig, is a small sheet of water called the Dow, or Dhu Loch, i.e., Black Loch. Till towards the end of last century the spot was much frequented for its healing water. A personal visit was not essential. When a deputy was sent he had to bring a portion of the invalid's clothing and throw it over his left shoulder into the loch. He then took up some water in a vessel which he carefully kept from touching the ground. After turning himself round sun-ways he carried the water home. The charm would be broken if he looked back or spoke to anyone by the way. Among the people of the district it was a common saying, when anyone did not respond to the greeting of a passer-by, that he had been at the Dow Loch. Pilgrimages to the loch seem to have been specially popular towards the close of the seventeenth century, for in the year 1695 the Presbytery of Penpont consulted the Synod of Dumfries about the superstitious practices then current. The Synod, in response to the appeal, recommended the clergy of the district to denounce from their pulpits such observances as heathenish in character. There were persons still alive in the beginning of the present century who had seen the offerings, left by the pilgrims, floating

on the loch or lying on its margin. To the passer-by,
ignorant of the superstitious custom, it might seem
that a rather untidy family washing was in progress.

The Church of St. Vigeans, in Forfarshire, is well
known to antiquaries in connection with its interesting
sculptured stones. An old tradition relates that the
materials for the building were carried by a water-
kelpie, and that the foundations were laid on large
bars of iron. Underneath the structure was said to
be a deep lake. The tradition further relates that
the kelpie prophesied that an incumbent of the church
would commit suicide, and that, on the occasion of the
first communion after, the church would sink into
the lake. At the beginning of the eighteenth century
the minister of the parish did commit suicide, and so
strong was the superstition that the sacramental rite
was not observed till 1736. In connection with the
event several hundred people took up a position on a
neighbouring rising ground to watch what would
happen. These spectators have passed away, but
the church remains.

St. Tredwell's Loch in Papa-Westray, Orkney, was
at one time very famous, partly from its habit of
turning red whenever anything striking was about
to happen to a member of the Royal Family, and
partly from its power to work cures. On a small
headland on the east of the loch are still to be
seen the ruins of St. Tredwell's Chapel, measuring
twenty-nine feet by twenty-two, with walls fully
four feet in thickness. On the floor-level about

thirty copper coins were found some years ago, the majority of them being of the reign of Charles the Second. At the door of the chapel there was at one time a large heap of stones, made up of contributions from those who came to pay their vows there. Mr. R. M. Fergusson, in his "*Rambles in the Far North*," gives the following particulars about the loch:—"In olden times the diseased and infirm people of the North Isles were wont to flock to this place and get themselves cured by washing in its waters. Many of them walked round the shore two or three times before entering the loch itself to perfect by so doing the expected cure. When a person was engaged in this perambulation nothing would induce him to utter a word, for, if he spoke, the waters of this holy loch would lave his diseased body in vain. After the necessary ablutions were performed they never departed without leaving behind them some piece of cloth or bread as a gift to the presiding genius of the place. In the beginning of the eighteenth century popular belief in this water was as strong as ever."

Superstitions had a vigorous life last century. Pennant, who made his first tour in Scotland in 1769, mentions that the wells of Spey and Drachalday, in Moray, were then much visited, coins and rags being left at them as offerings. Nowadays holy wells are probably far from the thoughts of persons living amid the stir and bustle of city life, but in rural districts, where old customs linger, they are not yet forgotten. In the country, amidst the sights and

sounds of nature, men are prone to cherish the beliefs
and ways of their forefathers. Practices born in
days of darkness thus live on into an era of greater
enlightenment. "The adoration of wells," remarks
Sir Arthur Mitchell in his "*Past in the Present*," "may
be encountered in all parts of Scotland from John o'
Groats to the Mull of Galloway," and he adds, "I
have seen at least a dozen wells in Scotland which
have not ceased to be worshipped." "Nowadays,"
he continues, "the visitors are comparatively few, and
those who go are generally in earnest. They have a
serious object which they desire to attain. That
object is usually the restoration to health of some
poor little child—some 'back-gane bairn.' Indeed
the cure of sick children is a special virtue of many
of these wells. Anxious mothers make long journeys
to some well of fame, and early in the morning of
the 1st of May bathe the little invalid in its waters,
then drop an offering into them by the hands of the
child—usually a pebble, but sometimes a coin—and
attach a bit of the child's dress to a bush or tree
growing by the side of the well. The rags we see
fastened to such bushes have often manifestly been
torn from the dresses of young children. Part of a
bib or little pinafore tells the sad story of a
sorrowing mother and a suffering child, and makes
the heart grieve that nothing better than a visit
to one of these wells had been found to relieve
the sorrow and remove the suffering." Mr. Campbell
of Islay bears witness to the same fact. In

his "*Tales of the West Highlands*" he says, "Holy healing wells are common all over the Highlands, and people still leave offerings of pins and nails and bits of rag, though few would confess it. There is a well in Islay where I myself have, after drinking, deposited copper caps amongst a hoard of pins and buttons and similar gear placed in chinks in the rocks and trees at the edge of the 'Witches' well.'"

A striking testimony to the persistence of faith in such wells is borne by Mr. J. R. Walker in volume v. (new series) of the "*Proceedings of the Society of Antiquaries of Scotland*," where he describes an incident that he himself witnessed about ten years ago on the outskirts of Edinburgh. Mr. Walker writes, "While walking in the Queen's Park about sunset, I casually passed St. Anthony's Well, and had my attention attracted by the number of people about it, all simply quenching their thirst, some probably with a dim idea that they would reap some benefit from the draught. Standing a little apart, however, and evidently patiently waiting a favourable moment to present itself for their purpose, was a group of four. Feeling somewhat curious as to their intention I quietly kept myself in the background, and by-and-by was rewarded. The crowd departed and the group came forward, consisting of two old women a younger woman of about thirty, and a pale sickly-looking girl—a child three or four years old. Producing cups from their pockets, the old women dipped them in the pool, filled them, and drank the contents.

A full cup was then presented to the younger woman and another to the child. Then one of the old women produced a long linen bandage, dipped it in the water, wrung it, dipped it in again, and then wound it round the child's head, covering the eyes, the youngest woman, evidently the mother of the child, carefully observing the operation and weeping gently all the time. The other old woman not engaged in this work was carefully filling a clear glass bottle with the water, evidently for future use. Then, after the principal operators had looked at each other with an earnest and half solemn sort of look, the party wended its way carefully down the hill."

Agricultural improvements, particularly within the present century, have done much to abolish the adoration of wells. In many cases ancient springs have ceased to exist through draining operations. In the parish of Urquhart, Elginshire, a priory was founded in 1125. Towards the end of last century the site was converted into an arable field. The name of Abbey Well, given to the spring whence the monks drew water, long kept alive the memory of the priory; but in recent times the well itself was filled up. St. Mary's Well, at Whitekirk, in Haddingtonshire, has also ceased to be, its water having been drained off. Near Drumakill, in Drymen parish, Dumbartonshire, there was a famous spring dedicated to St. Vildrin. Close to it was a cross two feet and a half in height, with the figure of the saint incised on it. About thirty years ago, however, the relic was broken up

C

and used in the construction of a farmhouse, and not long after, the well itself was drained into an adjoining stream. In the middle ages the spring at Restalrig, near Edinburgh, dedicated to St. Margaret, the wife of Malcolm Canmore, was a great attraction to pilgrims. The history of the well is interesting. There is reason to believe that it was originally sacred to the Holy Rood; and tradition connects it with the fountain that gushed out at the spot where a certain hart suddenly vanished from the sight of King David I. Mr. Walker, in the volume of the *"Proceedings of the Society of Antiquaries of Scotland"* already referred to, throws out the suggestion that the well may have had its dedication changed in connection with the translation of Queen Margaret's relics about 1251, on the occasion of her canonization. With regard to the date of the structure forming the covering of the well, Mr. Walker, as an architect, is qualified to give an opinion, and from an examination of the mason marks on it he is inclined to think that the building was erected about the same time as the west tower of Holyrood Abbey Church, viz., about 1170. The late Sir Daniel Wilson, in his *"Memorials of Edinburgh in the Olden Time,"* gives the following account of the structure, which, however, he by mistake describes as octagonal instead of hexagonal:—"The building rises internally to the height of about four and a half feet, of plain ashlar work, with a stone ledge or seat running round seven of the sides, while the eighth is occupied by a pointed arch which forms the entrance to the well. From the centre of the water which fills the whole area of the building, pure as in the days of the pious queen, a decorated pillar rises to the same height as the walls, with grotesque gurgoils, from which the water has originally been made to flow. Above this springs a beautifully groined roof, presenting, with the ribs that rise from corresponding corbels at each of the eight angles of the building, a singularly rich effect when illuminated by the reflected light from the water below. A few years since, this curious fountain stood by the side of the ancient and little frequented cross-road leading from the Abbeyhill to the village of Restalrig. A fine old elder tree, with its knotted and furrowed branches, spread a luxuriant covering over its grass-grown top, and a rustic little thatched cottage stood in front of it, forming altogether a most attractive object of antiquarian pilgrimage." The spot, however, was invaded by the North British Railway Company, and a station was planted on the site of the elder tree and the rustic cottage, the spring and its Gothic covering being imbedded in the buildings. Some years later the water disappeared, having found another channel. The structure was taken down stone by stone and rebuilt above St. David's Spring, on the north slope of Salisbury Crags, where it still stands.

In cases like the above, man interfered with nature and caused the disappearance of venerated springs. But it was not always so. In the parish of Logierait, in Perthshire, there was a spring that took the matter

into its own hands, and withdrew from public view.
This was the spring called in Gaelic Fuaran Chad,
i.e., Chad's Well. An annual market used to be held
close by in honour of the saint, on the 22nd August.
The spring was gratified and bubbled away merrily.
The market, however, was at length discontinued.
In consequence Fuaran Chad took offence, and sent
in its resignation. In one instance, at least, the belief
in the efficacy of a spring survived the very existence
of the spring itself. This was so in the case of a healing
well near Buckie, in Banffshire, filled up some years
ago by the tenant on whose farm it was situated.
So great was its fame that some women whose infants
were weakly went to the spot and cleared out the
rubbish. Water again filled the old basin, and there
the infants were bathed. While being carried home
they fell asleep, and the result was in every way to
the satisfaction of the mothers.

Certain characteristics of water specially recommended it as an object of worship in primæval times.
Its motion and force suggested that it had life, and
hence a soul. Men therefore imagined that by due
attention to certain rites it would prove a help to
them in time of need. What may be called the
anthropomorphism of fountains has left traces on
popular superstitions. The interest taken by St.
Tredwell's Loch in the national events has been
already alluded to, and other examples will be noticed
in future chapters.

One point may be mentioned here, viz., the power

possessed by wells of removing to another place. St. Fillan's Spring, at Comrie, in Perthshire, once took its rise on the top of the hill Dunfillan, but tradition says that it quitted its old site for the present one, at the foot of a rock, a quarter of a mile further south. In the article on Comrie in the "*Old Statistical Account of Scotland*," the well is described as "*humbled* indeed, but not forsaken." A more striking instance of flitting is mentioned by Martin as having occurred in the Hebrides. In his account of Islay, he says, "A mile on the south-west side of the cave Uah Vearnag is the celebrated well Toubir-in-Knahar, which, in the ancient language, is as much as to say, 'the well has sailed from one place to another'; for it is a received tradition of the vulgar inhabitants of this isle, and the opposite isle of Colonsay, that this well was first at Colonsay until an impudent woman happened to wash her hands in it, and that immediately after, the well, being thus abused, came in an instant to Islay, where it is like to continue, and is ever since esteemed a catholicon for diseases by the natives and adjacent islanders." Perhaps the instance that puts the greatest strain on credulity is that of the spring dedicated to St. Fergus on the hill of Knockfergan, in Banffshire. Tradition reports that this spring came in a miraculous manner from Italy, though how it travelled to its quiet retreat in Scotland we do not know. There must have been some special attraction about the well, for a market known as the Well-Market used to

be held beside it every year.   On one occasion a fight
took place about a cheese.   In consequence the
market was transferred to the neighbouring village
of Tomintoul, where it continues to be held in August,
under the same name.

In his "*Romances of the West of England*," the late
Mr. Robert Hunt puts in a plea for the preservation
of holy wells and other relics of antiquity, though he
allows " that it is a very common notion amongst the
peasantry that a just retribution overtakes those who
wilfully destroy monuments, such as stone circles,
crosses, wells, and the like," and he mentions the case
of an old man who altered a holy well at Boscaswell,
in St. Just, and was drowned the following day
within sight of his house.   Mr. Hunt is speaking
of Cornish wells; but the same is doubtless true of
those north of the Tweed.   Springs that can fly
through the air and go through certain other wonderful performances can surely be trusted to look after
themselves.

In hot Eastern lands, fountains were held in special
reverence.   This was to be expected, as their cooling
waters were there doubly welcome.   In accounting
for the presence of the cult in the temperate zones of
Europe, we do not need to trace it to the East as
Lady Wilde does in her "*Ancient Legends of Ireland*."
" It could not have originated," she says, " in a humid
country   .   .   .   where wells can be found at every
step, and sky and land are ever heavy and saturated
with moisture.   It must have come from an Eastern

people, wanderers in a dry and thirsty land, where
the discovery of a well seemed like the interposition
of an angel in man's behalf." In our own land there
are no districts where well-worship has held its
ground so firmly as those occupied by peoples of
Celtic blood, such as Cornwall, Wales, Ireland, the
Isle of Man, and the Scottish Highlands. A curious
instance of the survival of water-worship among our
Scottish peasantry was seen in the custom of going at
a very early hour on New-Year's morning to get a
pailful of water from a neighbouring spring. The
maidens of the farm had a friendly rivalry as to
priority. Whoever secured the first pailful was said
to get *the flower* of the well, otherwise known as
the *ream* or *cream* of the well. On their way to the
spring the maidens commonly chanted the couplet—

> "The *flower o' the well* to our house gaes,
> An' I'll the bonniest lad get."

This referred to the belief that to be first at the well
was a good omen of the maiden's matrimonial future.
It is a far cry from archaic water-worship to this
New-Year's love charm, but we can traverse in
thought the road that lies between.

CHAPTER II.

How Water became Holy.

Change from Paganism to Christianity — Columba — Spirits of Fountains — Hurtful Wells — Stone Circles — Superstitions regarding them—Standing Stones and Springs—Innis Maree—Maelrubha—Influence of early Saints—Names of Wells—Stone-coverings—Sacred Buildings and Springs—Privilege of Sanctuary — Some Examples — Freedstoll — Preceptory of Torphichen and St. John's Well—Cross of Macduff and Nine-wells.

WE come next to ask how water became holy in the folklore sense of the word. Fortunately we get a glimpse of springs at the very time when they passed from pagan to Christian auspices. The change made certain differences, but did not take away their miraculous powers. We get this glimpse in the pages of Adamnan, St. Columba's biographer, who narrates an incident in connection with the saint's missionary work among the Picts in the latter half of the sixth century. Adamnan tells us of a certain fountain "famous among the heathen people, which the foolish men, having their senses blinded by the devil, worshipped as God. For those, who drank of this fountain, or purposely washed their hands or feet in it, were allowed by God to be struck by

demoniacal art, and went home either leprous or pur-
blind, or at least suffering from weakness or other
kind of infirmity. By all these things the pagans
were seduced and paid divine honour to the fountain."
Columba made use of the popular belief in the
interests of the new faith, and blessed the fountain
in the name of Christ in order to expel the demons.
He then took a draught of the water and washed
his hands and feet in it, to show that it could no
longer do harm. According to Adamnan the demons
deserted the fountain, and many cures were afterwards wrought by it. In Ireland more than a
century earlier, St. Patrick visited the fountain of
Findmaige, called Slan. Offerings were wont to be
made to it, and it was worshipped as a god by the
Magi of the district.

It is difficult to determine exactly from what
standpoint our pagan ancestors regarded wells. The
nature-spirits inhabiting them, styled *demons* by
Adamnan, were malignant in disposition, if we judge
by the case he mentions; but we must not therefore conclude that they were so in every instance.
Perhaps it is safe to infer that most of them were
considered favourable to man, or the reverse, according as they were or were not propitiated by him.
Even in modern times, some springs have been
regarded as hurtful. The well of St. Chad, at Lich-
field, for instance, causes ague to anyone drinking
its water. Even its connection with the saint has
not removed its hurtful qualities. In west Highland

Folk-Tales allusion is made to poison wells, and such
are even yet regarded with a certain amount of fear.
In the article on the parish of Kilsyth in the " *Old
Statistical Account of Scotland,*" it is stated that
Kittyfrist Well, beside the road leading over the hill
to Stirling, was believed to be noxious. Successive
wayfarers, when tired and heated by their climb up
hill, may have drunk injudiciously of the cold water,
and thus the superstition may have originated.

Stone circles have given rise to much discussion.
They are perhaps best known by their popular name
of Druidical temples. Whatever were the other
purposes served by them, there is hardly any doubt
that they were primarily associated with interments.
Dr. Joseph Anderson has pointed out that a certain
archæological succession can be traced. Thus we find
first, burial cairns *minus* stones round them, then
cairns *plus* stones, and finally, stones *minus* cairns.
At one time there was a widely-spread belief that
men could be transformed into standing stones by
the aid of magic. This power was attributed to the
Druids. There are also traditions of saints thus
settling their heathen opponents. When speaking
of the island of Lewis, Martin says, " Several other
stones are to be seen here in remote places, and some
of them standing on one end. Some of the ignorant
vulgar say that they were men by enchantment turned
into stones. Such monoliths are still known to the
Gaelic-speaking inhabitants of Lewis as Fir Chreig,
i.e., false men. We learn from the " *New Statistical*

Account of Scotland" that the two standing stones at West Skeld, in Shetland, were believed by the islanders to have been originally wizards or giants. Close to the roadside on Maughold Head, in the Isle of Man, stands an ancient runic cross. A local tradition states that the cross was once an old woman, who, when carrying a bundle of wool, cursed the wind for hindering her on her journey, and was petrified in consequence.

With superstitions thus clinging to standing-stones it is not to be wondered that springs in their neighbourhood should have been regarded with special reverence. In the *"Old Statistical Account of Scotland"* allusion is made to Tobir-Chalaich, *i.e.*, Old Wife's Well, situated near a stone circle in the parish of Keith, Banffshire, and to another well not far from a second circle in the same parish. The latter spring ceased to be visited about the middle of last century. Till then offerings were left at it by persons seeking its aid. The writer of the article on the island of Barry, Inverness-shire, in the same work, says, " Here, *i.e.*, at Castle-Bay, there are several Druidical temples. Near one of these is a well which must have been once famous for its medicinal quality, as also for curing and preventing the effects of fascination. It is called Tobbar-nam-buadh or the Well of Virtues." Under the heading " Beltane," in " *Jamieson's Scottish Dictionary,"* the following occurs:—"A town in Perthshire, on the borders of the Highlands, is called Tillie (or Tullie) Beltane, *i.e.*, the eminence or rising ground

of the fire of Baal. In the neighbourhood is a
Druidical temple of eight upright stones, where it is
supposed the fire was kindled. At some distance
from this, is another temple of the same kind, but
smaller, and near it a well still held in great veneration. On Beltane morning, superstitious people go to
this well and drink of it, then they make a procession
round it, as I am informed, nine times; ·after this,
they in like manner go round the temple." Gallstack
Well, at Drumlanrig, in Dumfriesshire, is near a group
of standing stones. From examples like the above,
we may infer that some mysterious connection was
supposed to exist between standing stones and their
adjacent wells. In the Tullie Beltane instance indeed, stones and well were associated together in the
same superstitious rite.

A striking instance of Christianity borrowing
from paganism is to be seen in the reverence paid
to the well of Innis Maree, in Loch Maree, in Ross-
shire. This well has been famous from an unknown
past. It is dedicated to St. Maelrubha, after whom
both loch and island are named. Maelrubha belonged
to the monastery of Bangor, in Ireland. In the year
673, at the age of thirty-one, he settled at Apple-
crossan, now Applecross, in Ross-shire, and there
founded a church as the nucleus of a conventual
establishment. Over this monastery he presided for
fifty-one years, and died a natural death in 722.
A legend, disregarding historical probabilities, relates
that he was slain by a band of pagan Norse rovers,

and that his body was left in the forest to be
devoured by wild beasts. His grave is still pointed
out in Applecross churchyard, the spot being marked
by a pillar slab with an antique cross carved on it.
For centuries after his death he was regarded as
the patron saint, not only of Applecross, but of a
wide district around.   Pennant, who visited Innis
Maree in 1772, thus describes its appearance: "The
shores are neat and gravelly; the whole surface
covered thickly with a beautiful grove of oak, ash,
willow, wicken, birch, fir, hazel, and enormous hollies.
In the midst is a circular dike of stones, with a
regular narrow entrance, the inner part has been
used for ages as a burial-place, and is still in use.
I suspect the dyke to have been originally Druidical,
and that the ancient superstition of Paganism had
been taken up by the saint, as the readiest method
of making a conquest over the minds of the inhabitants.   A stump of a tree is shown as an altar,
probably the memorial of one of stone ; but the
curiosity of the place is the well of the saint; of
power unspeakable in cases of lunacy."   Whatever
Pennant meant by Druidical, there is reason to
believe that the spot was the scene of pre-Christian
rites. In the popular imagination the outlines of
Maelrubha's character seem to have become mixed
up with those of the heathen divinity worshipped
in the district.   Two circumstances point to this.
Firstly, as Sir Arthur Mitchell remarks in the fourth
volume of the "*Proceedings of the Society of*

Antiquaries of Scotland," " The people of the place speak often of the God Mourie instead of St. Mourie, which may have resulted from his having supplanted the old god." Secondly, as the same writer shows, by reference to old kirk session records, it was customary in the parish to sacrifice a bull to St. Mourie. This was done on the saint's day, the 25th of August. The practice was still in existence in the latter half of the 17th century, and was then denounced as idolatrous.

We thus see that the sacredness of springs can be traced back through Christianity to paganism, though there is no doubt that in some instances it took its rise from association with early saints. In deciding the question of origin, however, care must be taken, for, as already indicated, the reverence anciently paid to wells led to their selection by the early missionaries. The holy wells throughout the land keep alive their names. An excellent example of a saint's influence on a particular district is met with in the case of St. Angus, at Balquhidder, in Perthshire. In his " Notes in Balquhidder" in the " *Proceedings of the Society of Antiquaries of Scotland,*" vol. ix. (new series), Mr. J. Mackintosh Gow remarks, " Saint Angus, the patron saint of the district, is said to have come to the glen from the eastward, and to have been so much struck with its marvellous beauty that he blessed it. The remains of the stone on which he sat to rest are still visible in the gable of one of the farm build-

ings at Easter Auchleskine, and the turn of the
road is yet called 'Beannachadh Aonghais' (Angus's
blessing). At this spot it was the custom in the
old days for people going westward to show their
respect for the saint by repeating, 'Beannaich
Aonghais ann san Aoraidh' (Bless Angus in the
oratory or chapel), at the same time reverently
taking off their bonnets. The saint, going west,
had settled at a spot below the present kirk, and
near to a stone circle, the remains of which, and
of the oratory, persons now living remember to
have seen." After alluding to another stone circle
in a haugh below the parish church manse, Mr.
Gow mentions that this haugh is the stance of the
old market of Balquhidder, long a popular one in
the district. It was held on the saint's day in
April and named Feill-Aonghais, after him. In the
immediate neighbourhood there is a knoll called "Tom
Aonghais," i.e., Angus's hillock. In the grounds of
Edinchip there is a curing well called in Gaelic,
"Fuaran n'druibh chasad," i.e., the Whooping-cough
Well, beside the burn "Alt cean dhroma." "It is
formed of a water-worn pot hole in the limestone
rock which forms the bed of the burn, and is ten
or twelve inches in diameter at the top and six
inches deep. There must be a spring running into
the hollow through a fissure, as no sooner is it
emptied than it immediately refills, and contains
about two quarts of water. The well can easily
be distinguished by the large moss-covered boulder,

round and flat, like a crushed ball, and about seven
feet in diameter, which overshadows it, and a young
ash tree of several stems growing by its side." This
well was famous for the cure of whooping-cough,
and children were brought to it till within recent
years. The water was given in a spoon made from
the horn of a living cow. When the patients could
not visit the spring in person, a bottleful of the
healing liquid was taken to their homes, and there
administered. The district round the lower waters
of Loch Awe, now comprising the united parishes
of Glenorchy and Inishail was held to be under the
patronage of Connan. There is a well at Dalmally
dedicated to him. According to a local tradition
he dwelt beside the well and blessed its water.

In addition to springs named after particular saints,
there are some bearing the general appellation of
Saints' Wells or Holy Wells. There are Holy Rood
and Holy Wood Wells, also Holy Trinity and Chapel
Wells. There are likewise Priors', Monks', Cardinals',
Bishops', Priests', Abbots', and Friars' Wells. Various
springs have names pointing to no ecclesiastical connection whatever. To this class belong those known
as Virtue Wells, and those others named from the
various diseases to be cured by them. On the Ruther-
ford estate, in the parish of West Linton, Peeblesshire, there is a mineral spring called Heaven-aqua
Well. Considering the name, one might form great
expectations as to its virtues. There is much force in
the remarks of Dr. J. Hill Burton, in his *Book Hunter*."

He says, "The unnoticeable smallness of many of these consecrated wells makes their very reminiscence and still semi-sacred character all the more remarkable. The stranger in Ireland, or the Highlands of Scotland, hears rumours of a distinguished well, miles on miles off. He thinks he will find an ancient edifice over it, or some other conspicuous adjunct. Nothing of the kind. He has been lured all that distance, over rock and bog, to see a tiny spring bubbling out of the rock, such as he may see hundreds of in a tolerable walk any day. Yet, if he search in old topographical authorities, he will find that the little well has ever been an important feature of the district; that century after century it has been unforgotten; and, with diligence he may perhaps trace it to some incident in the life of the saint, dead more than 1200 years ago, whose name it bears." There are a few wells with a more or less ornamental stone covering, such as St. Margaret's Well, in the Queen's Park, Edinburgh, and St. Michael's Well, at Linlithgow. St. Ninian's Well, at Stirling, and also at Kilninian, in Mull; St. Ashig's Well, in Skye; St. Peter's Well, at Houston, in Renfrewshire; Holy Rood Well, at Stenton, in Haddingtonshire; and the Well of Spa, at Aberdeen, also belong to this class.

As already indicated, standing stones and the wells near them were associated together in the same ritual act. A curious parallelism can be traced between this practice and one connected with Christian places of worship. Near the Butt of Lewis are the ruins of a

D

chapel anciently dedicated to St. Mulvay, and known in the district as Teampull-mor. The spot was till quite lately the scene of rites connected with the cure of insanity. The patient was made to walk seven times round the ruins, and was then sprinkled with water from St. Ronan's Well hard by. In Orkney it was believed that invalids would recover health by walking round the Cross-kirk of Wasbister and the adjoining loch in silence before sunrise. In some instances sacred sites were walked round without reference to wells, and, in others, wells without reference to sacred sites. But when the two were neighbours they were often included in the same ceremony. In the early days when Christianity was preached, the structures of the new faith were occasionally planted close to groups of standing stones, and it may be assumed that in some instances, at least, the latter served to supply materials for building the former. Even in our own day it is not uncommon for Highlanders to speak of going to the clachan, i.e., the stones, to indicate that they are going to church. The reverence paid to the pagan sites was thus transferred to the Christian, and any fountain in the vicinity received a large share of such reverence.

In former times, both south and north of the Tweed, churches and churchyards were regarded with special veneration as affording an asylum to offenders against the law. In England the Right of Sanctuary was held in great respect during Anglo-Saxon times, and after the Norman Conquest laws were passed regulating the privileges of such shelters. When a robber or murderer was pursued, he was free from capture if he could reach the sacred precincts. But he had to enter unarmed. His stay there was only temporary. After going through certain formalities he was allowed to travel, cross in hand, to some neighbouring seaport to quit his country for ever. In the reign of Henry VIII., however, a statute was passed forbidding criminals thus to leave their native land on the ground that they would disclose state secrets, and teach archery to the enemies of the realm. In the north of England, Durham and Beverley contained noted sanctuaries. In various churches there was a stone seat called the Freedstoll or Stool of Peace, on which the criminal, when seated, was absolutely safe. Such a seat, dating from the Norman period, is still to be seen in the Priory Church at Hexham, where the sanctuary was in great request by fugitives from the debatable land between England and Scotland. The only other Freedstoll still to be found in England is in Beverley Minster. The Right of Sanctuary was formally abolished in England in the reign of James I., but did not cease to be respected till much later. Such being the regard in the middle ages for churches and their burying-grounds, it is easy to understand why fountains in their immediate neighbourhood were also reverenced. Several sanctuaries north of the Tweed were specially famous. In his "*Scotland in the Middle Ages*," Professor Cosmo Innes remarks,

"Though all were equally sacred by the canon, it would seem that the superior sanctity of some churches, from the relics presented there, or the reverence of their patron saints, afforded a surer asylum, and thus attracted fugitives to their shrines rather than to the altars of common parish churches." The churches of Stow, Innerleithen, and Tyningham were asylums at one time specially favoured. The church on St. Charmaig's Island, in the Sound of Jura —styled also *Eilean Mòr* or the *Great Island*—was formerly a noted place of refuge among the Inner Hebrides. So much sanctity attached to the church of Applecross that the privileged ground around it extended six miles in every direction. In connection with his visit to Arran, Martin thus describes what had once been a sanctuary in that island: "There is an eminence of about a thousand paces in compass on the sea-coast in Druim-cruey village, and it is fenced about with a stone wall; of old it was a sanctuary, and whatever number of men or cattle could get within it were secured from the assaults of their enemies, the place being privileged by universal consent." The enclosure was probably an ancient burying-ground.

The Knights of St. John of Jerusalem, otherwise known as the Knights of Rhodes, and also as the Hospitallers, received recognition in Scotland as an Order about the middle of the twelfth century. They had possessions in almost every county, but their chief seat was at Torphichen, in Linlithgow-

shire, where the ruins of their preceptory can still
be seen. This preceptory formed the heart of the
famous sanctuary of Torphichen. In the graveyard
stands a stone, resembling an ordinary milestone with
a Maltese cross carved on its top. All the ground
enclosed in a circle, having a radius of one mile from
this stone, formed a sanctuary for criminals and
debtors. Other four stones placed at the cardinal
points showed the limits of the sanctuary on their
respective sides. At some distance to the east of
the preceptory is St. John's Well, "to which," the
writer of the article in the "*New Statistical Account
of Scotland*" says, "the Knights of St. John used
to go in days of yore for a morning draught;" and
he adds, "whether its virtues were medicinal or of
a more hallowed character tradition can not exactly
inform us, but still its waters are thought to possess
peculiar healing powers, if not still rarer qualities
which operate in various cases as a charm."
Perhaps no Scottish sanctuary has been more talked
about than the one at Holyrood Abbey, intended
originally for law-breakers in general, but latterly
for debtors only. De Quincey found a temporary
home within its precincts. Through recent legisla-
tion, chiefly through the Debtors (Scotland) Act of
1880, the sanctuary has been rendered unnecessary,
and its privileges, though never formally abolished,
have accordingly passed away.

In a pass of the Ochils, near Newburgh, overlooking Strathearn, is a block of freestone three

and a half feet high, four and a half feet long,
and nearly four feet broad at the base.   This
formed the pedestal of the celebrated cross of
Macduff, and is all that remains of that ancient
monument.   The shaft of the cross was destroyed
at the time of the Reformation, in the sixteenth century.   In former days the spot was
held to be a privilege and liberty of girth.   When
anyone claiming kinship to Macduff, Earl of Fife,
within the ninth degree committed slaughter in hot
blood and took refuge at the cross, he could atone
for his crime by the payment of nine cows and a
colpindach or year-old cow.   Those who could not
make good their kinship were slain on the spot.
Certain ancient burial mounds, at one time to be
seen in the immediate neighbourhood, were popularly
believed to be the graves of those who thus met
their death, and a local superstition asserted that
their shrieks could be heard by night.   A fountain,
known as the Nine Wells, gushes out not far from
the site of the cross, and in it tradition says that the
manslayer who was entitled to claim the privilege of
sanctuary washed his hands, thereby freeing himself
from the stain of blood.

CHAPTER III.

SAINTS AND SPRINGS.

THE annals of hagiology are full of the connection
between saints and springs. On one occasion a child
was brought to Columba for baptism, but there was
no water at hand for the performance of the rite.
The saint knelt in prayer opposite a neighbouring
rock, and rising, blessed the face of the rock. Water
immediately gushed forth, and with it the child was

baptised. Adamnan, who tells the story, says that
the child was Lugucencalad, whose parents were
from Artdaib-muirchol (Ardnamurchan), where there
is seen even to this day a well called by the
name of St. Columba. There are many wells in
Scotland named after him. As might be expected,
one of these is in Iona. Almost all are along the
west coast and in the Hebrides. The name of
Kirkcolm, in Wigtownshire, signifies the Church of
Columba. The parish contains a fountain dedicated
to him, known as Corswell or Crosswell, from which
the castle headland and lighthouse of Corsewall
have derived their name. A certain amount of
sanctity still clings to the fountain. Macaulay, in
his "*History of St. Kilda*" published in 1764,
describes a spring there called by the inhabitants
Toberi-Clerich, the cleric in question being, according to him, Columba. "This well," he says, "is
below the village, . . . and gushes out like a
torrent from the face of a rock. At every full tide
the sea overflows it, but how soon that ebbs away,
nothing can be fresher or sweeter than the water.
It was natural enough for the St. Kildians to
imagine that so extraordinary a phenomenon must
have been the effect of some supernatural cause, and
one of their teachers would have probably assured
them that Columba, the great saint of their island
and a mighty worker of miracles, had destroyed the
influence which, according to the established laws of
nature, the sea should have had on that water."

This spring resembles one in the parish of Tain, in Ross-shire, known as St. Mary's Well. The latter is covered several hours each day by the sea, but when the tide retires its fresh, sweet water gushes forth again.

According to an old tradition, Drostan, a nephew of Columba, accompanied the latter when on a journey from Iona to Deer in Buchan, about the year 580, and was the first abbot of the monastery established there. The name of the place according to the "*Book of Deer*," was derived from the tears (in Gaelic, der or deur, a tear), shed by Drostan on the departure of his uncle. In reality, the name comes from the Gaelic dair, signifying an oak. There are five springs dedicated to Drostan. They are all in the east country, between Edzell and New Aberdour. At the latter place his relics were preserved, and miracles of healing were wrought at his tomb. The spring near Invermark Castle is popularly known as Droustie's Well. A market, called St. Drostan's Fair, is still held annually at Old Deer in December. Insch, in Aberdeenshire, has also a St. Drostan's Fair. Drostan was reverenced in Caithness, where he was tutelar saint of the parishes of Halkirk and Canisbay. In "*The Early Scottish Church*" the Rev. Dr. M'Lauchlan mentions that Urquhart in Inverness-shire, was called Urchudain, Maith Dhrostan, *i.e.*, St. Drostan's Urquhart.

Adamnan, Columba's biographer, became abbot of Iona in 679, and died there in 704. There are wells to him at Dull, in Perthshire, and at Forglen in Banffshire. His name occurs in Scottish topography, but shortened, and under various disguises. In the form of St. Oyne he has a well in Rathen parish, Aberdeenshire, where there is a mound—probably an ancient fortified site—also called St. Oyne's. About six miles north-east of Kingussie, in Inverness-shire, is the church of the *quoad sacra* parish of Inch, on a knoll projecting into the loch of the same name. The knoll is called Tom Eunan, *i.e.*, the hill of Adamnan, to whom the church was dedicated. Within the building is still to be seen a fine specimen of the four-cornered bronze bell used in the early Celtic church. According to a local tradition it was once carried off, but kept calling out, "Tom Eunan! Tom Eunan!" till brought back to its home. We find that Adamnan and Columba were associated together in the district. An annual gathering, at one time held there in honour of the latter, was named Feil Columcille, *i.e.*, Columba's Fair, and was much resorted to. Women usually appeared on the occasion in white dresses in token of baptism. An old woman, who died in 1882, at the age of ninety, was in the habit of showing the white dress worn by her in her young days at the fair. It finally served her as a shroud. Adamnan visited the Northumbrian court when Egfrid was king. His errand was one of peace-making; for he went to procure the release of certain Irish captives who had been made prisoners by Egfrid.

During his stay in Northumbria he became a convert
to the Roman view as against the Celtic in the two
burning questions of that age, viz., the time for
holding Easter, and the nature of the tonsure.
Though he did not get his friends in Scotland to see
eye to eye with him on these points, he seems to have
been generally popular north of the Tweed. Eight
churches at least were dedicated to him, mainly in
the east country between Forvie, in Aberdeenshire,
and Dalmeny, in West Lothian. One of these dedications was at Aboyne. Skeulan Well there contains
Adamnan's name in a corrupted form.

Kieran, belonging like Columba to the sixth century, was also like him from Ireland. He selected
a cave some four miles from Campbeltown as his
dwelling-place, and there led the life of an ascetic.
He died in 543 in his thirty-fourth year. Pennant
thus describes the cave:—"It is in the form of a
cross, with three fine Gothic porticoes for entrances,
. . . had formerly a wall at the entrance, a second
about the middle, and a third far up, forming different apartments. On the floor is the capital of a
cross and a round basin cut out of the rock, full of
fine water, the beverage of the saint in old times,
and of sailors in the present, who often land to dress
their victuals beneath this shelter." This basin is
more minutely described by Captain T. P. White in
his "*Archæological Sketches in Scotland.*" He says,
"There is a small basin, nearly oval in shape, neatly
scooped out of a block, two feet long by one and a half

wide, which exactly underlies a drip of water from the
roof of the cave.   The water supply is said never to have
failed and always to keep the little basin full.   Tradition calls it the saint's font or holy well."   Kieran
is commemorated in Kinloch-Kilkerran, the ancient
name of the parish of Campbeltown.   The word
means literally the head of the loch of Kieran's
cell.   On one occasion Kieran dropped his book of
the Gospels into a lake.   Sometime after it was
recovered in an uninjured state through the instru-
mentality of a cow.   The cow went into the water
to cool itself, and brought out the volume attached
to its hoof.   Another bovine association is connected
with the building of St. Kieran's Church on a hill at
Errigall-keroge, in County Tyrone, Ireland.   The
saint had an ox which, during the day, drew the
materials for the building, and in the evening was
slaughtered to feed the workmen.   The bones were
thrown each evening into a well at the foot of the
hill, and, morning by morning, the accommodating
animal appeared ready for the day's work.   The
well is still held to be miraculous.   There is a spring
dedicated to Kieran at Drumlithie, in Glenbervie
parish, Kincardineshire, and another at Stonehaven,
in the same county.   There is one in Troqueer parish,
Kirkcudbrightshire, locally known as St. Jergon's
or St. Querdon's Well, these names being simply an
altered form of Kieran.

Bridget or Bride, an Irish saint, was popular in
Scotland.   She received baptism from Patrick, and

died in 525 after a life of great sanctity. She was celebrated as a worker of miracles. She made a cow supply an enormous quantity of milk to satisfy the wants of three thirsty bishops who came to visit her. She also cured diseases. On one occasion two men suffering from leprosy came to her to be healed. She made the sign of the cross over water, and told them to wash in it. One of the two did so and was instantly restored to health; but, refusing to help the other, he at once became leprous again, while his companion was as suddenly made whole. On another occasion she used the sign of the cross to stay a company bent on the capture of a maiden who had sought refuge in the saint's nunnery. Perhaps her most wonderful miracle was the hanging of her gown on a sunbeam, a somewhat unusual cloak-peg, and one that, from the nature of the case, had not to be sought in a dark press. Her principal monastery was at Kildare, so named after the oak (dair) under whose shade her cell was built. Adjoining St. Bride's Churchyard in London is a spring dedicated to the saint, and popularly styled Bride's Well. The palace built in the immediate neighbourhood went by the name of Bridewell. It was handed over by Edward VI. to the city of London as a workhouse and place of correction. At a later date the name became associated with other houses used for a similar purpose. " Hence it has arisen," remarks Chambers in his "*Book of Days*," "that the pure and innocent Bridget, the first of Irish nuns,

is now inextricably connected in our ordinary
national parlance with a class of beings of the
most opposite description." There are fully a dozen
wells in Scotland bearing her name. These are
chiefly to be found in the counties of Wigtown,
Dumfries, Peebles, Lanark, Renfrew, Dumbarton,
Perth, Fife, and Aberdeen. A monastery was
founded in Bridget's honour at Abernethy, in Perthshire, probably in the eighth century, and she had
churches on the mainland and among the Western
Islands. A curious superstition connected with
Bridget has survived to the present time, at least
in one of these islands. It has to do with a certain
magical flower styled torranain, that must be
plucked during the influx of the tide, and is of
virtue to protect cows from the evil eye, and to
make them give a plentiful supply of milk. The
Rev. Dr. Stewart, in his "'Twixt Ben Nevis and
Glencoe," quotes the incantation associated with it
forwarded to him by a correspondent in Uist. The
following is one of the stanzas :—

> " Let me pluck thee, Torranain !
> With all thy blessedness and all thy virtue.
> The nine blessings came with the nine parts.
> By the virtue of the Torranain.
> The hand of St. Bride with me
> I am now to pluck thee."

A saint who could give efficacy to a spell was quite
the sort of person to be entrusted with the custody
of springs.

Ninian, popularly called Ringan, devoted his life

mainly to missionary work among the Picts of Galloway, although he extended his influence as far north
as the Tay. He seems to have been honoured in
Aberdeenshire, if we may judge by a fresco, representing him, discovered about thirty years ago in the
pre-Reformation Church of Turriff, and regard was
had for him as far north as the Shetland Isles. Even
the Scot abroad did not forget him. Chalmers, in his
"*Caledonia*," says that, "in the church of the Carmelite
Friars of Bruges in Flanders, the Scottish nation
founded an altar to St. Ninian, and endowed a chap-
lain who officiated at it." A cave by the sea in the
parish of Glasserton, in Wigtownshire, was his favourite retreat. This cave was explored about ten years
ago, and several stones, marked with incised crosses,
were discovered. Ninian brought masons from France,
and at Whithorn built Candida Casa—the first
stone church in Scotland. It was in course of construction in the year 397. Ninian then heard of the
death of Martin of Tours, and to the latter the new
church was dedicated. These two saints are found
side by side in the matter of church dedications.
Thus, Martin was patron of Ulbster, in Caithness:
not far off was a church to Ninian. Strathmartin,
in Forfarshire, was united in 1799 to the parish of
Mains, the latter claiming Ninian as its tutelar saint.
Sinavey Spring, in Mains parish, near the site of
the ancient Castle of Fintry, is believed to represent
St. Ninian's name in a corrupted form. His springs
are numerous, and have a wide range from the

counties of Wigtown and Kirkcudbright to those of
Forfar and Kincardine. There is a well to him near
Dunnottar Castle, in the last-mentioned county. In
the island of Sanda, off the Kintyre coast, is a spring
named after him. It had a considerable local celebrity in former times. St. Ninian's Well in Stirling
is a familiar spot in the district. There is a well
sacred to Martin in the Aberdeenshire parish of
Cairnie. Martinmas (November 11th) came long ago
into our land as a church festival. It still remains
with us as a familiar term-day.

An incident in Martin's biography has a bearing on
our subject, through the connection between the name
of the festival commemorating it and certain of our
place-names. In Scotland, the fourth of July used to
be known as Martin of Bullion's Day, in honour of
the translation of the saint's body to a shrine in the
cathedral of Tours. There is some uncertainty about
the origin of the term Bullion, though, according to
the likeliest etymology, it is derived from the French
bouiller, to boil, in allusion to the heat of the
weather at that time of the year. There is an old
proverb that if the deer rise up dry and lie down dry
on Martin of Bullion's Day, there will be a good
gose-harvest, *i.e.*, an early and plentiful one. An
annual fair was appointed to be held at Selkirk and
in Dyce parish, Aberdeenshire, in connection with the
festival. There are traces of both Martin and Bullion
in Scottish topography. In Perthshire there is the
parish of St. Martin's, containing the estate of St.

Martin's Abbey. Some miles to the east is Strath-martin in Forfarshire, already alluded to, and not far from it in the same county we find Bullionfield in the parish of Liff and Benvie. It is probable that these names are in some way connected together. In Eccles-machan parish in Linlithgowshire, there is, as far as we know, no trace of Martin in any dedication of chapel or spring; but Bullion is represented. There is a spring of this name issuing from the trap rocks of the Tor Hill. It is a mineral well. The water is slightly impregnated with sulphuretted hydrogen. In former times it was much resorted to by health-seekers, but it is now neglected.

Ninian consecrated a graveyard beside the Molen-dinar at Cathures, now Glasgow. About a hundred years later Kentigern, otherwise Mungo, bishop of the Strathclyde kingdom, brought to this cemetery from Carnock the body of Fergus, an anchorite, on a cart drawn by two wild bulls. Over the spot where Fergus was buried was built, at a later date, the crypt of what was to have been the south transept of the cathedral, had that portion of the structure ever been reared. The crypt is now popularly called Blackadder's Aisle, though, as Dr. Andrew MacGeorge points out in his "*Old Glasgow*," it ought to be called Fergus' Isle. It was so named in a minute of the kirk-session in 1648, and an inscription in long Gothic letters on a stone in the roof of the aisle tells the same tale. Kentigern took up his abode on the banks of the Molendinar, and gathered round him a company

E

of monks, each dwelling in a separate hut.   In the
twelfth century the spot was surrounded by a dense
forest, and in 1500 the "Arbores sancti Kentigerni"
were landmarks in the district.   Kentigern's Well, now
in the lower church of the cathedral, must, from the
very fact of its inclusion within the building, have
been deemed sacred before the cathedral was reared.
Other examples of wells within churches are on
record, though not in Scotland.   There is a spring in
St. Patrick's Cathedral, Dublin.   The cathedrals of
Carlisle, Winchester, and Canterbury, and the minsters
of York and Beverley, as well as one or two English
parish churches, either now have or once had wells
within their walls.   The Rev. T. F. Thiselton Dyer
gives several examples in his "*Church Lore Gleanings*,"
and remarks, "Such wells may have been of special
service in Border churches, which, like the cathedral
of Carlisle, served as places of refuge for the inhabitants in case of sudden alarm or foray."

Besides his well in the cathedral, Kentigern had
another dedicated to him at Glasgow, close to Little
St. Mungo's Church, in the immediate neighbourhood
of the trees already mentioned.   There are fully a
dozen wells sacred to him north of the Tweed.   As
might be expected, these are almost all to be found
in the counties south of the Forth and Clyde, and
particularly in those to the west of that district.
There is one in Kincardineshire, at Kinneff, locally
known as Kenty's Well.   Under the name of St.
Mongah's Well there is a spring dedicated to him in

Yorkshire at Copgrove Park four miles from Borough-bridge. A bath close by, supplied with water from this spring, was formerly much frequented by invalids of all ages, who remained immersed for a longer or shorter time in its intensely cold water. Other wells to Kentigern are to be met with in the north of England. The parish of Crossthwaite in Cumberland has its church dedicated to him. The spot was the thwaite or clearing in the wood where he set up his cross. Thanet Well, in Greystoke parish in the same county, is believed to have derived its name from Tanew or Thenew, Kentigern's mother, familiar to the citizens of Glasgow as St. Enoch. St. Enoch's Well, close to St. Enoch's Square in that burgh, used to be a favourite resort of health-seekers. It has now no existence.

Cuthbert, besides a well at St. Boswell's, in Rox-burghshire, had a bath in Strath Tay a rock-hewn hollow full of water where he periodically passed several hours in devotion. This famous Northumbrian missionary was born about 635, and spent his early boyhood as a shepherd on the southern slopes of the Lammermoors. He lived for thirteen years as a monk in the monastery of Old Melrose, situated two miles east from the present Melrose on a piece of land almost surrounded by the Tweed. On the death of Boisil, Cuthbert was appointed prior. He afterwards became bishop of Lindisfarne. During his stay at Melrose he visited the land of the Niduarian Picts, in other words the Picts of Galloway, and left a record of his journey in the name of Kirkcudbright, *i.e.*, the Church of Cuthbert. Various other churches were dedicated to him in the south of Scotland and in the north of England. A well-known Edinburgh parish bears his name. He was honoured as far south as Cornwall. St. Cuby's Well, locally called St. Kilby's, between Duloe and Sandplace in that county is believed to have been dedicated to him.

There is a good deal of uncertainty about the history of Palladius. He is believed to have been a missionary from Rome to the Irish in the fifth century, and to have suffered martyrdom for the faith. It is recorded of him that on one occasion, by removing some turf in the name of the Holy Spirit, he caused a spring to gush forth to supply water for baptism. He is popularly associated with Kincardineshire, though there is reason to believe that he had no personal connection with the district. A spring in Fordoun parish is locally known as Paldy's Well, and an annual market goes by the name of Paldy's or Paddy's Fair. A chapel was dedicated to him there, and received his relics, brought thither by his disciple Terrananus, whose name is still preserved in Banchory-Ternan, and who seems to have belonged to the district. Ternan has a well at Banchory-Devenick, and another at Kirkton-of-Slains, in Buchan. The old church of Arbuthnot was dedicated to him. It was for this church that the Missal, Psalter, and Office of the Virgin, now in the possession of Viscount Arbuthnot, were written and illuminated towards the end of the fifteenth century, these being the only *complete* set of Service-Books of a Scottish Church that have come down to us from pre-Reformation times.

Brendan of Clonfert in Ireland, visited several of the Western Isles during the first half of the sixth century, and various churches were afterwards dedicated to him there. He is connected also with Bute. The name Brandanes, applied to its inhabitants, came from him, and he bids fair to be remembered in the name of Kilbrandon Sound, between Arran and Kintyre. He was patron of a well in the island of Barra and was tutelar saint of Boyndie and Cullen in Banffshire; but we are not aware that any well at either of these places was called after him.

A curious legend is related to account for the origin of the See of Aberdeen. According to it Machar or Macarius, along with twelve companions, received instructions from Columba to wander over Pictland, and to build his cathedral-church where he found a river making a bend like a bishop's staff. Such a bend was found in the Don at Old Aberdeen. St. Machar's Cathedral, built beside it, keeps alive the saint's memory. In the neighbouring grounds of Seton is St. Machar's Well. Though now neglected, it was honoured in former times, and its water was used at baptisms in the cathedral. Under the name of Mocumma or Mochonna, Macarius appears as one of the followers of Columba on his memorable voyage

from Ireland to Iona. He is said to have visited
Pope Gregory the Great at Rome, and to have been
for a time bishop of Tours. In Strathdon, Aberdeenshire, is a well sacred to him called Tobar-Mhachar,
pronounced in the district Tobar-Vacher.

Constantine, known also by his other names of
Cowstan, Chouslan, and Cutchou, was a prince of
Cornwall in the sixth century, and was acquainted
with Columba and Kentigern. He relinquished his
throne and crossed over to Ireland, where he turned
monk. At a later date he came to the west of
Scotland, and founded a monastery at Golvedir,
believed to be Govan, near Glasgow, and, according to
Fordun, became its abbot. Kilchouslan Church, on
the north side of Campbeltown Bay, Kintyre, was
built in his honour. In its graveyard there is, or was
till quite lately, a round stone about the size of a
grinding stone. In the centre is a hole large enough
to let the hand pass through. There is a tradition
that if a man and woman eloped, and were able to
join hands through this hole before being overtaken
by their kinsfolk they were free from further pursuit.
In the spring of 1892 an interesting find of old coins
was made in the same graveyard. These consisted of
groats and half-groats, some of English and some of
Scottish coinage, the earliest belonging to the reign of
Edward II. of England. According to Martin, the
well of St. Cowstan at Garrabost, in Lewis, was
believed never to boil any kind of meat, though its
water was kept over the fire for a whole day. This

well is on a steep slope at the shore. Not far off once stood St. Cowstan's Chapel, but its site is now under tillage.

Serf or Servanus, who flourished during the latter half of the seventh century, was connected with the district north of the Firth of Forth, particularly with Culross, and the island named after him in Loch Leven, where he founded a monastery. At Dysart, Serf had a cave, and in it tradition says that he held a discussion with the devil. The name of Dysart indeed, comes from this *desertum* or retreat. Serf had a cell at Dunning, in Strathearn, where he died in the odour of sanctity. He had also some link with the parish of Monzievaird, where the church was dedicated to him, and where a small loch still goes by the name of St. Serf's Water. There is a well sacred to him at Alva. St. Shear's Well, at Dumbarton, retains his name in an altered form. Early last century this spring was put to a practical purpose, as arrangements were then made to lead its water across the Leven by pipes to supply the burgh.

CHAPTER IV.

MORE SAINTS AND SPRINGS.

IN any notice of early saints Ronan must not be
forgotten, especially when we remember that perhaps
no spring, thanks to Sir Walter Scott, is so familiar
to the general reader as St. Ronan's Well. It has
been commonly identified with the mineral well at
Innerleithen, in Peeblesshire for long held in much
favour in cases of eye and skin complaints, and also
for the cure of dyspepsia. The spring is situated a
short distance above the town on the skirt of Lee
Pen. The writer of the article on Innerleithen

parish in the "*New Statistical Account of Scotland*" says that this spring "was formerly called the 'Dow-well' from the circumstance that, long before the healing virtues of the water were discovered, pigeons from the neighbouring country resorted to it." The name, however, is more probably derived from the Gaelic *dhu* or *dubh*, signifying *black*. This is all the more likely when we remember that the ground around was wet and miry before the spring was put into order, and the present pump-room built, in 1826. We find marks of Ronan in Scottish topography. In Dumbartonshire is Kilmaronock, meaning, literally, the Church of my little Ronan; Kilmaronog near Loch Etive has the same signification. Dr. Skene refers to these two dedications, and adds, "Ronan appears to have carried his mission to the Isles. He has left his trace in Iona, where one of the harbours is Port Ronan. The church, afterwards the parish church, was dedicated to him, and is called Teampull Ronaig, and its burying-ground, Cladh Ronan. Then we find him at Rona, in the Sound of Skye, and another Rona, off the coast of Lewis; and, finally, his death is recorded in 737 as Ronan, abbot of Cinngaradh or Kingarth, in Bute." Ronan is patron of various springs. There is one sacred to him near Kilmaronock, another in the Aberdeenshire parish of Strathdon, and another, already referred to, beside Teampull Mòr, in the Butt of Lewis. The parish of Strowan, now joined to that of Monzievaird, has a well to the saint. This was to

be expected, since the name of the parish is merely
an altered form of St. Rowan or Ronan.   About a
hundred yards above the bridge of Strowan, there is
a deep pool in the river Earn, called Pol-Ronan, and
a piece of ground hard by was formerly the site of
the yearly gathering known as Feill-Ronan or St.
Ronan's Fair.

The parish of St. Fergus, in Buchan, known till
the year 1616 as Langley, commemorates an Irish
missionary of the eighth century, who led a roving
life, if we can believe the tradition, that he evan-
gelised Caithness, Buchan, Strathearn, and Forfarshire, as well as attended an Ecclesiastical Council
at Rome.   The legend that his well in Kirkmichael
parish, Banffshire, was at one time in Italy may be
connected with his visit to Rome.   Concerning this
spring, the Rev. Dr. Gregor gives the following
particulars :—" Fergan Well is situated on the south-
east side of Knock-Fergan, a hill of considerable
height on the west side of the river Avon, opposite
the manse of Kirkmichael.   The first Sunday of May
and Easter Sunday were the principal Sundays for
visiting it, and many from the surrounding parishes,
who were affected with skin diseases or running sores,
came to drink of its water, and to wash in it.   The
hour of arrival was twelve o'clock at night, and the
drinking of the water and the washing of the diseased
part took place before or at sunrise.   A quantity
of the water was carried home for future use.
Pilgrimages were made up to the end of September,

by which time the healing virtues of the water had
become less. Such after-visits seem to have begun
in later times." Fergus died at Glamis, and his
relics soon began to work cures. His head was
carried off to the monastery of Scone, and was so
much esteemed in later times that, by order of
James IV., a silver case was made for it. His cave
and well are to be seen at Glamis. There is a spring
dedicated to him near Montrose, and there is another
at Wick.

Various other saintly personages have left traces
of their names in holy wells. Chalmers, in his
"*Caledonia*," mentions that the ancient church of
Aldcamus, in Cockburnspath parish, Berwickshire,
was dedicated to Helen, mother of Constantine, and
that its ruins were known as St. Helen's Kirk. A
portion of the building still stands. To the north
of it is a burying-ground; but, curiously enough, as
Mr. Muir points out in his "*Ancient Churches of
Scotland*," the spot does not appear ever to have
been used for purposes of sepulture. We do not
know surely of any spring to Helen in the immediate
neighbourhood, but there is one at Darnick, near
Melrose. Another is in Kirkpatrick-Fleming parish,
Dumfriesshire. Perhaps the best known is St.
Helen's Well, beside the highway from Maybole
to Ayr, about two-and-a-half miles from the former
town. It was much resorted to on May Day for the
cure of sickly children. On Timothy Pont's map,
of date 1654, there is a "Helen's Loch" marked a

little to the south-west of Camelon, in Stirlingshire. Some writers have attempted to claim Helen as a native of Britain, and Colchester and York have, for different reasons, been fixed on as her birth-place. The circumstance that Constantine was proclaimed Emperor at the latter town, on the death there of his father, Constantius Chlorus, probably gave rise to the tradition. Anyhow, Helen seems to have been held in high honour in England. In an article in the "*Archæological Journal*" for December, 1891, Mr. Edward Peacock mentions that there are at least fifteen wells named after her south of the Tweed. He adds, "there are many churches dedicated to the honour of St. Helen in England, but they are very irregularly distributed. None seems to occur in Cumberland, Westmoreland, or Essex. The rest of the English shires, for which we have authentic information, give the following results :—Devonshire, three; Durham, two; Kent, one; Lincolnshire, twenty-eight ; Northumberland, three ; Nottinghamshire, fifteen; Yorkshire, thirty-two." Helen's name occurs in Welsh legends; but, as Mr. Peacock observes, "early history is so much distorted in them, that, if we did not know of her from more authentic sources, we might well believe Helen to have been a mere creation of the fervid Keltic imagination." As far as is known there are neither wells nor church dedications to her in the Principality.

At Ayton, in Berwickshire, we find St. Abb's Well, recalling Abb or Æbba, who, in the seventh century,

presided over a monastery on the headland still
bearing her name, and in whose honour the priory
at Coldingham was founded by Edgar, son of Malcolm
Canmore, some four centuries and a half later. Her
monastery on the headland was founded by Aidan,
who was sent from Iona to the North of England in
response to a request from King Oswald, of Bernicia,
for a missionary to preach Christianity to his pagan
subjects. This was about the year 635. Aidan made
the island of Lindisfarne, off the coast of Northumberland, his head-quarters. It is still known as Holy
Island. Aidan has not been forgotten in the matter
of wells. There are four to him, viz., at Menmuir
and at Fearn, in Forfarshire; at Balmerino, in Fife;
and at Cambusnethan, in Lanarkshire. This last,
called St. Iten's Well, was noted for the cure of
asthma and skin-disease.

Boisil, abbot of the monastery of Old Melrose,
about the middle of the seventh century, still lives
in the name of the Roxburghshire village and parish
of St. Boswell's. There is a spring in the parish
bearing the name of The Well-brae Wall. Boswell's
own spring is popularly styled the Hare-well. Not
far from both is St. Boswell's Burn, a tributary of the
Tweed. The local fair held on July 18th, in honour
of the saint, used to be a notable one in the border
counties, and was frequented by large numbers of
gipsies who set up booths for the sale of their wares.

Bathan, who flourished in the early seventh century,
had to do with Shetland, and with the region about

the Whittadder, in Berwickshire. Abbey St. Bathans, in the latter county, is named after him. His well is on one of the haughs beside the river, not far from the ruined nunnery. Its water is believed never to freeze.

Boniface belonged to the same century. He is said to have preached Christianity at Gowrie, in Pictavia, and afterwards at Rosemarkie, in the Black Isle, where he died at the age of eighty, and was buried in the church of St. Peter. A well and a fair at Rosemarkie still keep alive his memory.

The fame of Catherine of Alexandria travelled to Scotland at a comparatively early period. This holy maiden was noted for her learning, Indeed she was so wise that Maxentius the Emperor called her a "second Plato." The Emperor's compliments, however, stopped there, for he ordered her to be executed on account of her contempt for paganism. The wheel, her usual attribute in art, was not the instrument of her martyrdom, as it was miraculously destroyed. She met her death by being beheaded, and, immediately thereafter, her body was carried by angels to Mount Sinai. These and other legendary incidents must have conduced to make the saint popular. St. Catherine's Balm-well, at Liberton, Mid-Lothian, had a high reputation for curing skin-disease. Martin speaks of a well to St. Catherine on the south coast of Eigg, reckoned by the islanders a specific in all kinds of disease. He gives the following account of its dedication by Father Hugh, a priest, and of the respect paid to the spring in consequence:—" He (the priest) obliged all the inhabitants to come to this well, and then employed them to bring together a great heap of stones at the head of the spring by way of penance. This being done, he said Mass at the well, and then consecrated it; he gave each of the inhabitants a piece of wax candle, which they lighted, and all of them made the Dessil,—of going round the well sun-ways, the priest leading them; and from that time it was accounted unlawful to boil any meat with the water of this well." In the south-west of Scotland, Catherine has, or had, three wells, viz., at Stoneykirk, at Low Drumore, and at Old Luce, opposite the Abbey. In the north-east there are three, viz., at Fyvie, Aberdeenshire; and in Alvah parish, Banffshire; and at Banff itself. At Shotts, in Lanarkshire, the fountain by the roadside immediately below the parish church is, or at least was, locally known as Cat's or Kate's Well—a contraction of the Saint's name—reminding one of the Kate Kennedy celebration at St. Andrews University, which originated in connection with the gift of a bell by Bishop Kennedy in honour of the saint. The ruins of Caibeal Cairine, *i.e.*, Catherine's Chapel, are in Southend parish, Kintyre, and two farms called North and South Carine are in the immediate neighbourhood. Captain White, when exploring the district, sought for St. Catherine's Well in the adjoining glen, but failed to find it. A chapel to the saint once stood in the *quondam* town of

Kincardine in the Mearns. Its graveyard alone
remains. St. Catherine's Fair, held at Kincardine till
the year 1612, was then transferred to the neighbouring Fettercairn. There is perhaps no place-name
more familiar to visitors to Inveraray than St.
Catherine's, on the opposite shore of Loch Fyne.
It was in St. Catherine's Aisle, within the parish
church of Linlithgow, that James IV. saw the
mysterious apparation that warned him to beware of
Flodden. At Port-Erin, in the Isle of Man, is a
spring close to the beach, and on a stone beside it
in old lettering, can be read the piece of advice:—

> "St. Catherine's Well,
> Keep me clean."

Lawrence is represented by various springs, viz., by
one in Kirkcudbrightshire, at Fairgirth; by one in
Elginshire, at New Duffus; and by two in Aberdeenshire, at Kinnord; and at Rayne, where a horse
market, called Lawrence Fair, is still held annually in
August. Near the Fairgirth spring stand the ivy-clad
ruins of St. Lawrence's Chapel, at one time surrounded
by a graveyard. The parish of Slamannan, in
Stirlingshire, was anciently called St. Lawrence, its
pre-Reformation church having been dedicated to
him. An excellent spring, not far from the parish
church, is known as St. Lawrence's Well. There is
reason to believe that all these dedications relate to
Lawrence, who, about the middle of the third century,
suffered at Rome, by being broiled over a slow fire,
and in whose honour the Escurial in Spain was built

in the form of a gridiron—the supposed instrument of
his martyrdom. Laurencekirk, in Kincardineshire,
anciently called Conveth, received its name, not from
the martyr, but from Lawrence, archbishop of
Canterbury, successor of Augustine, early in the
seventh century. He is said to have visited the
Mearns. The church of Conveth was named in his
honour Laurencekirk. As far as we know, however,
there is no spring to him in the district.

Margaret, queen and saint, wife of Malcolm Canmore, was a light amid the darkness of the eleventh
century. Indeed she was a light to many later
centuries. The secret of her beneficial influence lay
in her personal character, and she undoubtedly did
much to recommend civilisation to a barbarous age.
At the same time it must not be forgotten that
through her English training she was unable to
appreciate either the speech or the special religious
institutions of her Scottish subjects, and that, accordingly, the changes introduced by her were not all
reforms. When sketching her influence on the history of her time, the Rev. Dr. M'Lauchlan, in his
"*Early Scottish Church*," observes, "She was somewhat unwillingly hindered from entering a monastery
by her marriage with Malcolm, and the latter repaid
the obligation by unbounded devotion to her and
readiness to fall in with all her schemes. She was
brought up in the Anglo-Saxon Church, as that
Church was moulded by Augustine and other emis-
saries of Rome, and was in consequence naturally

F

opposed to many of the peculiarities of the Scottish Church, which was still without diocesan bishops, and had many things in its forms of worship peculiar to itself." Dunfermline was Malcolm's favourite place of residence, and many were the journeys made by his wife between it and Edinburgh. The names of North and South Queensferry, where she crossed the Forth, tell of these royal expeditions. Malcolm and Margaret were associated with the town of Forfar. Local topography has still its King's Muir, and its Queen's Well to testify to the fact; and on the Inch of Forfar Loch, where Margaret had a residence, an annual celebration was long held in her honour. She had a spring at Edinburgh Castle, described as " the fountain which rises near the corner of the King's Garden, on the road leading to St. Cuthbert's Church." St. Margaret's Well—once at Restalrig, now in the Queen's Park—has already been referred to. At Dunfermline there is a spring in a cave where, according to tradition, she spent many an hour in pious meditation. The cave is about seven feet in height, fully eight in breadth, and varies in depth from eight to eleven. . "This cave," remarks the Rev. Peter Chalmers in his " *History of Dunfermline*," "is situated at a short distance north from the Tower Hill, and from the mound crossing the ravine on which part of the town stands. There is at present a small spring well at the bottom, the water of which rises at times and covers the whole lower space; but anciently, it is to be presumed, there was none, or at

least it must have been covered, and prevented from
overflowing the floor, which would either have been
formed of the rock or have been paved." A considerable amount of rubbish accumulated in the cave,
but this was removed in 1877. "During the process
of clearing out the cave," remarks Dr. Henderson in
his "*Annals of Dunfermline*," "two stone seats or
benches were discovered along the base of the north
and south sides, but there were no carvings or devices
seen on them. Near the back of the cave a small
sunk well was found, but it is now covered over with
a stone flag."

Several Scripture characters have wells named after
them. St. Matthew has springs at Kirkton, Dumfriesshire, and at Roslin, Midlothian. St. Andrew's name
is attached to wells at Sandal, in Kintyre; at North
Berwick, in East Lothian; at Shadar, in Lewis; and
at Selkirk—this last having been uncovered in 1892,
after remaining closed, it is believed, for fully three
hundred years. A spring at St. Andrews, called Holy
Well, is understood to have been dedicated either to
Andrew or to Regulus. St. Paul has springs at Fyvie
and at Linlithgow; St. Philip is patron of one in
Yarrow parish, Selkirkshire; St. James has one at Gar-
vock, in Aberdeenshire; St. Thomas has three—at Loch-
maben, Dumfriesshire; at Crieff, in Perthshire; and
near Stirling; and St. John has a considerable number
of springs. Some of these are to the Evangelist, and
some to the Baptist. It is often difficult to know
to which of the two the patronage of a given well

should be ascribed. Of the four chapels along the east wall of the *lower church* of Glasgow Cathedral, the one next to St. Mungo's Well was dedicated in pre-Reformation times to St. John the Evangelist. It would have been more appropriately dedicated to the Baptist. St. John's Wells are to be found at Moffat, in Dumfriesshire; at Logie Coldstone, in Aberdeenshire; near Fochabers, in Elginshire; at Inverkeithing, Balmerino; and Falkland, in Fife; at Kinnethmont, and in New Aberdour, in Aberdeenshire; at Marykirk, in Kincardineshire; at Kirkton of Deskford, at Ordiquhill, and also near the old church of Gamrie, in Banffshire; at Stranraer, in Wigtownshire; at Dunrobin, in Sutherland; and elsewhere. There are more than a dozen wells to St. Peter. These are to be found mainly in counties in the south-west, and in the north-east. In the latter district there is a well at Marnoch, in Banffshire, called Petrie's Well.

St Anne, the reputed mother of the Virgin, presided over wells at Ladykirk, in Berwickshire; near the old church of St. Anne, in Dowally parish, Perthshire; and at Glass, on the Deveron. The Virgin herself was specially popular as the patroness of fountains. There are *over seventy* dedicated to her under a variety of names, such as, St. Mary's Well, Maria Well, &c. The town of Motherwell, in Lanarkshire, was so called after a famous well to the Virgin. Tobermory, in Mull—literally, Well of Mary—was originally a fountain. A village was built beside it, in 1788, as a

fishing centre for the British Fisheries' Company. A
curious legend about the now ivy-clad ruins of the
church of St. Mary in Auchindoir parish, Aberdeenshire, is thus referred to by Mr. A. Jervise in the
"*Proceedings of the Society of Antiquaries of Scotland,*"
vol. viii. (old series):—"According to tradition, it
was originally proposed to rebuild the church at a
place called Kirkcairns (now Glencairns) to the
south of Lumsden village, and but for the warning
voice of the Virgin, who appears to have been a good
judge both of locality and soil, the kirk would have
been placed in an obscure sterile district. Besides
being in the neighbourhood of good land, fine views
of the upper part of Strathbogie and of the surrounding hills are obtained from the present site. . . .
St. Mary's Well is about a hundred yards to the
west."

If Michael the Archangel did not fold his wings
over any Scottish wells, he at least gave name to
several. There is a St. Michael's Spring in Kirkmichael parish, Banffshire, and another at Dallas in
Elginshire. In both cases, the ancient church was
dedicated to him. Culsalmond, in Aberdeenshire, and
Applegarth, in Dumfriesshire, have, and Edinburgh
once had, a St. Michael's Well. The best known is
probably the one at Linlithgow, with its quaint
inscription—"Saint Michael is kinde to straingers."
Mr. J. R. Walker—to whose list of Holy Wells in the
"*Proceedings of the Society of Antiquaries of Scotland,*"
vol. v. (new series), we have been indebted for various

useful hints—remarks, "The building covering this
well dates only from 1720. . . . It is conjectured
that the statue was taken from the Cross-well when
restored about that date and placed here to represent
St. Michael, who is the patron saint of Linlithgow
Church. . . . With the exception of the statue,
which is undoubtedly of much earlier date than 1720,
the structure shows the utter absence of architectural
knowledge—especially Gothic—characteristic of the
last century in Scotland. Michael was tutelar saint,
not only of the church, but also of the burgh of
Linlithgow. In the town Arms he is represented
with outspread wings, standing on a serpent whose
head he is piercing with a spear. He was also the
guardian of the burgh of Dumfries. At Inverlussa,
in North Knapdale parish, Argyllshire, may be seen
the ancient chapel and burying-ground of Kilmichael.
A well in the immediate neighbourhood is dedicated, not
to the archangel, but to some local ecclesiastic, whose
name is now forgotten. In reference to this spring,
Captain White says, "Trickling out from under a rock,
is the Priest's Well (Tobar-ant-Sagairt), famous, like
many another spring of so-called holy water, for its
miraculous healing virtues. I believe the country
people have by no means lost their faith in its
powers." The extent of the archangel's popularity
in Scotland is shown by his impress on topography.
Among place-names we find *at least three* Kilmichaels,
and there are *five* parishes called Kirkmichael,
respectively in the counties of Dumfries, Ayr, Perth,

Ross and Cromarty, and Banff. A chapel is said to have been dedicated to him at a very early date on the top of the Castle Rock at Edinburgh. Another once stood in the demesne of Lovat, where was founded, about 1232, a Priory for French monks, who were so struck with the beauty of the spot that they called it Beau-lieu, now Beauly. Far west, in the outer Hebrides, he had faithful votaries. On the island of Grimisay, close to North Uist, a chapel styled Team-pull Mhicheil was built in his honour towards the close of the fourteenth century. It was the work of Amie, otherwise Annie, wife of John of Isla, first Lord of the Isles, and was used by her as an oratory when prevented by rough weather from crossing the Minch to visit her friends in Lorne. That the archangel should have had wells named after him is therefore not surprising.

CHAPTER V.

STONE BLOCKS AND SAINTS' SPRINGS.

Stone Beds and Chairs — Cave Life — Dwarfie Stone — Stone Boats—Balthere—His Corpse—His Well and Cradle—Marnan —His Influence on Topography—His Head—St. Marnan's Chair and Well—Muchricha—Cathair Donan—St. Donan's Well—Patrick—His Wells—St. Patrick's Vat—Quarry at Portpatrick—Columbanus—Mark of his Hand—Kentigern's Chair and Bed—His connection with Aberdeenshire—The Lady's Bed — Thenew — Columba's Bed and Pillow—Holy Island — Traces of Molio — St. Blane's Chapel — Kilmun— Inan—St. Innian's Well—Tenant's Day—St. Inan's Chair and Springs—Kevin—Print of Virgin's Knee—Traces of Columba at Keil—St. Cuthbert's Stane—St. Madron's Bed—Mean-an-Tol—Morwenna—St. Fillan's Chair—St. Fillan's Spring— Water for Sore Eyes—The Two Fillans—Their Dedications— Queen Margaret's Seat—St. Bennet's Spring—The Fairies' Cradle — The Pot o' Pittenyoul — Church of Invergowrie — Greystane—Cadger's Bridge—Wallace's Seat and Well.

BEDS and Chairs of stone are connected with various early saints, and as such relics are often associated with holy wells, some notice of these may not be without interest. We have already seen that cave life was rather popular among these early missionaries. Anything of a rocky nature was therefore quite in line with their ascetic ways. Hoy, one of the Orkney Islands, famous for its wild scenery, and specially for the pillar of rock popularly

styled The Old Man, contains a curious monument
of antiquity in the shape of a large block of sandstone called The Dwarfie Stone, hollowed out long
ago by some unknown hand. The chamber, thus
excavated, contains two beds hewn out of the stone,
one of them having a pillow of the same hard
material. On the floor of the chamber is a hearth
where a fire had evidently burned, and in the roof
is a hole for the escape of the smoke. Legend
reports that a giant and his wife abode within;
but the hollow space was more probably the retreat
of some hermit—perhaps, of more than one, seeing
there are two couches; though, possibly, one of the
supposed couches may have been a table and the
other a bed. Perhaps the anchorite had his spring
whither he wandered daily to slake his thirst; but,
as far as we know, there is no tradition regarding
any holy well in the neighbourhood.

Martin, in connection with his visit to Orkney,
refers to a stone in the chapel of Ladykirk, in South
Ronaldshay, called St. Magnus's Boat. The stone
was four feet in length, and tapered away at both
ends; but its special feature was the print of two
human feet on the upper surface. A local tradition
affirmed that when St. Magnus wanted on one
occasion to cross the Pentland Firth to Caithness he
used this stone as his boat, and that he afterwards
carried it to Ladykirk. According to another tradition, the stone served in pre-Reformation times for
the punishment of delinquents, who were obliged to

stand barefooted upon it by way of penance. There
is a St. Magnus's Well, not in South Ronaldshay,
however, but at Birsay, in the mainland of Orkney.
When Conval crossed from Ireland to Scotland, in
the seventh century, he, too, made a block of stone
do duty as a boat. It found a resting-place beside
the river Cart, near Renfrew, and was known as
Currus Sancti Convalli. By its means miraculous
cures were wrought on man and beast. A rock
at the mouth of Aldham Bay, in Haddingtonshire,
is known as St. Baudron's Boat, and tradition
says that he crossed on it from the Bass, where
he had a cell. This saint—called also Balthere
and Baldred—founded the monastery of Tyningham,
and died early in the seventh century. He must
have been popular in the district, for, if we can
believe an old legend, the parishioners of the
churches of Aldham, Tyningham, and Prestonkirk
tried to get possession of his relics. To satisfy
their demands his body was miraculously multiplied
by three, and each church was thus provided with
one. Near Tantallon Castle is St. Baldred's Well,
and a fissure in the cliff at Whitberry, not far
from the mouth of the Tyne, is known as St.
Baldred's Bed or Cradle.

Marnan or Marnoch, besides giving name to the
town of Kilmarnock, in Ayrshire, and to the Island
of Inchmarnoch, off Bute, is remembered in the
name of the Banffshire parish of Marnoch, where
he laboured as a missionary in the seventh century.

His head was kept as a revered relic in the church
of Aberchirder, and solemn oaths were sworn by it.
Use was also made of it for therapeutic purposes.
It was periodically washed, and the water was given
to the sick for the restoration of their health. This
was not an isolated case.   Bede tells us, that after
Cuthbert's death, some of the water in which his
body was washed, was given to an epileptic boy
along with some consecrated earth, and brought
about a cure. A stone, called St. Marnan's Chair,
is, or was till lately, to be seen at Aberchirder;
and a spring, near the parish manse, bears the
saint's name. About a mile and a half from the
church of Aboyne, in Aberdeenshire, is St. Muchricha's
Well, and beside it is a stone marked with a
cross.   At one time, this stone was removed.
According to a local tradition, it was brought back
by Muchricha, the guardian of the well, who
seemed unwilling to lose sight of the lost property.
In the parish of Kildonan, Sutherland, two or three
blocks of stone, placed in the form of a seat, went by
the name of Cathair Donan, i.e., Donan's Chair.   In
his *cille* or church, Donan taught the truths of Christianity; and, seated in his *cathair*, he administered
justice to the people of the district. There is a St.
Donan's Well in Eigg, the island where the saint and
his companion clerics were murdered by the natives
early in the seventh century.

Patrick, the well-known missionary of Ireland,
was reverenced also in Scotland.   There is a well

dedicated to him in the parish of Muthill, Perthshire, and close to it once stood a chapel, believed
to have borne his name. From the article on
Muthill parish, in the "*New Statistical Account of
Scotland*," we learn that in former times the inhabitants of the district held the saint's memory "in such
veneration that, on his day, neither the clap of the
mill was heard nor the plough seen to move in the
furrow." There is a well dedicated to him in Dalziel
parish, Lanarkshire. About sixty yards from St.
Patrick's temple, in the island of Tyree, is a rock,
with a hollow on the top, two feet across and four feet
deep, known to the islanders as St. Patrick's Vat. At
any rate it was so named at the end of last century.
In a quarry at Portpatrick, Wigtownshire, used in
connection with the harbour works, once flowed a
spring dedicated to the saint. On the rock below were
formerly to be seen certain marks, said, by tradition,
to be the impression made by his knees and left hand.

Columban or Columbanus, belonged, like Columba,
to the sixth century. Ireland was also his native
land. When he left it he travelled, not north like
Columba, but south, and sought the sunny lands of
France and Italy. In the latter country he founded the
monastery of Bobbio among the Apennines. A writer·
in the "*Antiquary*" for 1891 remarks, in connection
with a recent visit to this monastery, " I was taken to
see a rock on the summit of a mountain called La
Spanna, near the cave to which the saint is said to
have retired for prayer and meditation. The im-

pression of the saint's left hand is still shown upon
the face of this rock. The healing power of the
patron's hand is believed by the peasantry of the
surrounding country to linger still in the hollow
marking, and many sufferers, climbing to this spot, have
found relief from laying their hand within its palm."

In addition to his well beside the Molendinar, at
Glasgow, Kentigern had a chair and bed, both of
stone. Concerning the latter, Bishop Forbes, in his
"*Kalendars of Scottish Saints,*" says, "Kentigern's
couch was rather a sepulchre than a bed, and was of
rock, with a stone for a pillow, like Jacob. . He rose
in the night and sang psalms and hymns till the
second cock-crowing. Then he rushed into the cold
stream, and with eyes fixed on heaven he recited the
whole psalter. Then, coming out of the water he
dried his limbs on a stone on the mountain called
Galath, and went forth for his day's work." Kentigern's work took him beyond the limits of Strathclyde.
He seems to have visited the uplands of Aberdeenshire. The church of Glengairn, a parish now incor-
porated with Tullich and Glenmuick, was probably
founded by him. At any rate, it was dedicated to him.
A tradition of his untiring zeal survived in Aberdeenshire down to the beginning of last century. According
to a proverb then current, systematic beneficence was
said to be "like St. Mungo's work, which was never
done." The Isle of May, in the Firth of Forth, has,
on one of its rocky sides, a small cave called The
Lady's Bed, containing a pool in its floor. As Mr. Muir

points out in his "*Ecclesiological Notes,*" it is traditionally associated with Thenew, Kentigern's mother,
"who," according to the legend, "after being cast
into the sea at Aberlady, was miraculously floated to
the May, and thence, in the same manner, to Culross,
where she was stranded and gave birth to the saint."
Columba, when in Iona, had a stone slab as a bed,
and a block of stone as a pillow. Adamnan mentions
that, after the saint's death, this pillow stone was
placed as a monument over his grave.

Guarding Lamlash Bay, where Haco gathered his
shattered fleet after the battle of Largs, in 1263, is
Holy Island, known to the Norsemen as Melansay.
In this island is a cave, at one time inhabited by the
hermit Molio, and below it, near the beach, is his
Holy Well, for centuries reckoned efficacious in the
cure of disease. A large block of sandstone, flat on
the top, with a series of recesses like seats cut
round its margin, constitutes the saint's chair and
table combined. Molio was educated in Bute by his
uncle Blane, to whom the now ruined St. Blane's Chapel
was dedicated. He afterwards went to Ireland, and
was placed under Munna, who is still remembered in the
name of Kilmun, on Holy Loch, in the Firth of Clyde.

Inan, probably the same as Finan, gave name to
Inchinnan, in Renfrewshire, though the ancient church
of the parish was dedicated, not to him, but to
Conval. The church at Lamington, in Lanarkshire,
was dedicated to Inan. St. Innian's Well is in the
parish. He is the patron saint of Beith, in Ayrshire.

The annual fair held there in August is popularly called Tenant's Day—Tenant being a corruption of St. Inan. St. Inan's Well and St. Inan's Chair keep his memory fresh in the district. Some particulars about them are given by Mr. Robert Love in the "*Proceedings of the Society of Antiquaries of Scotland*, vol. xi.:—" This chair is in the rocky hill-face at the west end of the Cuff hills, and from its elevated position a wide tract of country from south to north is overlooked. At the base of the hill, and distant from the chair some hundred yards, is a well called St. Inan's Well, a double spring, which issues from the rock at two points close by each other, and which is almost unapproachable in respect of its abundance and purity. This chair is formed in part, possibly by nature, out of the rock of the hill. Its back and two sides are closed in, while, in front, to the west, it is open. The seat proper is above the ground in front about two feet two inches, is two feet four inches in breadth, and one foot four inches in depth backwards." Visitors to the seven churches at Glendalough, in county Wicklow, Ireland, are usually shown St. Kevin's Seat on a block of rock. As a proof of its genuineness the mark made by the saint's leg and the impression of his fingers are duly pointed out by the local guide.

In Kirkmaiden parish, Wigtownshire, the print of the Virgin's knee was at one time shown on a stone where she knelt in prayer. There was a chapel dedicated to her in the neighbourhood.

In Southend parish, Kintyre, are the remains of St. Columba's Chapel, standing in the ancient burying-ground of Keil. In his " *Ecclesiological Notes* " Mr. Muir observes, " Under an overhanging rock, close by on the roadside, is St. Columba's Well, and on the top of a hillock, overlooking the west end of the burial ground there is a flat rock bearing on its top the impress of two feet, made, it seems, by those of the saint whilst he stood marking out and hallowing the spot on which his chapel should rest." In Bromfield parish, Cumberland, is a piece of granite rock called St. Cuthbert's Stane, and near it is a copious spring of remarkably pure water. Brand, in his "*Popular Antiquities*," says that "this spring, probably from its having been anciently dedicated to the same St. Cuthbert, is called Helly Well, *i.e.*, Haly or Holy Well."

Mr. R. C. Hope, in his "*Holy Wells*," refers to a block of stone near St. Madron's Spring, in Cornwall, locally known as St. Madron's Bed. We are told that "on it impotent folk reclined when they came to try the cold water cure." In the same parish is a pre-historic relic in the form of a granite block with a hole in the centre of it. It is known in Cornish as Mean-an-Tol, *i.e.*, the Stone of the Hole. Its name in English is The Creeping Stone. Sickly children were at one time passed through the hole a certain number of times, in the belief that a cure would follow. This superstitious custom recalls what was at one time done beside St. Paul's Well, in the parish of Fyvie, Aberdeenshire. Close to the well were the ruins of an old church. One of its stones was supported on other two with a space below. It went by the name of The Shargar Stone—shargar signifying a weakly child. The stone, in this instance, got its name from the custom in the district of mothers passing their ailing children through the space below the stone, in the belief that whatever hindered their growth would thereby be removed. Mr. Hope recounts a tradition concerning Morwenstowe, in Devon, and its patron saint, Morwenna, to the effect that when the parishioners wished to build a church, Morwenna brought a large stone from the foot of the cliff to form the font. Feeling fatigued by the climb she laid down the stone to rest herself, and from the spot a spring gushed forth.

On the top of green Dunfillan, in the parish of Comrie, is a rocky seat known in the district as Fillan's Chair. Here, according to tradition, the saint sat and gave his blessing to the country around. Towards the end of last century, and doubtless even later, this chair was associated with a superstitious remedy for rheumatism in the back. The person to be cured sat in the chair, and then, lying on his back, was dragged down the hill by the legs. The influence of the saint lingering about the spot was believed to insure recovery. St. Fillan's Spring, at the hillfoot, has already been referred to, in connection with its mysterious change of site. It was much frequented at one time by old and young, especially on

G

1st May and 1st August. The health seekers walked
or were carried thrice round the spring from east to
west, following the course of the sun. The next part
of the ritual consisted in the use of the water for
drinking and washing, in throwing a white stone on
the saint's cairn, near the spring, and in leaving a
rag as an offering before departing. In 1791 not
fewer than seventy persons visited the spot at the
dates mentioned. The writer of the article on
Comrie in the "*Old Statistical Account of Scotland*" supplies these particulars, and adds, "At
the foot of the hill there is a basin made by the
saint on the top of a large stone, which seldom wants
water, even in the greatest drought, and all who are
distressed with sore eyes must wash them three times
with this water." Fillan, to whom Comrie parish is
thus so much indebted, flourished about the sixth
century, and must not be confounded with the other
missionary of the same name, who dwelt more than a
century later, in the straths of the Fillan and the
Dochart, between Tyndrum and Killin. Concerning
the former, Dr. Skene writes in his "*Celtic Scotland*":
"Fillan, called Anlobar or 'the leper,' whose day
is 20th June, is said in the Irish calendar to have
been of *Rath Erenn in Alban*, or the fort of the
Earn in Scotland, and St. Fillans, at the east end of
Loch Earn, takes its name from him; while the
church of Aberdour, on the northern shore of the
Firth of Forth, is also dedicated to him." The other
Fillan had his Chapel and Holy Pool halfway between

Tyndrum and Crianlarich.   He is also connected with
Fife.   At Pittenweem, in that county, his cave is to
be seen, and in it is his holy well, supplied with
water from crevices in the rock.   At the mill of
Killin, in Perthshire, once stood a block of stone,
known as St. Fillan's Chair.   Close to the spot flows
the Dochart, and some person or persons, whose
muscles were stronger than their antiquarian in-
stincts, sought not unsuccessfully to throw the relic
into the river.   The Renfrewshire parish of Killallan,
united in 1760 to that of Houston, got its name from
Fillan.   Its ancient church, now ruined, was dedicated to him.   Near the ruins, are a stone with a
hollow in it and a spring, called respectively St.
Fillan's Seat and St. Fillan's Well.

About two miles and a half to the south-east of
Dunfermline, is a block of stone, believed to be the
last remnant of a group of pre-historic Standing
Stones.   According to tradition, it was used by
Queen Margaret, as a seat where she rested, when
on her way to and from the ferry over the Forth.
A farm in the immediate neighbourhood is called St.
Margaret's Stone Farm, after the block in question.
In his "*Annals of Dunfermline*" Dr. Henderson says,
" In 1856 this stone was removed to an adjacent site,
by order of the road surveyor, in order to widen the
road which required no widening, as no additional
traffic was likely to ensue, but the reverse ; it is
therefore much to be regretted that the old landmark
was removed.   It is in contemplation to have the

old stone replaced on its old site (as nearly as
possible) and made to rest, with secure fixings,
on a massive base or plinth stone." Not far
from the town of Cromarty is St. Bennet's Spring,
beside the ruins of St. Bennet's Chapel. Close
to the spot once stood a stone trough, termed The
Fairies' Cradle. Hugh Miller, in his *Scenes and
Legends of the North of Scotland*," says that this
trough was "famous for virtues derived from the
saint, like those of the well. For, if a child was
carried away by the fairies and some mischievous
imp left in its place, the parents had only to lay
the changeling in this trough, and, by some invisible
process, their child would be immediately restored to
them. The Fairies' Cradle came to a sudden end
about the year 1745. It was then broken to pieces
by the parish minister, with the assistance of two of
his elders, that it might no longer serve the purposes
of superstition."

The following, from the Rev. Dr. Gregor's "*Folklore
of the North-East of Scotland*," has certainly nothing
to do with a saint, but in other respects, has
a bearing on the subject in hand :—"The Pot o'
Pittenyoul is a small but romantic rock-pool in a
little stream called the 'Burn o' the Riggins,' which
flows past the village of Newmills of Keith. On the
edge of the pool are some hollows worn away by
the water and the small stones and sand carried
down by the stream. These hollows to a lively
imagination have the shape of a seat, and the story

is, that the devil, at some far-back time, sat down
on the edge of the pool and left his mark." Probably
at an equally distant date, the devil made his
presence felt, further south, though in a different
way. He had great objections to a church built at
Invergowrie, in Perthshire, and, in order to knock
it down, hurled a huge boulder across the Tay from
the opposite coast of Fife. We are not aware that
the stone struck the church. At any rate it can be
seen in the grounds of Greystane, a property to
which, according to local tradition, it gave name.
Sir William Wallace, though never canonized, had
certainly more of the saint about him than the last-
mentioned personage. We find various traditions
concerning him in the Upper Ward of Lanarkshire.
His connection with Lanark is well known. At
Biggar, he is said, by Blind Harry, to have defeated
the English, who greatly outnumbered his forces.
This battle took place on Biggar Moss. A few days
before the fight, he entered the enemy's camp, dis-
guised as a cadger or pedlar, to discover the
strength of the English army. Being pursued, he
turned on his assailants while crossing a bridge over
Biggar Water, a little to the west of the town. A
foot-bridge there still goes by the name of The
Cadger's Bridge. A rock with a hollow in it, lying
to the north of Vizzyberry, is locally styled Wallace's
Seat, and a spring near the spot is still known as
Wallace's Well.

CHAPTER VI.

HEALING AND HOLY WELLS.

HEALING and holy have an etymological kinship. The one is commonly associated with matters relating to the body, and the other with those relating to the soul. If the body is healed, it is said to be whole and its owner hale; and if the soul is healed, it is said to be holy. All these words have one idea in common, and hence we need not wonder that healing wells were, as a rule, reckoned holy wells, and *vice versa*. When speaking of the virtues of such wells, Mrs. Stone, in her "*God's Acre*," puts the point exactly, if somewhat quaintly, when she says, "Before chemistry was born, when medical science was little known, these medical virtues, so plainly and indis-

putably ostensible, were attributed to the beneficence
of the saint or angel to whom the spring had been
dedicated." Many still go to Moffat, Bridge-of-Allan,
and Strathpeffer to drink the waters, but probably,
none of those health-seekers now rely on magic for
a cure. It was quite otherwise in former times.
Cures wrought at Lourdes are still believed, by many,
to be due to the blessing of the water by the
Virgin Mary.

Not far from the highway between Ayr and
Prestwick once stood a lazar-house called King's
Ease or King's Case, known in the sixteenth
century as Kilcaiss. Its ruins were to be seen till
well on in the present century. According to
tradition, the hospital was founded for lepers by
King Robert Bruce, who was himself afflicted with
a disease believed to be leprosy. This was done as
a thank-offering, for benefit received from the water
of a neighbouring well. The spring was doubtless
sacred to some saint, probably to Ninian, to whom
the hospital was dedicated, and we can safely infer
that the patron got the credit of the cure. To
maintain the lepers the king gifted various lands
to the hospital, among others, those of Robertlone, in
Dundonald parish, and of Sheles and Spital-Sheles,
in Kyle Stewart. The right of presentation to the
hospital was vested in the family of Wallace of
Craigie. At a later date the lands belonging to the
charity passed into other hands. In the third
volume of his "*Caledonia,*" published in 1824,

Chalmers remarks, "The only revenue that remained
to it was the feu-duties payable from the lands
granted in fee-firm, and these, amounting to 64
bolls of meal and 8 marks Scots of money, with
16 threaves of straw for thatching the hospital, are
still paid. For more than two centuries past the
diminished revenue has been shared among eight
objects of charity in equal shares of 8 bolls of
meal and 1 mark Scots to each. The leprosy
having long disappeared, the persons who are now
admitted to the benefit of this charity are such
as labour under diseases which are considered as
incurable, or such as are in indigent circumstances."
In the time of Charles I., the persons enjoying
the benefit of the charity lived in huts or cottages
in the vicinity of the chapel. In 1787 the right
of presentation was bought from the Wallaces by
the burgh of Ayr, and the poorhouse there is thus
the lineal descendant of King Robert's hospital.
Mr. R. C. Hope, in his "*Holy Wells*," alludes to
the interesting fact that Bruce had a free pass from
the English king to visit Muswell, near London,
close to the site of the Alexandra Palace. This
well, dedicated to St. Lazarus, at one time belonged
to the hospital order of St. John's, Clerkenwell,
and was resorted to in cases of leprosy. Bruce's
foundation at Ayr recalls another at Stony Middleton,
in Derbyshire. The latter, however, was a chapel,
and not a hospital. Tradition says that a crusader,
belonging to the district, was cured of leprosy by

means of the mineral water there, and that in gratitude he built a chapel and dedicated it to his patron saint, Martin.

In glancing at the history of holy wells, it is not difficult to understand why certain springs were endowed with mysterious properties. When there were no chemists to analyse mineral springs, anyone tasting the water would naturally enough think that there was something strange about it, a notion that would not vanish with the first draught. The wonder, too, would grow if the water was found to put fresh vigour into wearied frames. Alum wells, like the one in Carnwath parish, Lanarkshire, would, through their astringent qualities, arrest attention. A well at Halkirk, Caithness, must have been a cause of wonder, if we judge by the description given of it in the "*Old Statistical Account of Scotland*," where we read, that "on its surface lies always a thin beautiful kind of substance, that varies like the plumage of the peacock displayed in all its glory to the rays of the sun."

The petrifying power of certain springs would also tend to bring them into notice. There is a famous well of this kind near Tarras Water, in Canonbie parish, Dumfriesshire. In Kirkmaiden parish, Wigtownshire, is a dropping cave, known as Peter's Paps. In former times it was resorted to by persons suffering from whooping-cough. The treatment consisted in standing with upturned face below the drop, and allowing it to fall into the open mouth. For more than two centuries and a half, the mineral waters of Peterhead have been famous for both internal and external use, though their fame is not now so great as formerly. Towards the end of the seventeenth century, they were spoken of as one of the six wonders of Buchan. The principal well is situated to the south of the town, and is popularly called the Wine Well. Its water is strongly impregnated with carbonic acid, muriate of iron, muriate of lime, and muriate of soda. The chalybeate spring in the Moss of Melshach, in Kennethmont parish, had at one time a considerable local reputation for the cure of man and beast. Clothes of the former and harness of the latter were left beside the well. Visits were paid to it in the month of May. Another Aberdeenshire health - resort formerly attracted many visitors, viz., Pannanich, near Ballater, with its four chalybeate springs. These are said to have been accidentally discovered, about the middle of last century, but were then probably only rediscovered. They were at first found beneficial in the case of scrofula, and were afterwards deemed infallible in all diseases. In his "*Antiquities and Scenery of the North of Scotland*," Cordiner, under date 1776, writes: "In coming down these hilly regions, stopped the first night at ' Pananach-lodge :' an extensive building opposite to the strange rocks and pass of Bolliter. There, a mineral well and baths, whose virtues have been often experienced, are become much frequented by the infirm. The lodge, containing a number of bed-chambers, and a spacious public room, is fitted up for the accommodation of those who come to take the benefit of the waters. Goat whey is also there obtained in the greatest perfection." Almost a century later, another visitor to the spot, viz., Queen Victoria, thus writes, in her "*More Leaves from the Journal of a Life in the Highlands*": "I had driven with Beatrice to Pannanich wells, where I had been many years ago. Unfortunately, almost all the trees which covered the hills have been cut down. We got out and tasted the water, which is strongly impregnated with iron, and looked at the bath and at the humble, but very clean, accommodation in the curious little old inn, which used to be very much frequented." The Well of Spa, at Aberdeen, was more famous in former times than it is now. There are two springs, both of them chalybeate. The amount of iron in the water, however, diminished very considerably more than fifty years ago—a change due to certain digging operations in the neighbourhood. The present structure connected with the well was renovated in 1851. It was built in 1670 to replace an earlier one, repaired by George Jamieson, the artist, but soon afterwards completely demolished by the overflowing of the adjoining Denburn. The present building, according to Mr. A. Jervise, in the fourth volume of the "*Proceedings of the Society of Antiquaries of Scotland*," "bears representations of the Scottish Thistle, the Rose of England, and the

Fleur-de-lis of France, surmounting this inscription:—

> ' As heaven gives me
>   So give I thee.'

Below these words is a carving of the rising sun, and the following altered quotation from Horace :—

> ' Hoc fonte derivata Salus
>   In patriam populumque fluat.'

" It appears," continues Mr. Jervise, " that the virtues of this Spa were early known and appreciated, for in 1615 record says that there was 'a long wyde stone which conveyed the waters from the spring, with the portraicture of six Apostles hewen upon either side thereof.' It is described as having then been 'verie old and worne.'"

An unusual kind of holy well, viz., one, in which salt water takes the place of fresh, is to be found in the case of the Chapel Wells in Kirkmaiden parish, Wigtownshire, half way between the bays of Portan-kill and East Tarbet. About thirty yards to the north-west are the ruins of St. Medan's Chapel, partly artificial and partly natural, a cave forming the inner portion. In days gone by, the spot was much frequented on the first Sunday of May (O.S.), called Co' Sunday, after this cave or cove. Dr. Robert Trotter, who examined the chapel and the wells in 1870, gives the results of the observations in the eighth volume of the " *Proceedings of the Society of Antiquaries of Scotland*" (new series). He says, "These wells—three natural cavities in a mass of

porphyritic trap—are within the tide mark, and are
filled by the sea at high water of ordinary tides.
The largest is circular, five feet in diameter at the
top, and four feet at one side, shelving down to five
feet at the other, and is wider inside than at the top,
something like a kailpot in fact, and it is so close to
the edge of the rock that at one place its side is not
two inches thick. The other wells almost touch it,
and are about one foot six inches wide and deep
respectively." Sickly children were brought to be
bathed, the time selected being just before sunrise.
Dr. Trotter mentions that children are still brought
occasionally, sometimes from long distances. The
ceremony described to him by an eyewitness was
as follows:—"The child was stripped naked, and
taken by the spaul—that is, by one of the legs—
and plunged headforemost into the big well till
completely submerged; it was then pulled out, and
the part held on by was dipped in the middle well,
and then the whole body was finished by washing
the eyes in the smallest one, altogether very like
the Achilles and Styx business, only much more
thorough. An offering was then left in the old
chapel, on a projecting stone inside the cave behind
the west door, and the cure was complete."

Much uncertainty attaches to Medan or Medana,
the tutelar saint of the spot. One legend makes her
a contemporary of Ninian. According to another, she
lived about one hundred years later. Dr. Skene
thinks she is probably the same as Monenna, other-

wise Edana, who is said to have founded churches in
Galloway, and at Edinburgh, Stirling and Longforgan.
Kirkmaiden parish, at one time called Kirkmaiden *in
Ryndis*, is believed to be named after her, like the
other parish known as Kirkmaiden *in Farnes*, now
united to the parish of Glasserton.   An incident in
her history has a bearing on the present subject.
According to the Aberdeen Breviary, she fled from
her home in Ireland to escape from the importunities
of a certain noble knight who sought to marry her.
Accompanied by two handmaidens, she crossed to
Galloway and took up her abode in the Rhinns.
The knight followed her.   When Medana saw him
she placed herself along with her maidens on a rock
in the sea.   By a miracle, this rock became a boat, and
she was conveyed over the water to Farnes.   Again
the knight appeared.   This time Medana sought
refuge among the branches of a tree, and, from this
coign of vantage, asked her lover what it was that
made him pursue her so persistently.   " Your face
and eyes," replied the knight.   Thereupon Medana
plucked out her eyes and threw them down at the
feet of her lover, who was so filled with grief and
penitence that he immediately departed.   On the
spot where her eyes fell a spring of water gushed
forth, and in it Medana washed her face, doubtless
thereby restoring her sight.   There is much to favour
the view taken by Dr. Trotter: that " possibly the
well was the original institution; the cave a shelter
or dwelling for the genius who discovered the

miraculous virtues of the water, and his successors;
and the chapel a later edition for the benefit of the
clergy, who supplanted the old religion by grafting
Christianity upon it, St. Medana being a still later
institution."

St. Catherine's Balm Well, at Liberton, near Edinburgh, is still considered beneficial in the treatment of
cutaneous affections. The spring is situated on a
small estate, called after it, St. Catherine's. Peter
Swave, who visited Scotland in 1535, on a political
mission, mentions that near Edinburgh there was a
spot in a monastery where oil flowed out of the ground.
This was his way of describing the Balm Well.
Bitumenous particles, produced by decomposition of
coal in seams beneath, intermittently appear on the
surface of the water. This curious phenomenon must
have attracted attention at a very early period, and
one can easily understand why the well was in
consequence regarded with superstitious reverence.
When speaking of this well, Brome, who visited
Scotland about 1700, observes, "It is of a marvellous
nature, for as the coal whereof it proceeds is very apt
quickly to kindle into a flame, so is the oil of a sudden
operation to heal all scabs and tumours that trouble
the outward skin; and the head and hands are speedily
healed by virtue of this oil, which retains a very sweet
smell." According to Boece, the fountain sprang from
a drop of oil, brought to Queen Margaret of Scotland,
from the tomb of St. Catherine on Mount Sinai. The
same writer mentions that Queen Margaret built a

chapel to St. Catherine, in the neighbourhood of the spring. In 1504 an offering was made by James IV. in this chapel, described as "Sanct Kathrine's of the oly, *i.e.*, oily well." The later history of the spring is thus referred to by Sir Daniel Wilson, in his "*Memorials of Edinburgh in the Olden Time*": "When James VI. returned to Scotland, in 1617, he visited the well, and commanded it to be enclosed with an ornamental building with a flight of steps to afford ready access to the healing waters; but this was demolished by the soldiers of Cromwell, and the well now remains enclosed with plain stone-work, as it was partially repaired at the Restoration." About three miles to the north of the well, once stood the Convent of St. Catherine of Sienna—a religious foundation which gave name to the part of Edinburgh still called "The Sciennes." What Sir Daniel Wilson describes as "an unpicturesque fragment of the ruins" served to the middle of the present century, and perhaps, even later, as a sheep-fold for the flocks pasturing in the adjoining meadow. Lord Cockburn, in his "*Memorials of His Time*," mentions that in his boyhood, about 1785, "a large portion of the building survived." Before the Reformation the nuns of this convent walked annually in solemn procession to the Balm Well. The saints to whom the convent and the spring were respectively dedicated were, of course, not identical, though bearing the same name. The coincidence of name, however, evidently led to these yearly visits. As it may be taken for granted that the two Catherines were on friendly terms, the pilgrimages doubtless proved a benefit to all who took part in them. At any rate, it is safe to assume that the health of the pilgrims would be the better, and not the worse, for their walk in the fresh country air.

In the valley below the Dean Bridge, Edinburgh, close to the Water of Leith, is the sulphur spring known as St. Bernard's Well—traditionally connected with Bernard the Abbot of Clairvaux. In his *"Journey through Scotland,"* about 1793, Heron remarks: "The citizens of Edinburgh repaired eagerly to distant watering-places, without inquiring whether they might find medicinal water at home. But within these few years, Lord Gardenstone became proprietor of St. Bernard's Well. His lordship's philanthropy and public spirit suggested to him the possibility of rendering its waters more useful to the public. He has, at a very considerable expense, built a handsome Grecian edifice over the spring, in which the waters are distributed by a proper person, and at a very trifling price. His lordship's endeavours have accomplished his purpose. The citizens of Edinburgh are now persuaded that these waters are salutary in various cases; and have, particularly, a singular tendency to give a good breakfasting appetite; in consequence of which, old and young, males and females, have, for these two or three last summers, crowded to pay their morning respects to Hygeia in the chapel which Lord Garden-

H

stone has erected to her." The last allusion is to
a statue of Hygeia placed within the building on
its erection, in 1789. The goddess of health, however,
eventually showed signs of decrepitude; and, about
a hundred years later, the original statue was replaced
by one in marble through the liberality of the late
Mr. William Nelson, who also restored the pump-room
and made the surroundings more attractive.

Coming next to consider the case of springs not
possessing medicinal qualities, in other words, such
as have no taste save that of clear and sparkling
water, we find here, too, many a trace of superstition.
Springs of this kind were probably *holy* wells first,
and then *healing* wells. We have already seen that,
in a large number of instances, fountains became
sacred through their connection with early saints.
It usually happened that the Christian missionary
took up his abode near some fountain, or river,
whence he could get a supply of water for his daily
needs. In later times the well or stream was endowed
with miraculous properties. Water was also used
for purposes of bodily discipline. It was a practice
among some of the early saints to stand immersed
in it while engaged in devotion. The colder the
water, the better was it for the purpose. Special
significance, too, was given to water through its
connection with baptism, particularly when the rite
was administered to persons who had only recently
emerged from heathenism.

At Burghead, in Elginshire, is an interesting

rock-cut basin supplied with water from a spring.
Burghead is known to have been the site of an
early Christian church, and Dr. James Macdonald
believes that the basin in question was anciently
used as a baptistery. All trace of it, and well-nigh
all memory of it, had vanished till the year 1809.
Extensive alterations were then in progress at the
harbour, and a scarcity of water was felt by the
workmen. A hazy tradition about the existence of
a well, where the ground sounded hollow when struck,
was revived. Digging operations were begun, and,
at a depth of between twenty and thirty feet below
the surface, the basin was discovered. We quote
the following details from Dr. Macdonald's article
on the subject in the "*Antiquary*" for April, 1892:—
" Descending into a hollow by a flight of twenty
well-worn steps, most of them also hewn out of the
solid rock, we come upon the reservoir. The dimensions of the basin or piscina are as follow—greatest
breadth of the four sides, ten feet eight inches, eleven
feet, ten feet ten inches, and ten feet seven inches
respectively; depth, four feet four inches. One part
of the smooth bottom had been dug up at the time
of the excavations, either because it had projected
above the rest, as if for some one to stand upon,
or because it was thought that by doing so the
capacity of the well and perhaps the supply of
the water would be increased. Between the basin
and the perpendicular sides of the reservoir a small
ledge of sandstone has been left about two feet six

inches in breadth. These sides measure sixteen feet three inches, sixteen feet seven inches, sixteen feet nine inches, and seventeen feet respectively; and the height from the ledge upwards is eleven feet nine inches. The angles, both of the basin and its rock walls, are well rounded. In one corner the sandstone has been left in the form of a semi-circular pedestal, measuring two feet nine inches by one foot ten inches, and one foot two inches in height; whilst in that diagonally opposite there is a circular hole, five inches in diameter and one foot four inches in depth. From the ledge, as you enter, two steps of irregular shape and rude workmanship lead down into the basin. The sides of the reservoir are fissured and rent by displacement of the strata; and portions of the rock, that have given way from time to time, have been replaced by modern masonry. The arched roof is also modern." An Irish legend accounts for the origin of Lough-shanan, in County Clare, by connecting it with the baptism of Senanus, from whom it derived its name. "The saint, while still an infant, was miraculously gifted with speech and told his mother to pluck three rushes in a valley near her home. When this was done, a lake appeared, and in it Senanus was baptised according to a form of words prescribed by himself."

In the eighth volume of the "*Proceedings of the Society of Antiquaries of Scotland*" (new series), Sir Daniel Wilson gives an account of the ancient burying-ground of Kilbride, some three miles from

Oban. " I had visited the venerable cemetery repeatedly," he tells us, " and had carefully investigated
its monuments, without heeding the sacred fountain
which wells up among the bracken and grass, about
a dozen yards from the gate of the churchyard, and
flows in a stream down the valley. Yet, on inquiry,
I learned that it was familiarly known as Tober-an-
easbuig, *i.e.*, The Bishop's Well or The Holy Well.
Here, as we may presume, the primitive missionary
and servant of St. Bridget, by whom Christianity was
introduced into the wild district of Lorne, baptised
his first converts ; and here, through many succeeding
generations, the neophytes were signed with the sign
of the cross, and taught the mystic significance of the
holy rite."

The thoughts suggested by the sight of a crystal
spring are alluded to by Mr. Hunt in his "*Romances
of the West of England*," where he says, "The tranquil
beauty of the rising waters, whispering the softest
music, like the healthful breathing of a sleeping
infant, sends a feeling of happiness through the soul
of the thoughtful observer, and the inner man is
purified by its influence, as the outer man is cleansed
by ablution." This is the poetic view ; but the
superstitious view is not far to seek.

In the "*Home of a Naturalist*," Mrs. Saxby thus
recounts a Shetland superstition of a gruesome kind :
—" There is a fine spring well near Watlie, called
Heljabrün, and the legend of it is this: A wandering
packman (of the Claud Halcro class) was murdered

and flung into Heljabrün. Its water had always been
known to possess healing power, and, after becoming
seasoned by the unfortunate pedlar's remains, the
virtue in the water became even more efficacious.
People came from far and near to procure the precious
fluid. All who took it away had to throw three
stones or a piece of ' white money ' into the well,
and the water never failed to cure disease."

On Soutra Hill, the most westerly ridge of the
Lammermoors, once stood the hospital built by
Malcolm IV., about 1164, for the reception of wayfarers. It was dedicated to the Holy Trinity. Every
vestige of the building was removed between forty
and fifty years ago except a small aisle, appropriated
in the seventeenth century by the Pringles of Beat-
man's Acre as a burial vault. A short distance below
the site of the hospital is a spring of pure water,
locally known as Trinity Well. In former times it
was much visited for its healing virtues. A similar
reputation was for long enjoyed by St. Mungo's Well,
on the west side of St. Mungo's Hill, in the parish
of Huntly, Aberdeenshire. In Fortingall parish,
Perthshire, on the hillside near the Old Castle of
Garth, is a limpid spring called by the natives Fuaran
n' Gruarach, and also Fuaran n' Druibh Chasad,
signifying the Well of the Measles and the Well
of the Whooping-Cough respectively. Mr. James
Mackintosh Gow describes the locality in an article in
the eighth volume of the "*Proceedings of the Society
of Antiquaries of Scotland*" (new series). He says,

" It was famous in the district for the cure of these infantile diseases, and nearly all I spoke to on the subject had themselves been taken to the well, or had taken their own children to drink the water; and when an epidemic of the maladies occurred my informant remarked on the curious and amusing spectacle the scene presented on a summer morning, when groups of children, with their mothers, went up the hill in procession. The last epidemic of whooping-cough occurred in 1882, when all the children of the neighbourhood were taken to the well." Some forty yards higher up the slope than the well, is an earth-fast boulder of mica schist, having on one of its sides two natural cavities. The larger of these holds about a quart and is usually filled with rain water. " It was the custom," Mr. Gow tells us, " to carry the water from the well (perhaps the well was at one time at the foot of the stone) and place it in the cavity, and then give the patients as much as they could take, the water being administered with a spoon made from the horn of a living cow, called a *beodhare* or living horn; this, it appears, being essential to effect a cure." On the farm of Balandonich, in Athole, is a spring famous, till a comparatively recent period, for the cure of various maladies. A story is told in the district of a woman, unable to walk through rheumatism, having been brought in a wheel-barrow from her home four miles away. She bathed her limbs in the spring, and returned home on foot.

Hugh Miller, in his "*Scenes and Legends of the
North of Scotland*," recounts a tradition concerning
a certain spring near the town of Cromarty known
as Fiddler's Well, from the name of the young man
who discovered its virtues. The water gushes out
from the side of a bank covered with moss and
daisies. The tradition, considerably abbreviated, is
as follows:—William Fiddler and a companion were
seized with consumption at the same time. The
latter died not long afterwards, and Fiddler, though
wasted to a shadow, was able to follow his friend's
body to the grave. That night, in a dream, he
heard the voice of his dead companion, who told
him to meet him at a certain spot in the neighbourhood of the town. Thither he went, still in his
dream, and seated himself on a bank to await his
coming. Then, remembering that his friend was
dead, he burst into tears. "At this moment a large
field-bee came humming from the west and began to
fly round his head. . . . It hummed ceaselessly
round and round him, until at length its murmur-
ings seemed to be fashioned into words, articulated
in the voice of his deceased companion—'Dig, Willie,
and drink!' it said, 'Dig, Willie, and drink!' He
accordingly set himself to dig, and no sooner had
he torn a sod out of the bank than a spring of
clear water gushed from the hollow." Next day he
took the bee's advice. He found a spring, drank
the water, and regained his health. Hugh Miller
adds, "its virtues are still celebrated, for though

the water be only simple water it must be drunk in the morning, and as it gushes from the bank; and, with pure air, exercise, and early rising for its auxiliaries, it continues to work cures."

We need not multiply examples of non-mineral healing wells. Whatever benefit may be derived from them cannot be ascribed to any specially medicinal quality in their waters. The secret of their popularity is to be sought for in the annals of medical folklore, and not in those of scientific medicine.

Certain springs got the credit of warding off disease. On the island of Gigha, near the west coast of Kintyre, is a farm called Ardachad or High Field. Tradition says that a plague once visited the island, but that the people, belonging to the farm, escaped its ravages. This immunity was ascribed to the good offices of a well, in an adjoining field. The high situation of the farm and the presence of good water would tend to prolong health, without the intervention of magic. The Rev. Dr. Gregor, in his *Folklore of the North-East of Scotland,*" alludes to St. Olaus' Well in Cruden parish, Aberdeenshire. Its virtues are recorded in the couplet—

"St. Olav's Well, low by the sea
Where pest nor plague shall never be."

On the top of the Touch Hills, in Stirlingshire, rises St. Corbet's Spring. The belief formerly

prevailed that whoever drank its water before
sunrise on the first Sunday of May would have
life prolonged for another year. As a consequence,
crowds flocked to the spot early on the day in
question. In 1840 some old people were still living
who, in their younger days, had taken part in these
annual pilgrimages. In mediæval times, the belief
prevailed that no one baptised with the water of
Trinity Gask Well, Perthshire, would be attacked
by the plague. When water for baptism was drawn
from some holy well in the neighbourhood, its use,
in most instances, was doubtless due to a belief in
its prophylactic power. As already mentioned,
baptisms in St. Machar's Cathedral, Old Aberdeen,
were at one time administered in water taken from
the saint's spring. Before the Reformation the
water used at the chapel of Airth, in Stirlingshire,
is believed to have been procured from a well,
dedicated to the Virgin, near Abbeyton Bridge.
We do not know of any spring in Scotland with
a reputation for the prevention of hydrophobia.
St. Maelrubha's Well, on Innis Maree, is said to
have lost its efficacy for a time through contact
with a mad dog. What happened, when a mad
bull was plunged into the Holy Pool at Strathfillan,
will be alluded to later. In the village of Les Saintes
Maries, in the south of France, is an interesting
twelfth-century church with a well in the crypt.
The water, when drunk, is said to prevent any evil
consequences from the bite of a mad dog. Mr. E. H.

Barker gives an account of this well in his "*Wayfaring in France.*"   He says, "The curé told me
that about thirty people, who had been bitten by
dogs said to be rabid, came annually to drink the
water; and, he added, 'not one of them has ever
gone mad.'   M. Pasteur had become a formidable
rival of the well."

CHAPTER VII.

WATER-CURES.

Trying different Springs—Curing all Diseases—Fivepennies Well
—Water and Dulse—Special Diseases—Toothache—Sore Eyes
—Blindness—Headaches and Nervous Disorders—Deafness—
Whooping-cough—Gout—Sores—Ague—Sterility—Epilepsy—
Sacrifice of a Cock — St. Tegla's Well — Insanity — Severe
Treatment — Innis-Maree — Struthill — Teampull-Mòr — Holy
Pool — Fillan's History and Relics — Persistence of Super-
stition.

SOME people apply to different doctors in succession,
in the hope that new professional advice may bring
the coveted boon of health.   For the same reason
visits were paid to different consecrated wells.   On the
principle that " far fowls have fair feathers," a more
or less remote spring was resorted to, in the hope that
distance might lend special enchantment to its water.
Certain springs had the reputation of healing every
ailment.   A spring of this kind is what Martin calls
"a catholicon for all diseases."   He so styles various
springs in the Western Isles, and one in the Larger
Cumbrae in the Firth of Clyde.   Fivepennies Well, in
Eigg, had some curious properties.   " The natives told
me," he says, " that it never fails to cure any person

of their first disease, only by drinking a quantity of
it for the space of two or three days; and that if a
stranger lie at this well in the night-time, it will
procure a deformity in some part of his body, but has
no such effect on a native; and this, they say, hath
been frequently experimented." A noted fountain in
the Orkney group was the well of Kildinguie in the
Island of Stronsay. It is situated not far from the
beach. To reach it one has to walk over a long
stretch of sand. Its fame at one time spread over
the Scandinavian world, and even Denmark sent can-
didates for its help. Besides drinking the water,
health-seekers frequently ate some of the dulse to be
found on the shore. A local saying thus testified to
the advantages of the combined treatment: "The
well of Kildinguie and the dulse of Guiyidn can cure
all maladies except black death." In the Island of
Skye is a spring called Tobar Tellibreck. The natives,
at one time, held that its water, along with a diet of
dulse, would serve for a considerable time instead of
ordinary food.

Other springs were resorted to for particular complaints. Toothache is distressingly common, and
commonly distressing; but, strange to say, very few
wells are specially identified with the ailment. Indeed,
we know of only three toothache wells in Scotland. One
is in Strathspey, and is known as Fuaran Fiountag,
signifying *the cool refreshing spring*. The second is
in the parish of Kenmore, at the foot of Loch Tay. The
third is in Glentruim, in Inverness-shire. Another

well at Kenmore was resorted to for the cure of sore
eyes.   In the parish of Glass, close to the river
Deveron, is an ancient church dedicated to St. Wallach.
Some thirty yards below its burying-ground is a well,
now dry, except in very rainy weather.   Its water
had the power of healing sore eyes.   The water of
St. John's Well, at Balmanno, in the parish of Marykirk, Kincardineshire, was a sovereign remedy for the
same complaint.   Beside the road close to the farmhouse of Wester Auchleskine, at Balquhidder, in Perthshire, once stood a large boulder containing a natural
cavity.   The water in this hollow was also noted for
the cure of sore eyes—the boulder being called in
consequence Clach-nan-Sul, *i.e.*, the stone of the eyes.
In 1878, by order of the road trustees, the boulder
was blasted, on the ground that it was a source of
danger to vehicles in the dark, and its fragments were
used as road metal.   The Dow Well, at Innerleithen,
was formerly much visited for the restoration of weak
sight.   A well in Cornwall, dedicated to St. Ludvan,
miraculously quickened the sense of sight.   In Ireland,
a spring at Gougou Barra, between Glengariff and Cork,
is believed by the peasantry to cure blindness.   In
1849, Miss Bessie Gilbert, a daughter of the late Bishop
Gilbert of Chichester, who had lost her sight when
a child, visited the spring along with some of her
relatives.   Curiosity, however, was her only motive.
Her biographer relates that " the guide besought Bessie
in the most earnest and pathetic manner to try the
water, saying that he was sure it would restore her

sight, and entreating her brothers and sisters to urge
her to make use of it."

Headaches and nervous disorders were cured by
water from Tobar-nim-buadh or the Well of Virtues
in St. Kilda. Deafness was also cured by it. At
the entrance to Munlochy Bay, in the Black Isle
of Cromarty, is a cave known in the neighbourhood
as Craig-a-Chow, *i.e.*, the Rock of Echo. Tradition
says that in this cave a giant once lived. If not the
retreat of a giant, it was, at any rate, of smugglers.
What specially concerns us is that it contains a
dripping well, formerly much in request. Its water
is particularly cold. Like the St. Kilda spring, it
was believed to remove deafness. Of Whooping-cough
Wells, a noted one was at Straid, in Muthill parish,
Perthshire. Invalids came to it from considerable
distances. Early in the present century a family travelled from Edinburgh to seek its aid. The water was
drunk immediately after sunset or before sunrise, and
a horn from a live ox had to convey it to the patient's
lips. This was not an uncommon practice. Perhaps
it may have been due to some vague notion, that life
from the animal, whence the horn came, would be
handed on, *via* the spoon and the water, to the
invalid. The Straid horn was kept by a woman in
the immediate neighburhood, who acted as a sort of
priestess of the well. A well at the Burn of Oxhill,
in the parish of Rathven, Banffshire, had a local
celebrity for the cure of the same complaint. Sufferers from gout tried the efficacy of a spring in

Eckford parish, Roxburghshire, styled Holy Well or
Priest's Well. A spring in the churchyard of Logie-
pert parish, Forfarshire, removed sores, and another
in Martin's Den, in the same parish, was reckoned
anti-scorbutic. Another noted Forfarshire spring was
in Kirkden parish, with the reputation of curing swell-
ings of the feet and legs. Lochinbreck Loch, in
Balmaghie parish, Kirkcudbrightshire, was visited
from time immemorial for the cure of ague. Indeed,
there was hardly a bodily ailment that could not be
relieved by the water of some consecrated spring.

Springs were sometimes believed to cure female
barrenness. Wives, anxious to become mothers, formerly visited such wells as those of St. Fillan at
Comrie, and of St. Mary at Whitekirk, and in the
Isle of May. In this connection, Mr. J. R. Walker,
in his article in the "*Proceedings of the Society of
Antiquaries of Scotland*," volume v. (new series),
observes, "Many of the wells dedicated to 'Our
Lady,' *i.e.*, St. Mary (Virgin Mary) and to St. Brigid,
the Mary of Ireland, were famous for the cure of
female sterility, which, in the days when a man's
power and influence in the land depended on the
number of his clan or tribe, was looked upon as a
token of the divine displeasure, and was viewed by
the unfortunate spouses with anxious apprehension,
dread, doubt, jealousy, and pain. Prayer and supplication were obviously the methods pursued by the
devout for obtaining the coveted gift of fertility,
looked upon, by females especially, as the most

valuable of heavenly dispensations; and making pilgrimages to wells under the patronage of the Mother
of our Lord would naturally be one of the most
common expedients."

Epilepsy, with its convulsions and cries, seldom
fails to arrest attention and call forth sympathy.
In times less enlightened than our own, the disease
was regarded with awe as of supernatural origin;
and remedies, always curious and sometimes revolting,
were tried in order to bring relief. We may assume
that the water of consecrated springs was used for
this purpose; but, as far as we know, no Scottish
fountain was systematically visited by epileptic
patients. After enumerating a variety of folk-cures
for the disease in question, Sir Arthur Mitchell,
in an article on Highland Superstitions bearing on
Lunacy in the "*Proceedings of the Society of Antiquaries of Scotland*," volume iv., remarks, "For
the cure of the same disease, there is still practised
in the North of Scotland a formal sacrifice—not an
oblique but a literal and downright sacrifice—to
a nameless but secretly acknowledged power, whose
propitiation is desired. On the spot where the
epileptic first falls a black cock is buried alive,
along with a lock of the patient's hair and some
parings of his nails. I have seen at least three
epileptic idiots for whom this is said to have been
done." The same writer adds, "Dr. G——, of
N——, informs me that some time ago he was
called on to visit a poor man belonging to the

I

fishing population who had suddenly died, and who had been subject to epileptic seizures. His friends told the doctor that at least they had the comfort of knowing that everything had been done for him which could have been done. On asking what remedies they had tried, he was told that, among other things, a cock had been buried alive below his bed, and the spot was pointed out." This sacrifice of a cock in Scotland is of special significance, for it formed a distinctive feature of the ritual once in vogue in Wales at the village of Llandegla, Denbighshire. St. Tegla's Well there, was believed to possess peculiar virtue in curing epilepsy. Pennant gives a minute account of the ceremony as practised in his days. The following is a summary:—"About two hundred yards from the church rises a small spring. The patient washes his limbs in the well, makes an offering into it of fourpence, walks round it three times, and thrice repeats the 'Lord's Prayer.' These ceremonies are never begun till after sunset. If the afflicted be of the male sex, he makes an offering of a cock; if of the fair sex, a hen. The fowl is carried in a basket, first round the well, after that into the churchyard, when the same orisons and the same circumambulations are performed round the church. The votary then enters the church, gets under the communion table, lies down with the Bible under his or her head, is covered with the carpet or cloth, and rests there till break of day, departing after

offering sixpence, and leaving the fowl in the
church. If the bird dies, the cure is supposed to
have been effected, and the disease transferred to
the devoted victim." As regards the cock or hen,
the ceremony in this case was quite as much a
sacrifice as in the Scottish example. St. Tegla
merely took the place of the pagan divinity who
had been first in the field, and to whom offerings
had been made. In former times, sacrificing a
living animal was also resorted to occasionally to
cure disease in cattle. An ox was buried alive in
a pit, and the pit having been filled with earth,
the other members of the herd were made to walk
over the spot. In 1629, Isabel Young, spouse to
George Smith, portioner of East Barnes, Haddingtonshire, was tried for witchcraft. From her indictment
we learn that she was accused, *inter alia*, of having
buried a " quick ox, with a cat and a quantity of
salt," in a pit as a sacrifice to the devil, the truth
being that a live ox had been so treated by her
husband as a charm to cure his cattle, which were
diseased. A remarkable circumstance bearing on
this point is alluded to by Mr. A. W. Moore in
his " *Surnames and Place-names of the Isle of
Man*," under the heading of Cabbal-yn-Oural-Losht,
i.e., Chapel of the Burnt Sacrifice. " This name,"
he tells us, " records a circumstance which took
place in the nineteenth century, but which, it is
to be hoped, was never customary in the Isle of
Man. A farmer, who had lost a number of his

sheep and cattle by murrain, burnt a calf as a
propitiatory offering to the Deity on this spot, where
a chapel was afterwards built. Such facts point to
the same notion as that already indicated in connection with St. Tegla's Well, viz., that disease is due to
some malignant being, whose favour is to be sought by
the offering up of a living creature.

In no department of medical science have methods
of treatment changed more within recent years than
in that of insanity. Enlightened views on the subject
now prevail among the educated classes of society; and
the old notion that a maniac can be restored to mental
health by treating him like a criminal, or by adminis-
tering a few shocks to his already excited nerves,
is fortunately a thing of the past. At least it no
longer holds sway in our lunatic asylums. In the
minds of the ignorant and credulous, however, the
old leaven still works. Lady Wilde, in her "*Ancient
Cures, Charms, and Usages of Ireland,*" alludes to
a method of treatment in fashion till lately among
the peasantry there. When anyone showed signs
of insanity 'a witch-doctor' was called in. This
potent individual sprinkled holy water about the
room and over the patient; and after uttering certain
incantations—understood by the by-standers to be
'Latin prayers'—proceeded to beat him with a stout
cudgel. In the end the ravings of the lunatic ceased,
or as it was put, "the devil was driven out of him."
In Cornwall, at St. Nun's Well, the expulsive power
of a new terror used to be tried. According to Carew,

the *modus operandi* was as follows:—"The water running from St. Nun's Well fell into a square and enclosed walled plat, which might be filled at what depth they listed. Upon this wall was the frantic person put to stand, his back towards the pool, and from thence, with a sudden blow in the breast, tumbled headlong into the pond; where a strong fellow, provided for the nonce, took him and tossed him up and down, alongst and athwart the water, till the patient, by foregoing his strength, had somewhat forgot his fury. Then was he conveyed to the church, and certain masses said over him, upon which handling, if his right wits returned, St. Nun had the thanks; but if there appeared small amendment, he was bowsened again and again, while there remained in him any hope of life or recovery." North of the Tweed the treatment was hardly less soothing. When a lunatic was being rowed over to Innis Maree to drink the water of St. Maelrubha's Well there, he was jerked out of the boat by the friends who accompanied him. A rope had previously been tied round his waist, and by this he was pulled back into the boat; but before he could gather together his all-too-scattered wits, he was in the water again. As a rule this was done, not once or twice, but repeatedly, and in the case of both sexes. Such was the method up to a comparatively recent date. Pennant thus describes what was done in 1772:— "The patient is brought into the sacred island; is made to kneel before the altar, viz., the stump of a

tree—where his attendants leave an offering in
money; he is then brought to the well and sips
some of the holy water; a second offering is made;
that done, he is thrice dipped in the lake; and the
same operation is repeated every day for some
weeks." This towing after a boat to cure insanity
was not an isolated instance. Early in the present
century, the wife of a man living at Stromness in
Orkney, went mad through the incantations of
another female believed to be a witch. The man
bethought him of the cure in question, and, out of
love for his afflicted wife, dragged her several times
up and down the harbour behind his boat. Mr.
R. M. Fergusson, who mentions this case in his
"*Rambles in the Far North*," says that the woman
"bobbed about behind the boat like a cork, and
remained as mad as ever."

The well at Struthill, in Muthill parish, Perthshire,
once had a considerable reputation for the cure of
insanity. It was customary to tie patients at night
to a stone near the spring, and recovery would
follow if they were found loose in the morning.
An adjoining chapel was ordered to be demolished
in 1650 by the Presbytery of Auchterarder, on the
ground of its being the scene of certain superstitious
rites, but the spring continued to be visited till a
much later date. At Teampull-mòr in Lewis, in
addition to walking round the ruins, and being
sprinkled with water from St. Ronan's Well, the
insane person was bound and left all night in the

chapel on the site of the altar. If he slept, he would recover; but if he remained awake, there was no hope of a cure. In the Struthill and Teampull-mòr instances, as well as that of Strath-fillan mentioned below, the binding of the patient was an essential part of the treatment; and in two at least of the cases the loosening of the bonds was reckoned an omen of good. The mysterious loosening of bonds used to be an article of common belief. Dalyell, in his "*Darker Superstitions of Scotland*," remarks, "Animals were sometimes liberated supernaturally. In the Isle of Enhallow, a horse tied up at sunset would wander about through the night; and while the kirk session took cognisance of a suspected witch who had exercised her faculties on a cow, the animal, though firmly secured, was found to be free, and in their vicinity when the investigation closed."

The Holy Pool of St. Fillan was famous for the cure of various diseases, but specially of insanity. It is referred to in "*Marmion*" as

"St. Fillan's blessed well
Whose springs can frenzied dreams dispel
And the craz'd brain restore."

It is not, however, a well, but a pool, in the river Fillan, about two miles lower down than Tyndrum. To correctly estimate the reverence paid to this sacred pool, we must glance at the influence, exerted by Fillan on the district during his life-time, and afterwards by means, of his relics. The saint flourished

in the early eighth century. He was born in Ireland.
His father was Ferodach, and his mother was
Kentigerna, daughter of a prince of Leinster. She
afterwards came to Scotland and led the life of a
recluse, on Inch Cailleach, an island in Loch Lomond.
According to the Aberdeen Breviary, Fillan was born
with a stone in his mouth, and was at once thrown
into a lake where he was ministered to by angels for
a year. He was then taken out and baptised by
Bishop Ybarus, and at a later date received the
monastic habit from Muna, otherwise called Mundus.
Devoting himself to solitary meditation he built a cell
close to Muna's monastery. On one occasion, a servant
went to call him to supper, and looking through a
chink in the wall, saw the saint busy writing, his
uplifted left hand throwing light over the book in
lieu of a candle. Whatever may be thought of the
incident, few will deny its picturesqueness. In
competent hands it might be made the subject of a
striking picture. Fillan afterwards went to Lochalsh,
where he dedicated a church to his uncle Congan, the
founder of the monastery of Turriff, in Aberdeenshire.
We next find Fillan in the principal scene of his
missionary work, viz., in Glendochart, in that portion
of the glen anciently called Siracht, and now Strathfillan. This area formed a separate parish till 1617,
but was then united to the parish of Killin. Fillan
arrived with seven serving clerics, and tradition says
that he built his church at a spot, miraculously pointed
out to him. The neighbourhood was, and is full of

interest. " Glendochart," writes Mr. Charles Stewart in "*An Gaidheal*," " is not celebrated for terrific mountain scenery like Glencoe or the Coolins, but has a grandeur of a different character. Lofty mountains, clothed, here in heather, there in green ; cloudy shadows frequently flitting across their sides, and serried ridges of multiplied lines and forms of varied beauty, and along their sides strangely shaped stones and boulders of rocks deposited by the ancient glaciers. Along the strath there are stretches of water, its course broken occasionally by lochs ; sometimes wending its way slowly and solemnly through green meadows, and anon rushing along as at the celebrated bridge of Dochart, at Killin, with fire and fury."

The same writer mentions that three spots, where Fillan was wont to teach the natives of the Strath, are still pointed out, viz., at the upper end of Glendochart, where the priory was afterwards built, halfway down the glen at Dun-ribin, and at the lower end at Cnoc-a-bheannachd, *i.e.*, Hill of the Blessing, near Killin. Fillan instructed the people in agriculture, and built mills for grinding corn. Out of compliment to him, the mill at Killin was idle on his festival, (Jan. 9th), as late as the middle of the present century. Indeed there was a superstition in the district that it would not be lucky to have it working on that day. Fillan also instituted fairs for the sale and barter of local produce. His fair is still held at Killin in January. The miraculous element in his history did not end

with his life.   He seems to have died somewhere
about Lochearn, and his body was brought back to
Glendochart, by way of Glen Ogle.   When the bearers
reached the point where Glendochart opens upwards
and downwards, a dispute arose as to the destination
of their burden.   Some wished the saint's body to be
buried at Killin and others at Strathfillan.   Behold a
marvel !   When they could not agree, they found that
instead of one coffin there were two, and so each party
was satisfied.

Robert Bruce's fight with the followers of Macdougall
of Lorne took place near St. Fillan's Church, at a spot,
afterwards named Dalrigh or the King's Field.   On
that occasion, an earnest prayer was addressed to the
saint of the district, and through his intercession
victory came to Bruce.   So at least runs the legend.
After his success at Bannockburn, the King in
gratitude founded St. Fillan's Priory, in Strathfillan,
and endowed it with the neighbouring lands of
Auchtertyre, and with the sheep-grazing of Bein-
mhannach or the Monk's Mountain, in Glenlyon.
Indeed, if tradition speaks truth, Bruce had a double
reason to be grateful to Fillan, for the victory at
Bannockburn, was attributed to the presence in the
Scottish camp, of a relic of the saint, said to be an
arm-bone set in silver.   The relic, however, as Dr.
John Stuart shows, in the twelfth volume of the
" *Proceedings of the Society of Antiquaries of
Scotland*," was probably his Coig-gerach or pastoral
staff, popularly, but erroneously called his Quigrich.

It is said to have been kept at Auchlyne, in a chapel called Caipal-na-Faraichd, and when the chapel was burnt to have been rescued by a person, either then, or afterwards, called Doire or Dewar, whose descendants became its custodiers. The subsequent history of the relic is curious. In 1782 it was at Killin in the keeping of Malice Doire. In 1818 it was taken to Canada, where it remained for some sixty years. Through the patriotic zeal of Sir Daniel Wilson it was then sent back to Scotland, and now forms one of the treasures in the National Museum of Antiquities, at Edinburgh.

The sanctity of Fillan thus distilled like a fertilising dew over the district of Glendochart. We need not, therefore, be surprised that, in days darker than our own, a thriving crop of superstitions was the result. It is certainly a striking testimony to the enduring influence of the saint, that the pool, believed to have been blessed by him, retained its fame till within the memory of persons still living. Possibly the pool was reverenced even before his time. Towards the end of last century, as many as two hundred persons were brought annually to the spot. The time selected was usually the first day of the quarter, (O.S.), and the immersion took place after sunset. The patients, with a rope tied round their waist, were thrown from the bank into the river. This was usually done thrice. According to previous instructions, they picked up nine stones from the bottom of the stream. After their dip they walked

three times round three cairns in the immediate
neighbourhood, and at each turn added a stone to
the cairn. An English antiquary, who visited the
spot in 1798, writes, "If it is for any bodily pain,
fractured limb or sore, that they are bathing, they
throw upon one of these cairns that part of their
clothing which covered the part affected; also, if they
have at home any beast that is diseased, they have
only to bring some of the meal which it feeds upon
and make it into paste with these waters, and afterwards give it to him to eat, which will prove an
infallible cure; but they must likewise throw upon
the cairn the rope or halter with which he was led.
Consequently the cairns are covered with old halters,
gloves, shoes, bonnets, nightcaps, rags of all sorts,
kilts, petticoats, garters, and smocks. Sometimes
they go as far as to throw away their halfpence."

After the ceremony at the cairns the patient was
led to the ruins of St. Fillan's Chapel, about half
a mile away, and there tied to a stone with a hollow
in it, large enough to receive the body, the unfortunate person being fastened down to a wooden
framework. The patient was then covered with
hay, and left in this condition all night. As at
Struthill, if the bonds were found loose in the
morning, he or she would recover; but if not, the
case was counted hopeless, or at least doubtful. As
the writer of the article on the parish, in the "*New
Statistical Account of Scotland*," shrewdly observes,
"The prospect of the ceremony, especially in a cold

winter evening, might be a good test for persons
pretending insanity." At the time when he wrote,
viz., in 1843, the natives of the parish had ceased to
believe in the efficacy of the holy pool, but it was
still visited by invalids from a distance. It was
usual, after the fastening process already described,
to place St. Fillan's bell on the head of the patient by
way of helping on the cure. This bell is quadran-
gular in shape. Its size and appearance are thus
described by Dr. Joseph Anderson in his "*Scotland
in Early Christian Times*": "It is an elegant casting
of bronze, stands twelve inches high and measures
nine by six inches wide at the mouth. The ends are
flat, the sides bulging, the top rounded. In the
middle of the top is the loop-like handle, terminating
where it joins the bell in two dragonesque heads
with open mouths." The bell weighs eight pounds
fourteen ounces. In the fifteenth century the relic
seems to have been held in special honour, for it
graced the coronation of James IV. in 1488. After
the Reformation, it was locked up for some time,
to prevent its use for the superstitious purpose
alluded to above. But, as a rule, it lay on a tombstone in the Priory graveyard, protected only by
the reverence paid to it in the district. There was
a belief that, if carried off, it would return of its
own accord, ringing all the way. In 1798 this belief
was put to a severe test, for in that year the English
antiquary, already quoted, removed the relic. "In
order," he says, "to ascertain the truth or falsehold

of the ridiculous story of St. Fillan's bell, I carried it off with me, and mean to convey it, if possible, to England. An old woman, who observed what I was about, asked me what I wanted with the bell, and I told her that I had an unfortunate relation at home out of his mind, and that I wanted to have him cured. 'Oh, but,' says she, 'you must bring him here to be cured, or it will be of no use.' Upon which I told her he was too ill to be moved, and off I galloped with the bell back to Tyndrum Inn." The bell was taken to England. About seventy years later, its whereabouts was discovered, and it was sent back to Scotland. Like the crozier of the same saint, it is now in the Antiquarian Museum at Edinburgh.

If we may believe a local tradition, the Holy Pool lost its miraculous virtue in the following manner, though, after what the English antiquary mentioned about its water being mixed with meal, and given to diseased cattle, we see no reason why it should have been so particular. A farmer who had a mad bull thought that, if the sacred water could heal human ills, it would be efficacious also in the case of the lower animals. So he plunged his infuriated beast into the stream. What was the effect on the bull we do not know: but since then the virtue has departed from the water. Except for a pleasure dip on a hot summer's day, no one need now apply at the Holy Pool.

The unbroken reputation of such health resorts, for centuries, is certainly remarkable. Strathfillan kept up its fame for over a thousand years. At Gheel, in Belgium, for fully twelve hundred years, successive generations of lunatics sought relief at St. Dympna's Well. We must not be too hard on the ages before our own; for, though in some respects dark, in other respects they had a good deal of light. Nevertheless, severe things might be said about them. From a present-day point of view, it might be argued that those, who took their insane friends to get cured in the manner described, required, like the patients themselves, a little rearrangement of their wits.

CHAPTER VIII.

Some Wonderful Wells.

THE epithet *wonderful* may fitly be applied to whatever springs are endowed by popular credulity with
mysterious properties. Those already considered have
been mainly associated with the removal or prevention
of disease. It is now proposed to glance at certain
other characteristics.

Some springs are wonderful as to their origin.
Who does not know the legend connected with Tre
Fontane, in the vicinity of Rome, where water
bubbled up at the three places touched by St. Paul's
severed head? We do not recollect any Scottish
instance of a well coming into being in this way;

but in England we have St. Osyth's Well in Essex, where that saint was beheaded by the Danes, and in Wales, St. Winifred's Well in Flintshire. Concerning the latter, Chambers, in his "*Book of Days*," thus writes:—"Winifred was a noble British maiden of the seventh century; a certain Prince Cradocus fell in love with her, and, finding his rough advances repulsed, cut off the lady's head. Immediately after doing this, the prince was struck dead, and the earth, opening, swallowed up his body. Meanwhile, Winifred's head rolled down the hill; where it stopped, a spring gushed forth—the blood from the head colouring the pebbles over which it flowed, and rendering fragrant the moss growing around." Sweden has its St. Eric's Spring at Upsala, marking the place where Eric, the king, was beheaded about the middle of the twelfth century. St. Oswald's Well at Winwick, in Lancashire, is said to indicate the spot where that famous Northumbrian king received his death-wound when fighting against Penda, the pagan ruler of Mercia. On a hill in Hertfordshire, a fountain arose to quench the thirst of Alban, England's proto-martyr, who suffered there about 300 A.D. According to a Kincardineshire tradition, a spring in Dunnottar Castle miraculously appeared for behoof of the Covenanters, who were confined there in 1685. In Holywood parish, Dumfriesshire, (so called from its oak forest, sacred even in pre-Christian times), a fountain sprang up at the intercession of Vynning, the patron of a

K

well at Kilwinning, in Ayrshire. In Scottish
hagiology, fountains usually gush forth to supply
water for baptism. In English legends they spring
up as a tribute to spots where the corpses of saintly
persons have rested. Thus, water issued from the
graves of Ethelbert at Marden, in Herefordshire,
and of Withburga at East Dereham, in Norfolk,
and also from that of Frideswide at Oxford. St.
Frideswide's Fair at the last-mentioned place was a
noted holiday in the middle ages. It lasted a
week, and, during its continuance, the keys of the
city were in the keeping of the prior, having been
handed over by the mayor, who ceased for the time
to be responsible for the peace of the burgh. At
Trondhjem, in Norway, a spring arose to mark the
spot where King Olaf was buried, about the middle
of the eleventh century.

Cuthbert was greatly honoured by the gushing
forth of springs, both during his lifetime and after
his death. While at Lindisfarne, he was seized
with a desire for still greater retirement, and accordingly withdrew to Farne Island, one of the Fern
group, two miles distant from Bamborough, and six
from Lindisfarne. This island was then haunted
by evil spirits; but these he drove away, as Guthlac
did from the marshes of Crowland, in Lincolnshire.
Cuthbert set about building a cell in Farne Island,
and, with the help of angels, the work was satisfactorily completed. Unfortunately, there was no
fresh water to be had; but the want was soon

supplied. In response to the saint's prayers, a spring arose in the floor of his cell. Bede says, "This water, by a most remarkable quality, never overflowed its first limits, so as to flood the floor, nor yet ever failed, however much of it might be taken out; so that it never exceeded or fell short of the daily wants of him who used it for his sustenance." The miracle did not end here. When Eistan of Norway was ravaging the coast of Northumberland in the twelfth century, he landed on Farne Island and destroyed the property of the hermits, whose retreat it then was. The spring, unwilling to give help to the robber bands, dried up. Thirst, accordingly, compelled them to quit the island. No sooner had they left than the spring reappeared and gladdened the spot once more. After Cuthbert's death, his body was carried from place to place for safety. In his "*History of St. Cuthbert*," Archbishop Eyre remarks, "There is a legendary tradition, that when the bearers of St. Cuthbert's body journeyed northwards from York-shire and came to Butterby, near Croxdale, they set down the coffin on the right bank before crossing the river, and immediately a saline spring burst out upon the spot. After fording the river they again rested the coffin, and a spring of chalybeate water rose up where they had laid down the body. A third time the weary travellers, struggling up the rugged pass, were compelled to lay their precious burden on the ground, and a sweet stream of water

gushed out of the rock to refresh them." Prior to
this, Cuthbert's relics had rested a while at Melrose.
Tradition says that, on resuming their wanderings,
they floated down the Tweed in a stone coffin as
far as Tillmouth, on the English Border. The
fragments of a sarcophagus, said to be the coffin
in question, are still to be seen there beside the
ruins of St. Cuthbert's Chapel. This incident is
thus referred to in " *Marmion* ":—

> " Seven years Saint Cuthbert's corpse they bore.
>   They rested them in fair Melrose :
>   But though, alive, he loved it well,
>   Not there his reliques might repose ;
>   For, wondrous tale to tell !
>   In his stone coffin forth he rides
>   (A ponderous bark for river tides),
>   Yet light as gossamer it glides,
>   Downward to Tillmouth cell."

A Shropshire legend narrates that, on one occasion,
Milburga, who is still remembered in the name of
Stoke St. Milborough, was riding in all haste to escape
from certain enemies. She fell at length exhausted
from her horse; but, at her command, the animal
struck a stone with his hoof, and water gushed out
for her refreshment. In a neighbouring field some
men were sowing grain, and the saint prophesied
that in the evening they would gather the ripe corn.
She instructed them to tell her enemies, on their
arrival, that she had passed when the crop was being
sown. The miracle duly happened, and Milburga's
foes were disconcerted in consequence. Shropshire and

Yorkshire have strange traditions about the sudden appearance of lakes, sometimes overwhelming human dwellings. In the latter case, the tops of houses are said to be visible through the water. Additional picturesqueness is occasionally given, by the introduction into the story of vanished bells, sending forth from the depths their soft cadences. At Tunstall, in Norfolk, a boggy piece of ground, locally known as Hell-Hole, is marked by frequently rising bubbles. The devil once carried off the bells of the church, and, when pursued, plunged into the marsh. The bubbles are due to the bells sinking lower and lower into the abyss. Such beliefs about lakes form an interesting supplement to Scottish superstitions.

When Henry VI. was in hiding in Bolton Hall, in Yorkshire, he wished to have a bath in the hot summer weather. His host, anxious to supply what was lacking to the comfort of the royal fugitive, used a hazel twig in his garden, in the hope of discovering water. The indications being favourable, a well was dug, and the king was enabled to cool himself to his heart's content. The spring still bears the king's name. Michael Scott, who was born in Fife in the thirteenth century, and was regarded by his contemporaries as a dabbler in the black art, had a pupil in the north of England who undertook a marvellous feat, viz., to bring the sea up the Wansbeck river to Morpeth. Certain incantations were gone through, and the magician started from the coast, followed by the tide. All went well till within about five miles from

the town, when he became alarmed by the roaring of
the water, and looked back. So the spell was broken,
and Morpeth remained inland. This recalls the story
accounting for the introduction of a good water-supply
into Plymouth. When there was a scarcity in the sixteenth century, Sir Francis Drake, the naval hero, rode
up to Dartmoor, and uttered some magical words over
a spring there. He immediately turned his horse and
galloped back to the town, followed by a copious stream.

Certain wells could put in a good claim to the title
of *wonderful* on the ground of the effects they
were able to produce. If a spring could act as a
sign-post to guide the wayfarer, who had strayed
from his path, it might surely be classed among
marvels! This is what a certain well on Dartmoor,
in Devonshire, could do, at least in the sixteenth
century. A man of the name of Fitz and his wife,
when crossing the moor in the year 1568, lost their
way. They lighted on the well in question, drank its
water, and found the lost track without the least
difficulty. In gratitude, Fitz afterwards raised a
memorial of stone over the well " for the benefit of
all pixy-led travellers." In Germany, before a meal,
the ceremony of wishing one's friend a good appetite
is still kept up. Such a salutation must have been
unnecessary in the Island of Harris, at least in
Martin's time, for he tells us of a spring, then lately
discovered, that could produce an appetite whenever
wanted. " The natives," he says, " find by experience
that it is very effectual for restoring lost appetite ; all

that drink of it become very soon hungry though they have eat plentifully but an hour before." A small quantity of its water might with advantage be added to the contents of the "loving cup" at the Lord Mayor's banquets, and on other festive occasions both in, and out of the Metropolis. Martin speaks of another marvel in Harris. "A large cave in the face of a hill hath," he says, "two wells in it, one of which is excluded from dogs, for they say that if a dog do but taste of the water, the well presently dryeth up; and for this reason, all such as have occasion to lodge there take care to tie their dogs that they may not have access to the water. The other well is called the Dogs' Well, and is only drunk by them." The student of folklore cannot fail to find Martin a congenial companion, as he records a variety of quaint Hebridean customs that might have been passed over in silence by a more matter-of-fact writer. When in the Island of Lewis, he was told of a fountain at Loch Carloway "that never whitened linen," though the experiment had been often tried. In connection with his visit to Barray, he says, "The natives told me there is a well in the village Tangstill, the water of which, being boiled, grows thick like puddle. There is another well, not far from Tangstill, which, the inhabitants say, in a fertile year, throws up many grains of barley in July and August. And they say that the well of Kilbar throws up embryos of cockles, but I could not discern any in the rivulet, the air being at that time foggy." This reminds one of the

Well in the Wall in Checkly parish, Staffordshire, said to throw out small bones like those of chickens and sparrows all the year round except in the months of July and August.   Toubir-ni-Lechkin, in Jura, rising on a hill near Tarbert, was a noted fountain. Martin mentions that its water was counted "lighter by one half" than any other water in the island, and that a great quantity of it might be drunk at one time without causing inconvenience.   He further says, "The river Nissa receives all the water that issues from this well, and this is the reason they give why salmons here are in goodness and taste far above those of any other river whatever."

The power of some wells over the lower animals was remarkable.   A spring at Harpham, in the East Riding of Yorkshire, dedicated to St. John of Beverley, was believed to subdue the fiercest animal. A raging bull, when brought to it, became as gentle as a lamb.   A spring of this kind would indeed be a great boon in the country to timid, town-bred tourists when crossing fields where there are cattle. To the margin of such a spring they could retreat and there feel safe.   Black Mere, at Morridge, near Leek, in Staffordshire, was credited with the power of frightening away animals.   Cattle would not drink its water, and birds would not fly over it.   A mermaid was believed to dwell in its depths.   A reminiscence of this belief is to be found in the name of "The Mermaid," a wayside inn in the neighbourhood frequented by sportsmen.   Some wells keep a sharp look-out on the use made of their water. A certain spring at Gilsland, in Cumberland, wished to dispense its favours freely, *i.e.*, without making the public pay for them. The proprietor of the ground, however, resolved to turn, what he counted, an honest penny, and built a house over the spring for the sale of the water. The fountain, much aggrieved at this, forthwith dried up. The house, not being required, was taken down, and the benevolent water once more made its appearance.

Intermittent springs have been observed from an early date, and strange notions have been formed about them. They are usually associated in their ebbing and flowing with some particular river. In some instances such a connection can be only imaginary, notably in the case of the Keldgate Springs at Cottingham, in Yorkshire, thought to be influenced by the river Derwent twenty miles away. An ebbing and flowing well at the foot of Giggleswick Scar, near Settle, in the same county, was represented by Michael Drayton under the poetic guise of a nymph flying from the pursuit of an unwelcome lover. Gough, in his edition of Camden's "*Britannia,*" of date 1806, has the following about a spring near Paisley:—"Bishop Gibson says that in the lands of Newyards, near Paisley, is a spring which ebbs and flows with the tide though far above any ground to which the tide comes. Mr. Crawford, in his '*History of the Shire of Renfrew,*' applies this to a spring in the lands of Woodside, which is three miles from the Clyde, and half-a-mile from Paisley bridge, and the ground much higher than the river." The name of Dozmare Lake, in Cornwall, signifies in Cornish a drop of the sea, the lake having been so called from a belief that it was tidal. The absurdity of the belief is proved by the fact that the sheet of water is eight hundred and ninety feet above the sea. The lake is said to be unfathomable, and has for a haunting spirit a giant who is doomed to empty it by means of a limpet shell.

A singular superstition is, or was till quite lately, cherished in Peeblesshire, that Powbate Well, close to Eddlestone, completely fills with its water the high hill on whose top it is situated. Chambers, in his "*Popular Rhymes of Scotland*," gives the following particulars about the spring:—"The mouth, called Powbate E'e, is covered over by a grate to prevent the sheep from falling into it; and it is supposed that, if a willow wand is thrown in, it will be found some time after, peeled at the water-laugh, a small lake at the base of the hill supposed to communicate with Powbate. Of course the hill is expected to break some day like a bottle and do a great deal of mischief. A prophecy, said to be by Thomas the Rhymer, and bearing evident marks of his style, is cited to support the supposition:

> ' Powbate, an ye break,
> Tak' the Moorfoot in yere gate ;
> Moorfoot and Mauldslie,
> Huntlycote, a' three,
> Five kirks and an Abbacie ! ' "

In explanation of this prophecy Chambers remarks:
"Moorfoot, Mauldslie, and Huntlycote are farm-
towns in the immediate neighbourhood of the hill.
The kirks are understood to have been those of
Temple, Carrington, Borthwick, Cockpen, and Dalkeith; and the abbacy was that of Newbottle, the
destruction of which, however, has been anticipated
by another enemy."

The Scottish imagination, in attributing wonderful
properties to springs, has not gone the length of
ascribing to any the power possessed by St. Ludvan's
Well in Cornwall. This fountain has been already
referred to as the giver of increased sight. But it
had the still more marvellous power of preventing
any one baptised with its water from being hanged
by a hempen rope. Nor have we heard of any spring
north of the Tweed that could be a match for another
Cornish well, viz., that of St. Keyne, familiar to readers
of Southey. Whoever, after marriage, first drank of
its water would be the ruler of the house. On one
occasion a bridegroom hurried to make sure of this
right, but was chagrined to find that he had been
anticipated: his bride had taken a bottleful of the
water with her to church.

CHAPTER IX.

WITNESS OF WATER.

Recovery from Illness—Hydromancy—Mirror—Juno's Pool—Prediction and Cure—Methods of Augury—Portents of Death—Water like Blood—Springs and National Annals—Heritable Jurisdictions — Water and Witchcraft — Devil's Mark — Water Ordeal—Abbey of Scone—Elgin Orderpot—Witch's Stone—Repeal of Penal Statutes—Witchcraft in the North—Insanity—Wild Murdoch.

"AM I likely to recover?" is a question on many a patient's lips. "Ask your doctor;" and if the case looks serious, "Have a consultation" is the answer nowadays. Formerly, the answer was "Go to a consecrated well," or "Get some one else to go in your stead, and you will get a reply." There is no reason to believe that *every* sacred spring was credited with this power; but *many* undoubtedly were. Hydromancy has been a favourite mode of divination. "The conscious water" could predict the future, and questions connected with health were laid before it for its decision. The Greeks dipped a mirror into a well, and foretold health or sickness from the appearance of the watery lines on its surface. A pool in Laconia, sacred to Juno, revealed approaching good or evil fortune respectively, by the sinking or floating of wheaten cakes thrown into it, and auguries were also drawn from the movements of stones when dropt into it. Springs, therefore, deserved the respect shown to them by the confiding public. Indeed they not only told of recovery; they supplied the medicine required to ensure it, and were thus doctors and druggists combined. Sometimes the omen was unpropitious. In many cases the prophecy would work out its own fulfilment. There was a well in the Island of Lewis that caused either instant death or recovery to the patient who tested its virtues: but a speedy fulfilment like this was exceptional. St. Andrew's Well at Shadar, in Lewis, was much esteemed for its power of augury. A tub, containing some of its water, was taken to the house of the patient, and a small wooden dish was placed on the surface of the water. If this dish turned sunways, it showed that the patient would recover; but if in an opposite direction, that he would die. In reference to this instance, Mr. Gomme, in his "*Ethnology in Folklore*," observes, "I am inclined to connect this with the vessel or cauldron so frequently occurring in Celtic tradition, and which Mr. Nutt has marked as 'a part of the gear of the oldest Celtic divinities' perhaps of divinities older than the Celts." On one occasion two parishioners of Fodderty, in Ross-shire, consulted Tobar-na-domhnuich in that parish in behalf of a sick friend. When they placed their pitcher on the surface of the water, the vessel moved round from south to west, as in the last

instance, and they hastened back to their friend with
the good news. This was in the year 1832. About
the same time, a woman brought her sick child to be
bathed in the well, but was surprised and not a little
terrified to see a strange creature, with glaring eyes,
leap into it as she approached. Love for her child
made her brave. Overcoming her fear, she dislodged
the creature, and bathed the little invalid. In the
end, however, she must have regarded the appearance
of the creature as a bad omen, for the child did
not recover. The usual way of consulting the spring
in question was to draw water from it before sunrise,
and to convey the water to the invalid's house. The
patient was then immersed in it, and if it remained
clear the circumstance pointed to recovery; but if it
assumed a brownish colour, the illness would end in
death. In former times a shirt was thrown into St.
Oswald's Well, in Yorkshire, by way of augury. The
floating of the shirt foretold returning health. The
sinking foretold death. When a portion of an
invalid's clothing was flung into the Dow Loch, in
Dumfriesshire, the same rule held good. As may be
noticed, the augury in these two cases was the *reverse*
of that in the case of Juno's pool above alluded to.

There were other ways in which wells acted the
prophet. If a certain worm in a spring on the top of
a particular hill in Strathdon was found alive, the
patient would recover. A well at Ardnacloich in
Appin contained a dead worm, if the patient's illness
would prove fatal; but a living one, if otherwise.

The Virgin's Well, near the ancient church of Kilmorie on the shores of Loch Ryan in Wigtownshire, had an ingenious way of predicting the future. If the patient, on whose account the water was sought, would recover, the fountain flowed freely; but if the malady would end in death, the water refused to gush forth. Montluck Well, in the grounds of Logan in the same county, got the credit of acting on a similar principle. When speaking of this spring, Symson says, "it is in the midst of a little bog to which several persons have recourse to fetch water for such as are sick, asserting (whether it be truth or falsehood I shall not determine) that if the sick person shall recover, the water shall so bubble and mount up when the messenger dips in his vessel, that he will hardly get out dry shod by reason of the overflowing of the well; but if the sick person be not to recover, there shall not be any such overflowing in the least." We find a belief in the south-west of England corresponding to this in the south-west of Scotland. Gulval Well, in Fosses Moor there, was resorted to by persons anxious to know the fate of absent friends. If the person inquired about was dead, the water remained perfectly still; if sick, it bubbled, though in a muddy fashion; but if well, it sent out a sparkling gush. Mr. Hunt mentions the case of a woman, who, with her babe in her arm, consulted the spring about her absent husband, under the guidance of an aged female who acted as the guardian of the well. "Obeying the old woman's directions, she knelt on the mat of bright

green grass which grew around, and, leaning over the
well so as to see her face in the water, she repeated
after her instructor:

> ' Water, water, tell me truly,
> Is the man I love truly
> On the earth, or under the sod,
> Sick or well,—in the name of God?'

Some minutes passed in perfect silence, and anxiety
was rapidly turning cheeks and lips pale, when the
colour rapidly returned.   There was a gush of clear
water from below, bubble rapidly followed bubble
sparkling brightly in the morning sunshine.   Full of
joy, the young mother rose from her knees, kissed
her child, and exclaimed, ' I am happy now!'"   At
Barenton in Brittany is a spring still believed in by
the peasantry.   A pin is dropt into the well, and if
good fortune is in store, the water sends up bubbles;
but if not, it remains quite still.   The quantity of
water in St. Maelrubha's Well on Innis-Maree varied
from time to time.   When a patient was brought for
treatment and there was a scanty supply, the omen
was considered unfavourable; but when the water
was abundant, the saint was deemed propitious, and
the hope of recovery was consequently great.

The fly at St. Michael's Well in Banffshire was
looked upon as a prophet.   In the "*Old Statistical
Account of Scotland*" we read, that, "if the sober
matron wished to know the issue of her husband's
ailment, or the love-sick nymph that of her languish-
ing swain, they visited the Well of St. Michael.   Every

movement of the sympathetic fly was regarded in silent awe; and as he appeared cheerful or dejected, the anxious votaries drew their presages." At Little Conan in Cornwall is a spring, sacred to Our Lady of Nants. It was at one time resorted to on Palm Sunday by persons anxious to know whether they would outlive the year. A cross, made of palm, was thrown into the water. If it floated, the thrower would survive the twelvemonth; but if it sank, he would die within that time. Maidens used to visit Madron Well in the same county on May morning to forecast their matrimonial fate. They took two pieces of straw, about an inch in length, and placing them crosswise fastened them together with a pin. The cross was then thrown into the spring. The rising bubbles were carefully counted, for they corresponded in number with the years that would elapse before the arrival of the wedding-day.

Portents of death were sometimes furnished by lochs and springs. At Harpham in Yorkshire there is a tradition that a drummer lad in the fourteenth century was accidentally drowned in a certain spring by a St. Quintin—Lord of the Manor. Ever afterwards the sound of a drum was heard in the well on the evening before the death of one of the St. Quintin family. Camden, in his "*Britannia*," tells of a sheet of water in Cheshire called Blackmere Lake, lying in the district where the Brereton family had lands, and records the local belief that, just before any heir of that house died, trunks of trees were seen floating

L

on its surface. Water occasionally gave warning by turning red like blood. A certain fountain, near the Elbe, in Germany, was at one time believed to do this, in view of an approaching war. St. Tredwell's Loch, in Papa-Westray, Orkney, has already been referred to, in connection with its habit of turning red, whenever anything remarkable was about to happen to a member of the Royal Family. When the Earl of Derwentwater was beheaded, in 1716, the news spread that the stream flowing past his estate of Dilston Hall in Northumberland ran with blood. The same was said of the river at Bothel, in the parish of Topenhow, in Cumberland, on the occasion of the execution of Charles I., in 1649. There was at one time a well in Canterbury Cathedral. After the assassination of Thomas à Becket the sweepings of his blood and brains from the floor were thrown into it, and more than once afterwards the water turned red and effected various miraculous cures. Lady Wilde, in her "*Ancient Legends of Ireland*," narrates how one of the holy wells of Erin lost its efficacy for curing purposes through having been touched by a murderer. The priest of the district took some of its water and breathed on it thrice in the name of the Trinity, when, lo! a mysterious change came over it, and it appeared red like blood! The murderer was captured and handed over to justice, and the well once more began to work cures.

Some springs seemed anxious to be behind the scenes (though before the event) in connection with

various incidents in British annals. A spring at
Warlingham, in Surrey, rises before any great event
in our country's history. At any rate it did so before three great events in the seventeenth century,
viz., the Restoration, the Plague, and the Revolution.
The famous Drumming Well at Oundle, in North-
amptonshire, was also specially active in the seventeenth century. By making a sound like the beating
of a drum, it announced the approach of a Scottish
army, and gave warning of the death of Charles II.
In the same century a pool in North Tawton parish,
Devonshire, even though dry in summer, became full
of water at the driest season before the death of
a prince, and remained so till the event happened.
Two centuries earlier a certain well at Langley Park,
in Kent, had a singular way of foretelling the future.
In view of a battle it became dry, though rain fell
heavily. If there was to be no fighting, it appeared
full of water, even during the greatest drought. A
spring at Kilbarry, in the island of Barra, Outer
Hebrides, served the same purpose, but its mode
of augury was different. In this case, as Dalyell
records in his "*Darker Superstitions*," drops of
blood appeared in prospect of war; but little
bits of peat, if peace was to remain unbroken.
Walcott mentions, in his "*Scoti-Monasticon*," that
there was at Kilwinning, in Ayrshire, "a sacred fountain which flowed in 1184, and at other times, before
a war or trouble, with blood instead of water for
eight successive days and nights." When Marvel-

sike Spring, near Brampton Bridge, in Northamp-
tonshire, overflowed its customary limits, people used
to interpret its conduct as signifying approaching
dearth, the death of some great person, or some
national disturbance. In these days, when so keen
an interest is taken in the proceedings of Parliament,
it is a pity that there is no spring in our land capable
of announcing the probable date of a dissolution.
Such a spring would relieve the public mind from
much uncertainty, and would benefit the trade and
commerce of the country.

Heritable jurisdictions were abolished in Scotland
soon after the Stuart rising of 1745. This privilege,
enjoyed till then by many landowners north of the
Tweed, was popularly known as the " right of pit and
gallows," the pit being for the drowning of women
and the gallows for the hanging of men. In 1679, a
certain woman, Janet Grant by name, was convicted
of theft in the baronial court of Sir Robert Gordon of
Gordonstone, held at Drainie, in Elginshire, and was
sentenced to be drowned in Spynie Loch. In this
and other similar cases water was used as a means of
execution. In the case of witchcraft it was called in
as a witness in the trial. The criminal proceedings
for the detection and punishment of so-called witches
form a painfully dark chapter in Scottish history.
As Mr. W. H. Davenport Adams pointedly puts it, in
his " *Witch, Warlock, and Magician,*" " The common
people for a time might have been divided into two
classes, ' witches and witchfinders.' " The same writer

observes, " Among the people of Scotland, a more
serious-minded and imaginative race than the English, the superstition of witchcraft was deeply rooted
at an early period. Its development was encouraged
not only by the idiosyncracies of the national character, but also by the nature of the country and
the climate in which they lived. The lofty mountains, with their misty summits and shadowy ravines,
their deep obscure glens, were the fitting homes of
the wildest fancies, the eeriest legends, and the
storm—crashing through the forests, and the surf
beating on the rocky shore, suggested to the ear
of the peasant or fisherman the voices of unseen
creatures—of the dread spirits of the waters and the
air." A favourite method of discovering whether an
accused person was guilty or not, was that technically
known as *pricking*. It was confidently believed that
every witch had the " devil's mark " somewhere on
her person. The existence of this mark could be
determined : for if a pin was thrust into the flesh
with the result that neither blood came, nor pain
was felt, the spot so punctured was the mark in
question. This showed, without doubt, that the
accused was guilty of the heinous crime laid to
her charge. Charles Kirkpatrick Sharpe, in his
" *History of Witchcraft in Scotland*," gives instances
of the finding of the " devil's mark." He mentions
the case of Janet Barker, a servant in Edinburgh,
who acknowledged that she possessed this particular
mark between her shoulders. A pin was stuck into

the spot and remained there for an hour without
her being aware of its presence, Such, at least, was
the way of stating the case in 1643. With this
simple test at command it is not easy to understand
why water should have been required to give
evidence. But so it was. Among various nations
the water-ordeal has been in fashion. It was
specially popular in Scotland a couple of centuries
ago. Part of the bay at St. Andrews is still styled
the Witches' Lake, recalling by its name the crude
notions and cruel practices of our ancestors. A
pool in the Carron, near Dunnottar Church in Kincardineshire, at one time served a similar purpose.

As we have seen, the sinking or the floating of
an object thrown into water in cases of sickness
told of death or recovery. In like manner innocence
or guilt could be determined in the case of persons
accused of sorcery. If the person sank, she was
innocent; but guilty, if she floated. King James
VI.—a great authority on the subject—explains why
this was so. In his "*Daemonologie*," he says,
"As in a secret murther, if the dead carcase be at
any time thereafter handled by the murtherer, it
will gush out of blood, as if the blood were raging
to the Heaven for revenge of the murtherer (God
having appointed that secret supernatural sign for
trial of that secret unnatural crime), so that it
appears that God hath appointed (for a supernatural
sign of the monstrous impiety of witches) that the
water shall refuse to receive them in her bosom

that have shaken off them the sacred water of
baptism and wilfully refused the benefit thereof."
The Abbey of Scone, in Perthshire, founded by
Alexander I., in 1114, received from him a charter
confirming the right of using the water-ordeal for
the detection of witchcraft. The place of trial was
a small island in the Tay, half-way between the
abbey and the bridge of Perth. According to the
practices, common at such trials, the accused was
thrown into the water, wrapped up in a sheet, and
having the thumbs and the great toes fastened
together. The chances of life were certainly not
great under the circumstances, for, if the poor
creature floated, she had soon to exchange water
for fire. The stake was her goal. If she sank,
the likelihood was that she would be drowned.
Bundled up in the manner described, she was
scarcely in a position to rescue herself; and the
bystanders were in no humour to give a helping
hand. Close to the town of Elgin was once a
witch-pool, known as the Order Pot, so called from
its having been the place of ordeal. Through time
it was filled up, mainly with rubbish from the
ruins of the cathedral, in fulfilment, it was believed,
of the prophecy of Thomas the Rhymer that

> "The Order Pot and Lossie grey
> Shall sweep the Chanonry kirk away."

In the seventeenth century a woman who was accused
of having brought disease on a certain man through
her sorceries was thrown into the pool. She sank,

and the crowd, who had collected to witness the
trial, exclaimed, "To Satan's kingdom, she hath gone."
The incident is of interest since the view of her
case, then taken, was contrary to the one usually
held, as explained above. Perhaps the people standing by thought that the devil was so eager to get
his own, that he would not lose the chance of securing
his victim at once. Elginshire has another memorial
of the black art in the form of The Witch's Stone
at Forres. It consists of a boulder about a yard
in diameter and probably marks the spot where
unhappy females convicted of witchcraft were executed. About the year 1790 some one wished to
turn the stone to good account for building purposes
and broke it into three pieces. The breaker, however,
was compelled to put it together again, and the
iron then used to clasp it is still in position. Legend
accounts for the breakage in a less prosaic way.
When the boulder was being carried by a witch
through the air in her apron, the apron-string broke,
and, as a result, the stone was broken too. The spot
was formerly reckoned ill-omened. It would be too
much to say that belief in the black art has vanished
from the Highlands; though, fortunately for the good
sense of our age, as well as for those who live in it,
witch pools are not now in requisition. Pennant
bears witness to the fact that belief in witchcraft
ceased in Perthshire soon after the repeal, in 1736,
of the penal statutes against witches. In more
northern districts it continued a vital part of the

popular creed till much later. The Rev. Donald
Sage mentions, in his "*Memorabilia Domestica,*"
that the Rev. Mr. Fraser, minister of Killearnan
in Ross-shire, about 1750, was much troubled with
somnolency even in the pulpit. He was in consequence thought to be bewitched—a notion that
he himself shared. Two women were fixed on, as
the cause of his unnatural slumbers. It was believed
that they had made a clay image representing the
minister and had stuck pins into it. Certain pains
felt by him were ascribed to this cause. Had it
not been for the Act of 1736, it would doubtless
have fared ill with the supposed witches.

Witches, however, were not alone in their power
of floating. According to a popular belief in the
north-west Highlands, insane people cannot sink in
water. Sir Arthur Mitchell, in the "*Proceedings of
the Society of Antiquaries of Scotland,*" volume iv.,
refers to the case of a certain madman—Wild
Murdoch by name—concerning whom strange stories
were told. He was born on the small island of
Melista, near the coast of Lewis, used only for
occasional habitation in connection with the pasturing
of cattle. Anyone born in the island is believed
to become insane. The superstition about not sinking was certainly put to a severe test in Wild
Murdoch's case. "It is said," remarks Sir Arthur,
"that his friends used to tie a rope round his body,
make it fast to the stern of the boat, and then pull
out to sea, taking the wretched man in tow. The

story goes that he was so buoyant that he could not sink; 'that they tried to press him down into the water;' that he could swim with a stone fastened to him; that when carried to the rocky holms of Melista or Greinan, round which the open Atlantic surges, and left there alone, he took to the water and swam ashore."

CHAPTER X.

WATER-SPIRITS.

"ONE of the great charms of Highland landscape is the gleam of still water that so often gives the element of repose in a scene of broken cliff and tumbled crag, of noisy cascade and driving cloud. No casual tourist can fail to notice what a wonderful variety of lakes he meets with in the course of any traverse he may take across the country. Among the higher mountains there is the little tarn nestling in a dark sunless corry, and half-encircled with grim snow-rifted crags. In the glen, there is the occasional broadening of the river into a lake that narrows again to let the stream rush down a rocky ravine.

In the wider strath there is the broad still expanse
of water, with its fringe of wood and its tree-covered
islets.   In the gneiss region of the North-West,
there is the little lochan lying in its basin of bare
rock   and   surrounded   with   scores   of   others   all
equally treeless and desolate." So writes Professor
Sir A. Geikie in his "*Scenery of Scotland.*" His point
of view is that of a scientific observer, keenly alive
to all the varied phenomena of nature.   But amid
the scenes described lived men and women who
looked at the outer world through the refracting
medium of superstition.   They saw the landscape, but
they saw also what their own imagination supplied.
In Strathspey, is a sheet of water bearing the Gaelic
name of Loch-nan-Spoiradan or the Lake of Spirits.
What shape these spirits assumed we do not know,
but there was no mistake about the form of the spirit
who guarded Lochan-nan-Deaan, close to the old
military road between Corgarff and Tomintoul.   The
appearance of this spirit may be gathered from the
Rev. Dr. Gregor's remarks in an article on " Guardian
Spirits of Wells and Lochs " in " *Folklore* " for March,
1892.   After describing the loch, he says, " It was
believed to be bottomless, and to be the abode of
a water-spirit that delighted in human sacrifice.
Notwithstanding this blood-thirsty spirit, the men of
Strathdon and Corgarff resolved to try to draw the
water from the loch, in hope of finding the remains of
those that had perished in it.   On a fixed day a
number of them met with spades and picks to cut a

way for the outflow of the water through the road.
When all were ready to begin work, a terrific yell
came from the loch, and there arose from its waters a
diminutive creature in shape of a man with a red cap
on his head. The men fled in terror, leaving their
picks and spades behind them. The spirit seized
them and threw them into the loch. Then, with a
gesture of defiance at the fleeing men, and a roar that
shook the hills, he plunged into the loch and disappeared amidst the water that boiled and heaved as
red as blood." Near the boundary, between the shires
of Aberdeen and Banff, is a small sheet of water
called Lochan-wan, i.e., Lamb's Loch. The district
around is now a deer forest, but at one time it was
used for grazing sheep. The tenants around had
the privilege of pasturing a certain number of sheep.
Dr. Gregor says, " Each one that sent sheep to this
common had to offer in sacrifice, to the spirit of the
loch, the first lamb of his flock dropped on the
common. The omission of this sacrifice brought
disaster; for unless the sacrifice was made, half of
his flock would be drowned before the end of the
grazing season." As in the case of Lochan-nan-Deaan,
an attempt was made to break the spell by draining
the loch, but this attempt, though less tragic in its
result, was equally unavailing. On three successive
days a channel was made for the outflow of the
water, but each night the work was undone. A
watch was set, and at midnight of the third day
hundreds of small black creatures were seen to rise

from the lake, each with a spade in his hand. They set about filling up the trench and finished their work in a few minutes. Mr. Charles Hardwick, in "*Traditions, Superstitions, and Folklore*," published in 1872, tells of a folk-belief, prevalent in the North of England, particularly in Lancashire. "I remember well," he says, "when very young, being cautioned against approaching to the side of stagnant pools of water partially covered with vegetation. At the time, I firmly believed that if I disobeyed this instruction a certain water 'boggart,' named Jenny Greenteeth, would drag me beneath her verdant screen and subject me to other tortures besides death by drowning."

Poetry and superstition regard external nature from the same standpoint, in as much as both think of it as animate. But there is a difference. The one endows nature with human qualities, and knows that it does so through the imagination; the other does the same, and believes that there is no imagination in the matter. The work of the former is well expressed by Dr. E. B. Tylor, when he observes, "In all that water does, the poet's fancy can discern its personality of life. It gives fish to the fisher and crops to the husbandman, it swells in fury and lays waste the land, it grips the bather with chill and cramp and holds with inexorable grasp its drowning victim." That rivers were monsters hungering, or perhaps, one should say, thirsting, for human victims is a fact borne witness to by poetry as well as by super-

stition. An example of this occurs in the following
popular rhyme connected with the Scottish Border:—

> " Tweed said to Till,
> ' What gars ye rin sae still ' ?
> Till said to Tweed,
> ' Though ye rin wi' speed,
> An' I rin slaw,
> Yet whare ye droon ae man,
> I droon twa.' "

Some Aberdeenshire lines have the same theme :—

> " Bloodthirsty Dee
> Each year needs three ;
> But bonny Don,
> She needs none."

According to folklore, there is no doubt that rivers are
" uncanny." Beneath their rippling surface dwells a
being who keeps a lookout for the unwary traveller
and seeks to draw him into the dark depths. A belief
in such a being is not always explicitly avowed. But
there are certain folk-practices undoubtedly implying
it. When anyone is drowned in a river, the natural
way to find the body is to drag the stream in the
neighbourhood of the accident. But superstition has
recourse to another method. A loaf of bread, with
or without quicksilver in it, is placed on the surface
of the water and allowed to drift with the current.
The place where the loaf becomes stationary marks
the spot where the body lies concealed. According
to another method, a boat is rowed up and down the
stream, and a drum is beat all the time. When the
boat passes over the resting place of the body the
drum will cease to sound. This was done in Derby-

shire no longer ago than 1882, in order to find the corpse of a young woman who had fallen into the Derwent. In such practices there is a virtual recognition of a water-spirit who can, by certain rites, be compelled to give up his prey, or at any rate to disclose the whereabouts of the victim. A Deeside tradition supplies a good illustration of this. A man called Farquharson-na-Cat, *i.e.*, Farquharson of the Wand, so named from his trade of basketmaking, had on one occasion to cross the river just above the famous linn. It was night. He lost his footing, was swept down into the linn, and there drowned. Search was made for his body, but in vain. His wife, taking her husband's plaid, knelt down on the river's brink, and prayed to the water-spirit to give her back her dead. She then threw the plaid into the stream. Next morning her husband's corpse, with the plaid wrapped round it, was found lying on the edge of the pool. Till quite lately, fishing on the Tweed was believed to be influenced by the fairies of the river. Salt was thrown into the water, and sprinkled on the nets to insure a plentiful catch of fish. This was really the offering of a sacrifice to the river-spirits.

Frequently the guardian of the flood appeared in distinctly human shape. An excellent example of this is to be found in Hugh Miller's "*My Schools and Schoolmasters*," where a picturesque description is given of the spirit haunting the Conan. Hugh Miller was an expert swimmer, and delighted to bathe in the pools of that Ross-shire stream. "Its goblin or water-wraith, he tells us, "used to appear as a tall woman dressed in green, but distinguished chiefly by her withered, meagre countenance, ever distorted by a malignant scowl. I knew all the various fords, always dangerous ones, where of old she used to start, it was said, out of the river before the terrified traveller to point at him as in derision with her skinny finger, or to beckon him invitingly on ; and I was shown the very tree to which a poor Highlander had clung when, in crossing the river by night, he was seized by the goblin, and from which, despite of his utmost exertions, though assisted by a young lad, his companion, he was dragged into the middle of the current, where he perished. And when in swimming at sunset over some dark pool, where the eye failed to mark, or the foot to sound, the distant bottom, the twig of some sunken bush or tree has struck against me as I passed, I have felt, with sudden start, as if touched by the cold, bloodless fingers of the goblin." At Pierse Bridge, in Durham, the water-spirit of the Tees went by the name of Peg Powler, and there were stories in the district, of naughty children having been dragged by her into the river.

In the Highlands and Lowlands alike, the spirit inhabiting rivers and lakes was commonly known as the water-kelpy. A south country ballad says:—

> " The side was steep, the bottom deep
> Frae bank to bank the water pouring ;
> And the bonnie lass did quake for fear,
> She heard the water-kelpie roaring."

M

Who does not remember Burns's lines in his "*Address
to the Deil*"?—

> " When thowes dissolve the snawy hoord,
>   An' float the jinglin' icy-boord,
>   Then water-kelpies haunt the foord
>   By your direction ;
>   An' 'nighted travellers are allur'd
>   To their destruction.
>
> An' aft your moss-traversin' spunkies
>   Decoy the wight that late and drunk is:
>   The bleezin', curst, mischievous monkeys
>   Delude his eyes.
>   Till in some miry slough he sunk is,
>   Ne'er mair to rise."

The kelpy corresponded in attributes with the
Icelandic Nikr; whence has come our term Old Nick,
popularly applied to the devil. A well-known picture by Sir Noel Paton has familiarised the story of
"Nickar, the soulless," who is there represented as
a creature with frog-like feet, but with a certain
human look about him, crouching among sedge by
the side of water, and playing his ghittern—an
instrument resembling a guitar. He appears, however, more melancholy and less mischievous than
the other members of his fraternity. A kelpy that
idled away his time with music and made no attempt
to drown anybody, was quite an exceptional being.
In Sweden, where Nikr was regarded with awe, ferry-
men at specially dangerous parts of rivers warned
those who were crossing in their boat not even to
mention his name, lest some mishap should follow.
In his "*Saxons in England*," Mr. J. M. Kemble

thus refers to other manifestations of the same
creature:—"The beautiful Nix or Nixie who allures
the young fisher or hunter to seek her embraces
in the wave which brings his death; the Neck who
seizes upon and drowns the maidens who sport
upon his banks; the river-spirit who still yearly, in
some parts of Germany, demands tribute of human
life, are all forms of the ancient Nicor." The same
writer continues:—"More pleasing is the Swedish
Stromkarl, who, from the jewelled bed of his river,
watches with delight the children gambol in the
adjoining meadows, and singing sweetly to them in
the evening, detaches from his hoary hair the sweet
blossoms of the water-lily, which he wafts over the
surface to their hands." In his *Folklore of East
Yorkshire,*" Mr. J. B. Nicholson alludes to a haunted
pool between Bewholme and Atwick, at the foot of
the hill on which Atwick Church stands. This pool
is shaded by willows, and is believed to be haunted
by a spirit known in the district as the Halliwell
Boggle. In connection with Robin Round Cap Well,
in the same district, Mr. Nicholson tells a story—
found also in the south of Scotland—of a certain
house-spirit or brownie, who proved so troublesome
to the farmer whom he served that his master resolved
to remove to other quarters. The furniture was
accordingly put in carts and a start was made for
the new home. On the way, a friend accosted the
farmer and asked if he was flitting. Before he could
reply, a voice came from the churn—"Ay, we're

flitting!" and, behold, there sat Robin Round Cap.
The farmer, seeing that he could not thus rid himself
of the spirit, returned to his old home; but, afterwards, he succeeded in charming the brownie into
a well, where he still remains.   The same writer
relates a superstition about a certain round hole near
Flamborough where a girl once committed suicide.
"It is believed," he says, "that anyone bold enough
to run nine times round this place will see Jenny's
spirit come out, dressed in white; but no one has
yet been bold enough to venture more than eight
times, for then Jenny's spirit called out:—

> 'Ah'll tee on my bonnet
> An' put on me shoe,
> An' if thoo's nut off
> Ah'll seean catch thoo!'

A farmer, some years ago, galloped round it on
horseback, and Jenny did come out, to the great
terror of the farmer, who put spurs to his horse and
galloped off as fast as he could, the spirit after him.
Just on entering the village, the spirit, for some
reason unknown, declined to proceed further, but
bit a piece clean out of the horse's flank, and the
old mare had a white patch there to her dying day."

In the "*Folklore Journal*" for 1889, Dr. Gregor
relates some kelpy legends collected by him in
Aberdeenshire.   On one occasion a man had to cross
the Don by the bridge of Luib, Corgarff, to get to
his wife who was then very ill.   When he reached
the river, he found that the bridge—a wooden one—

had been swept away by a flood. He despaired of
reaching the other bank, when a tall man suddenly
appeared and offered to carry him across. The man
was at first doubtful, but ere long accepted the
proffered help. When they reached the middle of
the river, the kelpy, who had hitherto shown himself
so obliging, sought to plunge his burden beneath the
water. A struggle ensued. The man finally found
a foothold, and, disengaging himself from the kelpy,
scrambled in all haste up the bank. His would-be
destroyer, disappointed of his victim, hurled a boulder
after him. This boulder came to be known as the
Kelpy's Stane. Passers-by threw a stone beside it
till eventually a heap was formed, locally styled the
Kelpy's Cairn. A Braemar kelpy stole a sackful of
meal from a mill to give it to a woman for whom he
had taken a fancy. As the thief was disappearing,
the miller caught sight of him and threw a fairy-
whorl at his retreating figure. The whorl broke
his leg, and the kelpy fell into the mill-race and
was drowned. Such was the fate of the last
kelpy seen in Braemar. Sutherland, too, abounded
in water-spirits. They used to cross the mouth of
the Dornoch Firth in cockle-shells, but, getting
tired of this mode of transit, they resolved to build
a bridge. It was a magnificent structure, the piers
being headed with pure gold. A countryman,
happening to pass, saw the bridge, and invoked a
blessing on the workmen and their work. Immediately, the workmen vanished, and their work

sank beneath the waves. Where it spanned the Firth there is now a sandbar dangerous to mariners. Miss Dempster, who recounts this legend in the "*Folklore Journal*" for 1888, supplies further information about the superstition of the district. A banshee, adorned with gold ornaments and wearing a silk dress, was seen hurrying down a hill near the river Shin, and finally plunging into one of its deep pools. These banshees were commonly web-footed, and seemed addicted to finery, if we may judge from the instance just given, and from another mentioned by Mr. Campbell in his "*Tales of the West Highlands.*" He there speaks of one who frequented a stream about four miles from Skibo Castle in Dornoch parish. The miller's wife saw her. "She was sitting on a stone, quiet, and beautifully dressed in a green silk dress, the sleeves of which were curiously puffed from the wrists to the shoulder. Her long hair was yellow like ripe corn, but on nearer view she had no nose." Miss Dempster narrates the following incident connected with the water-spirit haunting another Sutherland river:—"One, William Munro, and the grandfather of the person from whom we have this story, were one night leading half-a-dozen pack-horses across a ford in the Oikel, on their way to a mill. When they neared the river bank a horrid scream from the water struck their ears. 'It is the Vaicgh,' cried the lad, who was leading the first horse, and, picking up some stones, he sent a shower of them into the deep pool at his feet. She must have been repeatedly hit, as she emitted a series of the most piercing shrieks. 'I am afraid,' said Monro, 'that you have not done that right, and that she will play us an ugly trick at the ford.' 'Never mind, we will take more stones,' he answered, arming himself with a few. But the kelpy had had enough of stones for one night."

Off the Rhinns of Islay is a small island formerly used for grazing cattle. A strong tide sweeps past the island, making the crossing of the Sound dangerous. A story, related by Mr. Campbell, tells that on a certain boisterous night a woman was left in charge of a large herd of cattle on the island. She was sitting in her cabin, when all at once she heard strange noises outside, and, looking up, saw a pair of large eyes gazing in at her through the window. The door opened, and a strange creature strode in. He was tall and hairy, with a livid covering on his face instead of skin. He advanced towards the woman and asked her name. She replied in Gaelic, "Mise mi Fhin"— "Me myself." He then seized her. In her terror she threw a ladleful of boiling water on the intruder. Yelling with pain he bounded out of the hut. These unearthly voices asked what was the matter, and who had hurt him? "Mise mi Fhin" —"Me myself," replied the creature. The answer was received with a shout of laughter from his mysterious companions. The woman rushed out of the hut, and dislodging one of the cows lay down on the spot, at the same time making a magical circle round her on the ground. All night she heard terrible sounds mingling with the roaring of the wind. In the morning the supernatural manifestations disappeared, and she felt herself safe. It had not fared, however, so well with the cow, for, when found, it was dead.

In Chapter I. reference was made to mermen and mermaids, and little requires to be added in the present connection. In the south of Scotland the very names of these sea-spirits have a far-off sound about them. No one beside the Firths of Forth and Clyde expects nowadays to catch sight of such strange forms sitting on rocks, or playing among the breakers; but among our Northern Isles it is otherwise. Every now and again (at long intervals, perhaps) the mysterious mermaid makes her appearance, and gives new life to an old super-stition. About three years since, one was seen at Deerness in Orkney. She reappeared last year, and was then noticed by some lobstermen who were working their creels. She had a small black head, white body, and long arms. Somewhat later, a creature, believed to be this mermaid, was shot not far from the shore, but the body was not captured. In June of the present year another mermaid was seen by the Deerness people. At Birsay, recently, a farmer's wife was down at the sea-shore, and observed a strange creature among

the rocks. She went back for her husband, and
the two returned quite in time to get a good view
of the interesting stranger. The woman spoke of
the mermaid as "a good-looking person"; while
her husband described her as "having a covering
of brown hair." Curiosity seems to have been
uppermost in the minds of the couple, for they
tried to capture the creature. In the interests of
folklore, if not of science, she managed to escape,
and was quickly lost to sight beneath the waves.
Perhaps, as the gurgling waters closed over her,
she may have uttered an *au revoir*, or whatever
corresponds to that phrase in the language of the
sea. The following story about a mermaid, told by
Mr. J. H. Dixon in his "*Gairloch*," published in
1886, is fully credited in the district where the
incident occurred:—"Roderick Mackenzie, the elderly
and much respected boat-builder at Port Henderson,
when a young man, went one day to a rocky part
of the shore there. Whilst gathering bait he
suddenly spied a mermaid asleep among the rocks.
Rorie 'went for' that mermaid, and succeeded in
seizing her by the hair. The poor creature in great
embarrassment cried out that if Rorie would let go
she would grant him whatever boon he might ask.
He requested a pledge that no one should ever be
drowned from any boat he might build. On his
releasing her the mermaid promised that this should
be so. The promise has been kept throughout
Rorie's long business career—his boats still defy

the stormy winds and waves." Mr. Dixon adds, "I am the happy possessor of an admirable example of Rorie's craft. The most ingenious framer of trade advertisements might well take a hint from this veracious anecdote."

CHAPTER XI.

MORE WATER-SPIRITS.

Water-horses and Water-bulls—Highland Superstition—Spiritual
Water-demon and Material Water-monster—Water-bulls of
Loch Llundavrà and Loch Achtriachtan—Water-horses of Loch
Treig—Kelpy of Loch Ness—Water-horse Bridles—Pontage
Pool—Kelpy's Footprint—MacCulloch and Sir Walter Scott—
Recent Example of Belief in Water-monster—Tarroo-Ushtey
in the Isle of Man—Other Water-spirits—Dragon—Black-dog—
Fly—Fish—Demons—Origin of Well-worship.

So far we have been dealing with water-spirits more
or less human in form. Another class consists of
those with the shape and attributes of horses and
bulls. The members of this class are connected
specially with Highland districts. Lonely lochs were
their favourite haunts. In treeless regions, a belief
in such creatures would naturally arise. Any
ordinary animal in such an environment would
appear of a larger size than usual, and the eye of
the beholder would transmit the error to his imagination, thereby still further magnifying the creature's
bulk. In some instances, the notion might arise
even when there was no animal on the scene. A
piece of rock, or some other physical feature of the

landscape would be enough to excite superstitious
fancies.   Mr. Campbell remarks, "In Sutherland
and elsewhere, many believe that they have seen
these fancied animals. I have been told of English
sportsmen who went in pursuit of them, so circum-
stantial were the accounts of those who believed
they had seen them. The witnesses are so numerous,
and their testimony agrees so well, that there must
be some old deeply-rooted Celtic belief which clothes
every object with the dreaded form of the Each
Uisge, *i.e.*, Water-horse." When waves appeared
on a lake, and there seemed no wind to account for
them, superstitious people readily grasped at the
idea that the phenomenon was due to the action of
some mysterious water-spirit. As Dr. Tylor points
out, there seems to have been a confusion " between
the 'spiritual water-demon' and the 'material water-
monster.'" Any creature found in or near the water
would naturally be reckoned its guardian spirit.

The Rev. Dr. Stewart gives the following particulars about water-horses and water-bulls in his
"*'Twixt Ben Nevis and Glencoe.*" They are thought
of " as, upon the whole, of the same shape and form
as the more kindly quadrupeds after whom they
have been named, but larger, fiercer, and with an
amount of 'devilment' and cunning about them, of
which the latter, fortunately, manifest no trace.
They are always fat and sleek, and so full of strength
and spirit and life that the neighing of the one
and the bellowing of the other frequently awake

the mountain echoes to their inmost recesses for miles and miles around. . . . Calves and foals are the result of occasional intercourse between these animals and their more civilised domestic congeners, such calves bearing unmistakable proofs of their mixed descent in the unusual size and pendulousness of their ears and the wide aquatic spread of their jet black hoofs; the foals, in their clean limbs, large flashing eyes, red distended nostrils, and fiery spirit. The initiated still pretend to point out cattle with more or less of this questionable blood in them, in almost every drove of pure Highland cows and heifers you like to bring under their notice." The lochs of Llundavrà and Achtriachtan, in Glencoe, were at one time famous for their water-bulls; and Loch Treig for its water-horses, believed to be the fiercest specimens of that breed in the world. If anyone suggested to a Lochaber or Rannoch Highlander that the cleverest horse-tamer could "clap a saddle on one of the demon-steeds of Loch Treig, as he issues in the grey dawn, snorting, from his crystal-paved sub-lacustral stalls, he would answer, with a look of mingled horror and awe, 'Impossible!' The water-horse would tear him into a thousand pieces with his teeth and trample and pound him into pulp with his jet-black, iron-hard, though unshod hoofs!"

A noted demon-steed once inhabited Loch Ness, and was a cause of terror to the inhabitants of the neighbourhood. Like other kelpies, he was in the

habit of browsing along the roadside, all bridled
and saddled, as if waiting for some one 'to mount
him. When any unwary traveller did so, the kelpy
took to his heels, and presently plunged into
deep water with his victim on his back. Mr. W.
G. Stewart, in his "*Highland Superstitions and
Amusements*," tells a story to show that the kelpy
in question did not always have things his own way.
A Highlander of the name of MacGrigor resolved to
throw himself in the way of the water-horse in the
hope of getting the better of him. The meeting took
place in the solitary pass of Slochd-Muichd, between
Strathspey and Inverness. The kelpy looked as innocent as usual, and was considerably startled when
MacGrigor, sword in hand, struck him a blow on the
nose. The weapon cut through the bridle, and the
bit, falling to the ground, was instantly picked up
by MacGrigor. This was the turning point of the
encounter. The kelpy was powerless without his bit,
and requested to have it restored. Though a horse,
the kelpy had the power of human speech, and con-
versed, doubtless in excellent Gaelic, with his victor,
using various arguments to bring about the restoration of his lost property. Finding that these were
unavailing, he prophesied that MacGrigor would never
enter his house with the bit in his possession, and
when they arrived at the door he planted himself in
front of it to block the entrance. The Highlander,
however, outwitted the kelpy, for, going round to the
back of his house, he called his wife and flung the bit

to her through a window. Returning to the kelpy,
he told him where the bit was, and assured him that
he would never get it back again. As there was a
rowan cross above the door the demon-steed could
not enter the house, and presently departed uttering
certain exclamations not intended for benedictions.
Those who doubt the truthfulness of the narrative
may have their doubts lessened when they learn that
this was not the only case of a water-horse's bit becoming the property of a human being. The Rev.
Dr. Stewart narrates an anecdote bearing on this.
A drover, whose home was in Nether Lochaber, was
returning from a market at Pitlochry by way of the
Moor of Rannoch. Night came on; but, as the moon
was bright, he continued his journey without difficulty. On reaching Lochanna Cuile, he sat down
to refresh himself with bread, cheese, and milk.
While partaking of this temperate repast he caught
sight of something glittering on the ground, and,
picking it up, he found it to be a horse's bridle.
Next morning he was astonished to find that the
bit and buckles were of pure silver and the reins of
soft and beautifully speckled leather. He was still
more surprised to find that the bit when touched was
unbearably hot. A wise woman from a neighbouring
glen was called in to solve the mystery. She at once
recognised the article to be a water-horse's bridle, and
accounted for the high temperature of the bit on the
ground that the silver still retained the heat that it
possessed when in a molten state below ground. The

reins, she said, were made of the skin of a certain poisonous serpent that inhabited pools frequented by water-horses. According to her directions, the bridle was hung on a *cromag* or crook of rowan wood. Its presence brought a blessing to the house, and the drover prospered in all his undertakings. When he died, having no children of his own, he bequeathed the magical bridle to his grandnephew, who prospered in his turn.

A pool in the North Esk, in Forfarshire, called the Ponage or Pontage Pool, was at one time the home of a water-horse. This creature was captured by means of a magical bridle, and kept in captivity for some time. While a prisoner he was employed to carry stones to Morphie, where a castle was then being built. One day the bridle was incautiously removed, and the creature vanished, but not before he exclaimed—

> "Sair back an' sair banes,
> Carryin' the Laird o' Morphie's stanes;
> The Laird o' Morphie canna thrive
> As lang's the kelpy is alive."

His attempted verse-making seems to have gratified the kelpy, for when he afterwards showed himself in the pool he was frequently heard repeating the rhyme. The fate of the castle was disastrous. At a later date it was entirely demolished, and its site now alone remains. Some six miles from the Kirkton of Glenelg, in Inverness-shire, is the small sheet of water known in the district as John MacInnes' Loch. It was so called from a crofter of that

name who was drowned there. The circumstances
are thus narrated by Mr. J. Calder Ross in "*Scottish
Notes and Queries*" for February, 1893: "John
MacInnes found the labour of his farm sadly burden-
some. In the midst of his sighing an unknown
being appeared to him and promised a horse to him
under certain conditions. These conditions John
undertook to fulfil. One day, accordingly, he found a
fine horse grazing in one of his fields. He happened
to be ploughing at the time, and at once he yoked the
animal to the plough along with another horse. The
stranger worked splendidly, and he determined to
keep it, though he well knew that it was far from
canny. Every night when he stabled it he spread
some earth from a mole's hill over it as a charm;
according to another version he merely blessed the
animal. One night he forgot his usual precautions:
perhaps he was beginning to feel safe. The horse
noticed the omission, and seizing poor John in his
teeth, galloped off with him. The two disappeared
in the loch."

Water-horses were not always malignant in disposition. On one occasion an Aberdeenshire farmer
went with his own horse to a mill to fetch home
some sacks of meal. He left the horse at the door
of the mill and went in to bring out the sacks.
The beast, finding itself free, started for home.
When the farmer reappeared and found the creature
gone he was much disconcerted, and uttered the
wish that he might get any kind of horse to carry

N

his sacks even though it were a water-kelpy. To his surprise, a water-horse immediately appeared! It quietly allowed itself to be loaded with the meal, and accompanied the farmer to his home. On reaching the house he tied the horse to an old harrow till he should get the sacks taken into the house. When he returned to stable the animal that had done him the good turn, horse and harrow were away, and he heard the beast plunging not far off in a deep pool in the Don. If anyone refuses to believe in the existence of water-horses, let him go to the parish of Fearn, in Forfarshire, and there, near the ruined castle of Vayne, he will see on a sandstone rock the print of a kelpy's foot. Noran Water flows below the castle, and the mysterious creature had doubtless its home in one of its pools. In Shetland, such kelpies were known as Nuggles, and showed themselves under the form of Shetland ponies.

MacCulloch, the author of " *A Description of the Western Islands of Scotland*," found the belief in the water-bull a living faith among the people, notably among the dwellers beside Loch Rannoch and Loch Awe. He tells of a farmer who employed his sons to search a certain stream for one of these creatures, while the farmer himself carried a gun loaded with sixpences to be discharged when the monster appeared, silver alone having any effect on such beasts. The same writer, when speaking of the grandeur of the scenery about Loch Coruisk, remarks:—"It is not surprising that Coruisk should be considered by the natives as the haunt of the water-goblin or of spirits still more dreadful. A seaman, and a bold one, whom, on one occasion, I had left in charge of the boat, became so much terrified at finding himself alone that he ran off to join his comrades, leaving it moored to the rock, though in danger of being destroyed by the surge. I afterwards overheard much discussion on the courage of the Southron in making the circuit of the valley unattended. Not returning till it was nearly dark, it was concluded that he had fallen into the fangs of the kelpy." MacCulloch's " *Description* " consists of a series of letters to Sir Walter Scott. Sir Walter himself has an interesting reference to the same superstition in. his " *Journal,*" under date November 23rd, 1827. After enumerating the company at a certain dinner party at which he had been present, he continues : " Clanronald told us, as an instance of Highland credulity, that a set of his kinsmen—Borradale and others—believing that the fabulous ' water-cow ' inhabited a small lake near his house, resolved to drag the monster into day. With this view they bivouacked by the side of the lake in which they placed, by way of night-bait, two small anchors such as belong to boats, each baited with the carcase of a dog slain for the purpose. They expected the ' water-cow ' would gorge on this bait, and were prepared to drag her ashore the next morning, when, to their confusion

of face, the baits were found untouched. It is
something too late in the day for setting baits for
water-cows." If such conduct seemed wonderful in
1827, what would the author of "*Waverley*" have
thought had he known that more than half-a-century
later, people in the Highlands retained a thorough-
going belief in such monsters? No longer ago than
1884 rumours were current in Ross-shire that a
water-cow was seen in or near a loch on the
Greenstone Point, in Gairloch parish. Mr. J. H.
Dixon, in his "*Gairloch*," states that about 1840 a
water-cow was believed to inhabit Loch-na-Beiste,
in the same parish, and that a serious attempt was
then made to destroy the creature. The proprietor
tried to drain the loch, which, except at one point,
is little more than a fathom in depth; but when
his efforts failed he threw a quantity of quicklime
into the water to poison the monster. It is reasonable to hold that the trout were the only sufferers.
The creature in question was described by two men
who saw it as in appearance like "a good sized boat
with the keel turned up." Belief in the existence of
water-cows prevailed in the south as well as in the
north of Scotland. In the Yarrow district there was
one inhabiting St. Mary's Loch. Concerning this
water-cow, Hogg, the Ettrick Shepherd, writes:
"A farmer in Bowerhope once got a breed of her,
which he kept for many years until they multiplied
exceedingly; and he never had any cattle throve so
well, until once, on some outrage or disrespect on the

farmer's part towards them, the old dam came out
of the lake one pleasant March evening and gave
such a roar that all the surrounding hills shook
again, upon which her progeny, nineteen in number,
followed her all quietly into the loch, and were
never more seen."

In the Isle of Man the water-bull was, and perhaps
still is believed in by the peasantry. It is called in
Manx, tarroo-ushtey.   There is much force in Mr.
Campbell's conclusion that the old Celts reverenced
a destroying water-god, to whom the horse was
sacred, or who assumed the form of a horse.   A
similar notion may have originated the belief in
the water-bull.

Other creatures, besides those already mentioned,
acted in the capacity of water spirits. In Strath-
martin, in Forfarshire, is a spring styled the Nine
Maidens' Well.   These maidens were the daughters of
a certain Donewalde or Donald in the eighth century,
and led, along with their father, a saintly life in the
glen of Ogilvy in the same county.   Their spring at
Strathmartin must have been well looked after, for it
had as its guardian, no less formidable a creature than
a dragon.   We do not know whether there was any
St. George in the vicinity to dispute possession with
the monster.   In Kildonan parish, Sutherland, a
stagnant pool of water, some ten yards long by three
broad, was regarded by the inhabitants with superstitious dread.   According to tradition, a pot of gold
lay hidden below ; but no one could reach the treasure

as it was guarded by a large black dog with two heads. The Rev. Donald Sage, when noticing this superstition in his "*Memorabilia Domestica*," remarks, "It is said that a tenant once had attempted to drain the loch and had succeeded, so that the water was all carried off. The only remuneration the unfortunate agriculturist received was to be aroused from his midnight slumbers by a visit from the black dog, which set up such a hideous howl as made the hills reverberate and the poor man almost die with fright. Furthermore, with this diabolical music, he was regularly serenaded at the midnight hour till he had filled up the drain, and the loch had resumed its former dimensions." We do not know whether any later attempt was made to abolish the stagnant pool; but at any rate a dread of the black dog kept it from being again drained till well on in the present century. Sutherland, however, cannot claim a monopoly in the matter of a guardian spirit in the shape of a dog. Concerning Hound's Pool in Dean Combe parish, Devon, the tradition is that it is haunted by a hound doomed to keep guard till the pool can be emptied by a nutshell with a hole in it. Readers of "*Peveril of the Peak*" can hardly fail to remember the Moddey Dhoo — the black demon-dog — that roamed through Peel Castle, in the Isle of Man. St. Michael's Well in Kirkmichael parish, Banffshire, had for its guardian spirit a much smaller animal than any of the above. It showed itself in the form of a fly that kept skimming over the surface of the water.

This fly was believed to be immortal. Towards the end of last century the spring lost its reputation for its cures, and the guardian spirit shared in its neglect. The writer of the article on the parish, in the "*Old Statistical Account of Scotland*," mentions having met an old man who greatly deplored the degeneracy of the times. A glowing picture is given of this old man's desires. "If the infirmities of years and the distance of his residence did not prevent him, he would still pay his devotional visits to the well of St. Michael. He would clear the bed of its ooze, opening a passage for the streamlet, plant the borders with fragrant flowers, and once more, as in the days of youth, enjoy the pleasure of seeing the guardian fly skim in sportive circles over the bubbling waves, and with its little proboscis imbibe the panacean dews."

Consecrated fish have been reverenced, from of old, in East and West alike. In Syria, at the present day, such fish are preserved in fountains; and anciently certain pools in the stream, flowing past Ascalon, were the abodes of fish sacred to Derketo, the Phœnician Venus, who had a temple there. In our own land the same cult prevailed. A curious Cornish legend tells how St. Neot had his well stocked with fish by an angel. These fish were always two in number. Day by day, the saint had one for dinner, and its place was miraculously supplied to keep up the proper number. One day he fell sick, and his servant, contrary to all ascetic precedent, cooked both and set them before

his master. The saint was horrified, and had both
the fish—cooked though they were—put back into the
spring. He sought forgiveness for the rash act, and
lo! the fish became alive once more; and as a further
sign that the sacrilege was condoned, St. Neot, on
eating his usual daily portion, was at once restored
to health. In Scotland there were various springs
containing consecrated fish. Loch Siant, in the Isle
of Skye, described by MacCulloch as "the haunt of
the gentler spirits of air and water," abounded in
trout; but, as Martin informs us, neither the natives
nor strangers ever dared to kill any of them on
account of the esteem in which the water was held.
This superstition seems to have been specially cherished in the island, for Martin further says, "I saw a
little well in Kilbride, in the south of Skie, with one
Trout only in it; the natives are very tender of it,
and though they often chance to catch it in their
wooden pales, they are very careful to preserve it
from being destroyed; it has been there for many
years." In a well near the church of Kilmore, in
Lorne, were two fishes held in much respect in the
seventeenth century, and called by the people of the
district, Easg Seant, *i.e.*, holie fishes. From Dalyell's
"Darker Superstitions of Scotland" we learn that,
like those belonging to St. Neot, they were always
two in number: they never varied in size: in colour
they were black, and according to the testimony of
the most aged persons their hue never altered. In
Tober Kieran, near Kells, County Meath, Ireland,

were two miraculous trout which never changed their appearance. A Strathdon legend, narrated by the Rev. Dr. Gregor, thus accounts for the appearance of fish in Tobar Vachar, *i.e.*, St. Machar's Well, at Corgarff, a spring formerly held in high honour on account of its cures:—"Once there was a famine in the district, and not a few were dying of hunger. The priest's house stood not far from the well. One day, during the famine, his housekeeper came to him and told him that their stock of food was exhausted, and that there was no more to be got in the district. The priest left the house, went to the well, and cried to St. Machar for help. On his return he told the servant to go to the well the next morning at sunrise, walk three times round it, in the name of the Father, Son, and Holy Ghost, without looking into it, and draw from it a draught of water for him. She carried out the request. On stooping down to draw the water, she saw three fine salmon swimming in the well. They were caught, and served the two as food, till supply came to the famine-stricken district from other quarters." According to a Herefordshire tradition, a fish with a golden chain round it was caught in the river Dore, and was afterwards kept in the spring whence the river flows. At Peterchurch, in that county, is a sculptured stone bearing a rude representation of the fish in question.

Sometimes the guardian spirit of a loch or well was thought of in the vaguest possible way. In that case the *genius loci* had neither name nor shape of any kind, the leaving of an offering being the only recognition of his existence. Occasionally the presiding spirit was pictured in the popular imagination in the guise of a demon, commonly with a hazy personality. Callow Pit, in Norfolk, was believed to contain a treasure-chest guarded by such a being. On one occasion an attempt to raise the chest was made, and was on the verge of being successful, when one of the treasure-hunters defied the devil to get his own again. Suddenly the chest was snatched down into the pit, and the ring, attached to the lid, alone remained to tell its tale. This ring was afterwards fixed to the door of Southwood Church. At Wavertree, in Lancashire, once stood a monastery and beside it was a well. When pilgrims arrived, the occupants of the monastery received their alms. If nothing was given, a demon, chained to the bottom of the well, was said to laugh. This notion was either originated or perpetuated by a fifteenth century Latin inscription to this effect, " *Qui non dat quad habet. Daemon infra ridet.*" When wells were dedicated to Christian saints, the latter were usually considered the guardians of the sacred water. This was natural enough. If, for instance, St. Michael was supposed to watch over a spring, why should not his aid have been sought in connection with any wished-for cure ? It is interesting, however, to note that this was not so in every instance. In many cases the favourite, because favourable time for visiting a sacred spring, was not the festival of the saint to whom it was dedicated, but, as we shall see hereafter, a day quite distinct from such festival. Petitions, too, were frequently addressed not to the saint of the well, but to some being with a character possessing fewer Christian attributes. All this points to the fact that the origin of well-worship is to be sought, not in the legends of mediæval Christianity, but in the crude fancies of an earlier paganism.

CHAPTER XII.

Offerings at Lochs and Springs.

Offerings at lochs and springs have been incidentally
mentioned more than once, but the subject is one
deserving separate treatment. Wells were not merely
so much water, with stones and turf round them, and
lochs, sheets of water, encompassed by moorland or
forest. They were, as we have seen, the haunts of
spirits, propitious if remembered, but resentful if
neglected. Hence no one thought it proper to come
to them empty-handed. The principle was, no gift,
no cure. Classical literature contains allusions to

such votive offerings.   Numa sacrificed a sheep to
a fountain, and Horace promised to offer to his sweet
Bandusian spring a kid not without flowers.   Near
Toulouse, in France, was a sacred lake, into whose
water the neighbouring tribes anciently threw offerings of gold and silver.   In our own country, the
gifts were, as a rule, of small intrinsic value.   When
speaking of Toubir-nim-buadh, in St. Kilda, Macaulay
says:—" Near the fountain stood an altar on which
the distressed votaries laid down their oblations.
Before they could touch the sacred water with any
prospect of success, it was their constant practice
to address the genius of the place with supplication
and prayer.   No one approached him with empty
hands.   But the devotees were abundantly frugal.
The offerings, presented by them, were the poorest
acknowledgments that could be made to a superior
being, from whom they had either hopes or fears.
Shells and pebbles, rags of linen, or stuffs worn out,
pins, needles, or rusty nails, were generally all the
tribute that was paid ; and sometimes, though rarely
enough, copper coins of the smallest value."   The
appearance of this well is thus described by the
author of " *Ecclesiological Notes*":—"A low square-
shaped massy stone building with a stone roof, covers
the spring, which, after forming a pool in the floor of
the cell, runs down the russet slope like a thread of
silver to join the stream in the valley."

The offerings, made by the St. Kildians, were indeed
much the same as those commonly made in other

parts of the country. We get a glimpse of what was done in the south of Scotland from Symson, who, in his quaint " *Description of Galloway,*" remarks:—" In this parish of Bootle, about a mile from the kirk, towards the north, is a well called the Rumbling Well, frequented by a multitude of sick people for all sorts of diseases the first Sunday of May; lying there the Saturday night, and then drinking of it early in the morning. There is also another well, about a quarter of a mile distant from the former, towards the east. This well is made use of by the country people when their cattle are troubled with a disease called by them the Connoch. This water they carry in vessels to many parts and wash their beasts with it, and give it them to drink. It is, too, remembered that at both the wells they leave behind them something by way of a thank-offering. At the first, they leave either money or clothes; at the second, they leave the bands and shackles wherewith beasts are usually bound." The objects, commonly left on the cairns beside the Holy Pool in Strathfillan, have already been enumerated. In addition, bunches of heath, tied with worsted, were occasionally left. The Cheese Well, on Minchmoor, in Peeblesshire, was so called from the pieces of cheese thrown into it by passers-by as offerings to the fairies. Around a certain spring near Newcastle, in Northumberland, the bushes were so covered with shreds of clothing that the spring went by the name of the Rag Well. At St. Oswald's

Well, near the foot of Roseberry Topping, in Yorkshire, the pieces of cloth were so numerous that,
as a spectator once remarked, they "might have
made a fair ream in a paper-mill." A contributor
to "*Notes and Queries*," in 1876, observes:—"The
custom of hanging shreds of rags on trees as votive
offerings still obtains in Ireland. I remember as a
child to have been surreptitiously taken by an Irish
nurse to St. John's Well, Aghada, County Cork, on
the vigil of the saint's day, to be cured of whooping-
cough by drinking three times of the water of the
holy well. I shall never forget the strange spectacle
of men and women, creeping on their knees in volun-
tary devotion, or in obedience to enjoined penance,
so many times round the well, which was protected
by a grey stone hood, and had a few white thorn
trees growing near it, on the spines of which fluttered
innumerable shreds of frieze and vary-coloured rags,
the votive offerings of devotees and patients."

In the Isle of Man, also, the custom of hanging up
rags was at one time much in vogue. In Malew parish
there is Chibber-Undin, signifying the Foundation
Well, so called from the foundations of a now almost
obliterated chapel hard by. The ritual practised at
the well is thus described by Mr. A. W. Moore in
his "*Surnames and Place-names of the Isle of
Man*":—"The patients who came to it, took a
mouthful of water, retaining it in their mouths
till they had twice walked round the well. They
then took a piece of cloth from a garment which

they had worn, wetted it from the water from the
well, and hung it on the hawthorn tree which grew
there. When the cloth had rotted away the cure
was supposed to be effected." Evidence from Wales
to the same effect is furnished by Professor Rhys
in *"Folklore"* for September, 1892. He there
gives the following information, lately sent to him
by a friend, about a Glamorganshire holy well
situated between Coychurch and Bredgled:—"It is
the custom," he writes, "for people suffering from
any malady to dip a rag in the water, and bathe
the affected part. The rag is then placed on a tree
close to the well. When I passed it, about three
years ago, there were hundreds of these shreds
covering the tree, and some had evidently been
placed there very recently." Professor Rhys also
refers to other Glamorganshire springs where rags
are to be seen hanging on trees.

Scottish examples of the same superstition are
numerous. At Montblairie, in Banffshire, pieces of
linen and woollen stuffs were hung on the boughs
beside a consecrated well, and farthings and bodles
were thrown into the spring itself. The bushes
around a well at Houston, in Renfrewshire, were
at one time the recipients of many a rag. Hugh
Miller, who took so keen an interest in all such
relics of superstition, has not failed to notice the
custom as practised near his native town of Cromarty.
In his *"Scenes and Legends of the North of Scotland,"*
he says:—"It is not yet twenty years since a thorn

bush, which formed a little canopy over the spring of St. Bennet, used to be covered anew every season with little pieces of rag, left on it as offerings to the saint by sick people who came to drink of the water." St. Wallach's Bath, in Strathdeveron, was a popular health-resort till the beginning of the present century. Non-thriving children were brought to it annually in large numbers. No longer ago than 1874 an invalid from the seaside sought its aid. The bath—a cavity in the rock fully a yard in depth—is close to the river, and is supplied with water from a scanty spring, several yards higher up the slope. The supply trickles over the edge of the bath into the river, some four feet below. A bib or other part of the child's clothing was hung on a neighbouring tree or thrown into the bath. Sometimes when the Deveron was in flood, it submerged the bath, and swept these offerings down to the sea. As previously mentioned, St. Wallach's Well, hard by, was much resorted to for the cure of sore eyes. Pins were the usual offerings. They were left in a hole in a stone beside the well. May was the favourite season for visiting the spring, and by the end of the month the hole was often full of pins. This was the case down to a comparatively recent date.

Offerings, such as pins, were often thrown into the well itself instead of being left beside its margin. Near Wooler, in Northumberland, on the southern slopes of the Cheviots, is a spring locally styled the Pin Well. A fairy was believed to make it her

o

home, and maidens, as they passed, dropped in a
crooked pin to gain her good graces. Crooked pins
were rather popular, anything so bent—*e.g.*, a crooked
sixpence—being deemed lucky. In the case of more
than one English spring the notion prevailed that,
when a pin was thrown in, the votary would see the
pins already there rise to meet the newcomer. But
faith was essential. Otherwise the mysterious vision
would be withheld. We do not know that a corresponding belief prevailed north of the Tweed.
Between the glens of Corgarff and Glengairn in
Aberdeenshire, is the spring known as Tobar-na-Glas-
a-Coille or The Well in the Grey Wood. A pin or
other piece of metal had to be dropped into it by
anyone taking a draught of its water. Whoever
neglected this duty, and at any time afterwards again
drew water from the spring, was doomed to die of
thirst. Some of these votive pins were found at the
bottom of the well, no longer ago than the autumn of
1891.

Probably very few travellers by the Callander
and Oban railway are aware of the existence of
an interesting, but now neglected holy well, only a
few yards distant from the line. It is situated
at the entrance of rugged Glen Ogle, and from the
spot a fine view can be had of Ben Lawers, Ben
More, and Ben Loy. The well is on Wester Lix
farm, and is locally known as the Lix Well. The
spring rises in one of the many hillocks in the
neighbourhood. The top of the hillock had been

levelled. Round the spring is built a wall of stone and turf, about two feet in height, and shaped like a horse-shoe, the opening being to the east. The distance across the enclosed space is about fourteen feet. In the centre is the well, in the form of a parallelogram, two feet by one and a half, with a long drain leading from it through the opening of the horse-shoe. This drain was at one time covered with flagstones. Four shapely lintels of micaceous schist enclose the well. The spot used to be frequented at the beginning of May, the wall already referred to forming a convenient resting-place for visitors. Quartz pebbles were the favourite offerings on these occasions. Immediately behind the well, quite a small cairn of them can still be seen. Pebbles were among the cheapest possible offerings, the only cost being the trouble of picking them up. Coins were rather more expensive; but, as they were commonly of small value, the outlay was trifling even in their case. The more fervent the zeal of the votary, the greater would doubtless be the length he or she would go in the matter of expense. In the parish of Culsalmond, in Aberdeen-shire, a gold coin of James I. of Scotland was found associated with an ancient healing-well. Such liberality, however, was rare. After desribing St. Maelrubha's Well on Innis Maree in the " *Proceedings of the Society of Antiquaries of Scotland*," volume iv., Sir Arthur Mitchell observes, " Near it stands an oak tree, which is studded with nails. To each

of these was originally attached a piece of the
clothing of some patient who had visited the spot.
There are hundreds of nails, and one has still
fastened to it a faded ribbon.   Two bone buttons
and two buckles we also found nailed to the tree.
Countless pennies and halfpennies are driven edge-
ways into the wood—over many the bark is closing,
over many it has already closed." Within recent
years, another visitor from the south examined one
of the coins stuck into the tree.   It was ostensibly
silver, but proved on examination to be counterfeit.
The pilgrim, who left it as an offering, evidently
thought that the saint could be easily imposed upon.

As in the case of the pins, the coins, given as
offerings were, as a rule, thrown into the spring
itself.   As an example, we may cite the case of
St. Jergon's or St. Querdon's Well in Troqueer
parish, Kirkcudbrightshire.   In an article in the
"*Transactions of the Dumfries and Galloway Natural
History Society*" for 1870, Mr. Patrick Dudgeon
remarks, "Taking advantage of the very dry summer
of last year when the spring was unusually low,
I had the well thoroughly cleaned out and put in
order, it having been almost obliterated by cattle
being allowed to use it as a watering-place.   Several
hundreds of coins were found at the bottom—almost
all being of the smallest description of copper coin,
dating from the time of Elizabeth to that of
George III. . . .   None were of any particular
interest or value; the greatest number are Scottish,

and belong to the time of James VI., Charles I.,
and Charles II. The circumstance that no coins
were found of an older date than the reign of
Elizabeth is not at all conclusive that offerings of
a similar nature had not been made at much earlier
periods. It will be observed that the oldest coins
are the thinnest, and that, although many are as
thin as a sheet of writing paper, the legend on them
is perfectly distinct and legible; this, of course,
would not have been the case had the thinning
process been owing to wear and tear. When first
taken out, they were perfectly bright—as new
copper—and had all the appearance of having been
subjected to the action of an acid. Something in
the water has acted very slowly as a solvent on
the metal, and, acting quite equally over the whole
surface, has reduced the coins to their present state:
it is, therefore, reasonable to conclude that, owing
to the solvent properties of the water, any coins
thrown into the well anterior to the date of those
found may have been completely dissolved." Mr.
Dudgeon mentions having been told by old people
in the neighbourhood, that they remembered the
time, when rags and ribbons were hung on the
bushes around the well. It is a remarkable circumstance that even since the cleaning out of the spring
above referred to, coins have been thrown into it.
A recent examination of the spot brought these to
light, and showed the persistence of this curious
phase of well-worship.

What would be styled "a collection in silver" in modern ecclesiastical language was sometimes regarded with special favour. . The name of the Silver Wells in different parts of the country can thus be accounted for. There is a *Siller* Well in Walston parish, Lanarkshire. Arbroath, in Forfarshire; Alvah, in Banffshire; and Fraserburgh, in Aberdeenshire, have each their Silver Well. At Turriff, in the last-mentioned county, there is a farm on the estate of Gask called Silver Wells after a local spring. At Trelevean, in Cornwall, is a spring known as the Brass Well. Its name, however, is derived not from the nature of the offerings left there, but from the colour of the scum on its surface. Close to the ruins of Avoch Castle, in the Black Isle, is a well hollowed out of the conglomerate rock. Tradition says, that the treasures of the castle were thrown into it about the middle of the seventeenth century. This was done, not by way of offering a gift to the presiding spirit of the water, but to prevent the valuables from falling into the hands of Cromwell's troops. A diamond ring was dropped, not very long ago, into St. Molio's Well, on Holy Island, near Lamlash. It fell into the water by accident, and, after remaining in it for some time, was found and restored to its owner.

The present ample water-supply of Glasgow from Loch Katrine was introduced in 1859. For about fifty years before that date, the city looked mainly to the Clyde for the supply of its daily needs. Still

earlier, it depended entirely on its wells.   In 1736
these are believed to have numbered about thirty in all.
Among the best known were the Deanside or Meadow
Well, Bogle's Well, Barrasyett Well near the foot
of Saltmarket, the Priest's or Minister's Well and
Lady Well beside the Molendinar, the Arns Well in
the Green—so-called from the alders on its brink,
and St. Thenew's Well, near what is now St.
Enoch's Square.   Not far from the well was a chapel
dedicated to St. Thenew, with a graveyard round it.
Some remains of the chapel were to be seen in 1736,
when M'Ure wrote his history of the city.   Dr.
Andrew MacGeorge, in his " *Old Glasgow*," when
describing St. Thenew's Well, remarks, "It was shaded
by an old tree which drooped over the well, and
which remained till the end of the last century.
On this tree, the devotees, who frequented the well,
were accustomed to nail, as thank-offerings, small bits
of tin-iron—probably manufactured for that purpose
by a craftsman in the neighbourhood—representing
the parts of the body supposed to have been cured
by the virtues of the sacred spring, such as eyes,
hands, feet, ears, and others."   Dr. MacGeorge further
mentions that the well was cleaned out about a
hundred years ago.   On that occasion there were
" picked out from among the debris at the bottom
several of these old votive offerings which had
dropped into it from the tree, the stump of which was
at that time still standing."

Horace tells of a shipwrecked sailor, hanging up

his garments, as a thank-offering in the temple
of the divinity who delivered him from the angry
sea. In like manner, Pennant describes what he
saw at St. Winifred's Well, in 'North Wales. "All
infirmities," he says, "incident to the human body,
met with relief; the votive crutches, the barrows
and other proofs of cures, to this moment remain as
evidence pendent over the well." In his "*Spring
of Kinghorn Craig*," published in Edinburgh
in 1618, Dr. Patrick Anderson has some curious
remarks on the subject of votive offerings. He
speaks of wells as being "all tapestried about with
old rags, as certaine signes and sacraments wherewith
they arle the well with ane arls-pennie of their
health." He continues, "So suttle is that false knave
making them believe that it is only the virtue of the
water, and no thing else. Such people cannot say
with David, 'The Lord is my helper,' but the Devill."
What can still be seen on the other side of the English
Channel is thus described by the Rev. C. N. Barham,
in an article on Ragged Relics, in "*The Antiquary*"
for January, 1893 :—"At Wierre Effroy, in France,
where the water of St. Godeleine's Well is esteemed
efficacious for ague, rheumatism, gout, and all affections of the limbs, a heterogeneous collection of
crutches, bandages, coils of rags, and other rejected
adjuncts of medical treatment, is to be seen hanging
upon the surrounding shrubs. They are intended
as thankofferings and testimonies of restoration.
Other springs, famous for curing ophthalmia, abound

in the same district, and here too, bandages, shades,
guards, and rags innumerable are exhibited."

The leaving of offerings at wells finds a parallel in
the practice, at one time common, of depositing gifts
in consecrated buildings. The chapel of St. Tears, in
the parish of Wick, Caithness, used to be visited on
Childermas (December 28th) by devotees, who left in
it pieces of bread and cheese as offerings to the souls
of the Holy Innocents slain by Herod. This was done
till about the beginning of the present century. Till
even a later date it was customary for the inhabitants
of Mirelandorn to go to the Kirk of Moss, in the same
parish, on Christmas before sunrise. They took bread
and cheese as offerings, and placed them along with a
silver coin on a certain stone. The Kirk of Moss was
dedicated to Duthac, patron saint of Tain; and the
gifts were doubtless destined for him. On Eilean
Mòr is a chapel said to have been built by Charmaig,
the tutelar saint of the island. In a recess in this
building is a stone coffin, anciently used for the inter-
ment of priests. The following statement occurs in
the "*Old Statistical Account of Scotland*":—"The
coffin, also, for ages back, has served the saint as a
treasury; and this, perhaps, might be the purpose for
which it was originally intended. Till of late, not a
stranger set foot on the island who did not conciliate
his favour by dropping a small coin into a chink
between its cover and side."

When we examine the motives prompting to the
practice under review, we can discover the working

of a principle, vaguely grasped perhaps, but sufficiently
understood to serve as a guide to action. This crude
philosophy was two-fold. On the one hand, the gift
left at a loch or spring was what has been facetiously
styled a "retaining fee." It secured the goodwill of
the *genius loci*, and thereby guaranteed to a certain
extent the fulfilment of the suppliant's desire. This
desire, as we have seen, was commonly the removal of
a definite disease. On the other hand, the disease to
be removed was in some mysterious way identified
with the offering. The latter was the symbol, or
rather the embodiment of the former, and, accordingly,
to leave the gift was to leave the ailment—the patient
being thus freed from both. The corollary to this
was, that whoever removed the offering took away
also the disease represented by it. According to a
well-established law of medical science, infection is
transferred from one person to another by clothing,
or indeed by whatever comes into contact with the
morbid particles from the patient's body. But infection in folklore is something different from this.
Disease of any kind, whether usually reckoned infec-
tious or not, passed *via* the offering to the person
lifting it. Hence such gifts had a charmed existence,
and were as safe as if under the sweep of the "Ancient
Monuments Protection Act." The Rev. Dr. Gregor
thus expresses the feeling on this point, as it prevailed
till lately in the north-east of Scotland :—" No one
would have been foolhardy enough to have even
touched what had been left, far less to have carried

it off. A child, or one who did not know, was most carefully instructed why such things were left in and around the well, and strict charge was laid not to touch or carry any of them off. Whoever carried off one of such relics contracted the disease of the one who left it."

The notion that disease can be transferred lies at the root of various folk-cures. Dalyell, in his "*Darker Superstitions*," remarks, "It is said that, in the Highlands, a cat is washed in the water which has served for the ablution of an invalid, as if the disease absorbed from one living creature could be received by another, instead of being let free." In some parts of the Highlands, a common cure for an ailing cow was to make the animal swallow a live trout, so that the disease might pass from the one creature to the other. This was done not long ago, at a farm near Golspie, in Sutherland. In Norfolk, as a remedy for whooping-cough, a spider was caught, tied up in a piece of muslin, and pinned over the mantelpiece. The cough disappeared when the spider died. In Gloucester-shire, ague was cured in the following way:—A living snail was worn in a bag round the neck for nine days. The snail was then thrown upon the fire when it was believed to shake as if with ague, and the patient recovered. Many more illustrations of this principle might be given, but the above are sufficient to show how it was applied.

Symson records an instance in Galloway of swift

vengeance following the theft of certain votive offerings. He says, "Hereabout, *i.e.*, near Larg, in Minnigaff
parish, is a well called the Gout Well of Larg, of
which they tell this story—how that a piper stole
away the offering left at this well, but when he
was drinking of ale, which he intended to pay with
the money he had taken away, the gout, as they
say, seized on him, of which he could not be cured,
but at that well, having first restored to it the money
he had formerly taken away." Accident, rather than
disease, sometimes resulted from such sacrilegious
acts. The offerings were the property of the guardian spirit who was quick to resent their removal
and to punish the doer of the deed. In the district
of Ardnamurchan is a cave, associated with Columba,
who there baptised some freebooters. The water
used for the purpose lay in a hollow of the rock,
and, in after times, votive gifts were left beside it.
On one occasion, a young man stole some of these,
but he did not remain long unpunished, for before
reaching home he fell and broke his leg. Tobar-
fuar-Mòrie, *i.e.*, The big cold Well, situated at the foot
of a steep hill in the parish of Corgarff, Aberdeenshire, consists of three springs about a yard distant
from each other. Each spring formerly cured a
separate disease—one, blindness; the other, deafness;
and the third, lameness. The guardian spirit of
the springs lived under a large stone called the
kettle stone, because below it was a kettle where
she stored her votive offerings. She was somewhat

exacting in her demands, for no cure could be
expected unless gold was presented, These particulars were obtained in the district by the Rev.
Dr. Gregor, who records them in "*Folklore*" for
March, 1892, and adds, "If one tried to rob the
spirit, death by some terrible accident soon followed.
My informant, more than fifty years ago, when a
lad, resolved to remove the kettle stone from its
position, and so become possessor of the spirit's gold.
He accordingly set out with a few companions all
provided with picks and spades, to displace the stone.
After a good deal of hard labour the stone was moved
from its site, but no kettle full of gold was found.
An old woman met the lads on their way to their
homes, and when she learnt what they had been
doing, she assured them they would all die within
a few weeks, and that a terrible death would befall
the ring-leader."

That the guardians of springs look well after their
possessions in the new world, as well as in the old,
is proved by the following quotation from Sir J.
Lubbock's "*Origin of Civilisation*":—"In North
Mexico," he says, "Lieutenant Whipple found a sacred
spring which, from time immemorial 'had been held
sacred to the rain-god.' No animal may drink of its
waters. It must be annually cleansed with ancient
vases, which, having been transmitted from generation to generation by the caciques, are then placed
upon the walls, never to be removed. The frog, the
tortoise, and the rattlesnake represented upon them,

are sacred to Montezuma, the patron of the place,
who would consume by lightning any sacrilegious
hand that should dare to take the relics away."
With the growth of enlightenment men's minds
rose above such delusions. Had it not been so, the
Holy Wells in our land would still have presented
the appearance of rag fairs, or served as museums for
old coins. Holy Loch, in Dunnet, Caithness, used to
be much resorted to as a place of healing. The
invalids walked or were carried round the lake and
threw a penny into the water. Some of these
pennies have been picked up from time to time by
persons who have outgrown the old superstition.
The hollow in the Clach-nan-Sul at Balquhidder,
already referred to, contained small coins placed
there by those who sought a cure for their sore
eyes. Mr. J. Mackintosh Gow was told by some
one in the district, that "people, when going to
church, having forgotten their small change, used
in passing to put their hands in the well and find
a coin." Mr. Gow's informant mentioned that he
had done so himself.

In the ceremony known as "well-dressing" or "well-
flowering," the offerings took the form of blossoms
and green boughs. For different reasons Scotland
has not been abreast of England in floral matters.
Only in the latter country did the practice take root,
and even there only within a somewhat limited area.
We must seek for its home in Derbyshire and the
adjacent counties. At some places it has died out,

while at others it still survives, and forms the excuse
for a pleasant holiday.   At Bonchurch, Isle of Wight,
indeed, St.   Boniface's Well was decorated with
wreaths of flowers on the saint's day; but this
was an exceptional instance so far south.   Within
comparatively recent years well-flowering has, at
one or two places, been either instituted, as at
Belper, in Derbyshire, in 1838, or revived, as at
St. Alkmund's Well in Derby, in 1870.   The clergy
and choir of St. Alkmund's Church celebrate the
day by meeting at the church and walking in
procession to the well.   Writing in the seventeenth
century, Aubrey says, "In Cheshire, when they
went in perambulation, they did bless the springs,
i.e., they did read the Gospel at them, and did believe
the water was the better."   At Droitwich, in Wor-
cestershire, a salt spring, dedicated to St. Richard,
used to be annually adorned with flowers.

A correspondent of the "*Gentleman's Magazine*"
of 1794 remarks, "In the village of Tissington,
in the county of Derby, a place remarkable for
fine springs of water, it has been a custom, time
immemorial, on every Holy Thursday, to decorate
the wells with boughs of trees, garlands of tulips,
and other flowers, placed in various fancied devices,
and, after prayers for the day at the church, for
the parson and singers to pray and sing psalms
at the wells."   In Hone's "*Every Day Book*,"
under date 1826, are the following remarks by a
correspondent :—" Tissington ' well-dressing ' is a

festivity which not only claims a high antiquity,
but is one of the few country fêtes which are kept
up with anything like the ancient spirit. It is
one which is heartily loved and earnestly anticipated; one which draws the hearts of those who
were brought up there, but whom fortune has
cast into distant places, homewards with an irre-
sistible charm. I have not had the pleasure of
witnessing it, but I have had that of seeing the
joy which sparkled in the eyes of the Tissing-
tonians as they talked of its approach and of their
projected attendance." The festival is still held in
honour at Tissington, and elaborate preparations continue to be made for its celebration. Flowers are
arranged in patterns to form mottoes and texts of
Scripture, and also devices, such as crosses, crowns,
and triangles, while green boughs are added to complete the picture. A correspondent of " *Notes and
Queries* " thus describes the decorations on Ascension
Day in 1887 : "The name of 'well-dressing' scarcely
gives a proper idea of these beautiful structures. They
are rather fountains or cascades, the water descending
from above, and not rising as in a well. Their height
varies from ten to twelve feet, and the original stone
frontage is on this day hidden by a wooden erection in
the form of an arch or some other elegant design.
Over these planks a layer of plaster of Paris is spread,
and whilst it is wet, flowers without leaves are stuck
in it, forming a most beautiful mosaic pattern. On
one the large yellow field ranunculus was arranged in

letters, and so a verse of Scripture or of a hymn was recalled to the spectator's mind.   On another a white dove was sculptured in the plaster and set in a ground-work of the humble violet.   The daisy, which our poet Chaucer would gaze upon for hours together, formed a diaper-work of red and white; the pale yellow primrose was set off by the rich red of the 'ribes.'   Nor were the coral berries of the holly, mountain ash, and yew forgotten; they are carefully gathered and stored in the winter to be ready for the May Day fête.   It is scarcely possible to describe the vivid colouring and beautiful effect of these favourites of nature arranged in wreaths and gar-lands and devices of every hue.   And then the pure sparkling water, which pours down from the midst of them on to the rustic moss-grown stones beneath, completes the enchantment, and makes this feast of the 'well-flowering' one of the most beautiful of all the old customs that are left in Merrie England." Well-flowering also prevails at Buxton, and is a source of interest to the many visitors to that airy health resort.

Such floral devices do not now rank as votive gifts. They are merely decorations.   The custom may have originated in the Roman Fontinalia.   At any rate it had at one time a corresponding object.   The Fontinalia formed an annual flower-festival in honour of the nymphs inhabiting springs.   Joyous bands visited the fountains, crowned them with boughs, and threw nosegays into their sparkling water.   The parallelism

P

between the Roman and the English Fontinalia is too well marked to be overlooked. In Derbyshire and Staffordshire the ceremony of well-dressing is usually observed on Ascension Day. In more than one instance the festival has attracted to itself various old English sports commonly associated with May Day. Among these may be mentioned May-pole and Morris-dancing and crowning the May-queen.

At Endon, in Staffordshire, the festival is celebrated on Royal Oak Day (May 29th), or on the following day if the 29th is a Sunday. The following account—somewhat abbreviated—is from the "*Staffordshire Evening Post*" of 31st May, 1892, and gives some interesting particulars about the festival: "The secluded village of Endon yesterday celebrated the well-dressing feast. This institution, dear to the heart of every loyal inhabitant, holds foremost rank in the local calends, for it is not a holiday of ordinary frivolous significance, but a thanksgiving festival. The proceeds, which generally amount to some hundreds of pounds, are divided between the poor of the parish and the parochial schools. There are two wells at Endon. One is very old and almost dry, and has long since fallen into disuse. The other alone supplies the village with water. From a very early hour in the morning the whole village was astir, and those people who were gifted with taste and a delicate touch busied themselves in bedecking the wells for the coming ceremony. As the day advanced, crowds of visitors

poured in from all parts of the potteries; and
towards evening the village green probably held no
fewer than two thousand people. The proceedings,
which were under the personal guidance of the
vicar, commenced a little before two o'clock. A
procession of about a hundred and twenty Sunday-
school children was formed at the new well, with
the Brownedge village brass band at its head. The
children carried little flags, which they vigorously
waved in excess of glee. The band struck up
bravely, and the procession marched in good order
up the hill to the old parish church, where a solemn
service was conducted. The villagers attended in
overwhelming numbers, and completely thronged
the building. There was a fully surpliced choir,
whose singing, coupled with the music of the organ,
greatly added to the impressiveness of the service.
Hymns and psalms, selected by the vicar as appli-
cable to a thanksgiving service for water, were sung
by the congregation in spirited style. At the
conclusion of the service the procession was reformed, the band leading the way back to the new
well. Upon arrival, the clergy and choir, who had
retained their surplices, walked slowly round the
well, singing 'Rock of Ages' and 'A living stream
as crystal clear.' Both wells were very beautifully
decorated; but the new well was a masterpiece of
elaborated art. A large wooden framework had been
erected in front of the well, and upon this a smooth
surface of soft clay had been laid. The clay was

thickly studded with many thousands of flower heads in great variety of kind and hue, and in pictorial as well as geometrical arrangement. There were two very pretty figures of peacocks in daisies, bluebells, and dahlias, and a resplendent motto, 'O, ye wells! bless ye the Lord!' (from the Benedicite) garnished the summit. The old well was almost deserted, although its decorations were well worthy of inspection. Its motto, 'Give me this water' (from the fourth chapter of St. John) was very finely traced, and its centre figures—two white doves and a crown—were sufficiently striking.. May-pole dances, including the crowning of the May-queen, occupied the greater part of the afternoon. In the evening the band played for dancing, and there was a repetition of the May-pole dances. After dusk there was a display of fireworks."

Though, as already stated, well-dressing was un-known north of the Tweed, any account of votive offerings would be incomplete without a reference to the picturesque ceremony.

CHAPTER XIII.

WEATHER AND WELLS.

Importance of Weather—Its Place in Folklore—Raising the Wind—
Witches and Wind-charms—Blue-stone in Fladda—Well in
Gigha — Tobernacoragh — Routing-well—Water Cross—Stone
in British Columbia—Other Rain-charms—Survivals in Folk-
customs — Sympathetic Magic — Dulyn — Barenton — Tobar
Faolan—St. Fumac's Image at Botriphnie—Molly Grime.

IN all ages much attention has been given to the
weather, with special reference to its bearings on
human well-being. As Mr. R. Inwards truly
observes, in his *"Weather-lore,"* "From the earliest
times hunters, shepherds, sailors, and tillers of the
earth have from sheer necessity been led to study
the teachings of the winds, the waves, the clouds,
and a hundred other objects from which the signs
of coming changes in the state of the air might be
foretold. The weather-wise amongst these primitive
people would be naturally the most prosperous, and
others would soon acquire the coveted foresight by
a closer observance of the same objects from which
their successful rivals guessed the proper time to
provide against a storm, or reckoned on the prospects
of the coming crops." Hence, naturally enough, the

weather has an important place in folklore. Various
prognostications concerning it have been drawn from
sun and moon, from animals and flowers; while
certain meteorological phenomena have, in their turn,
been regarded as prophetic of mundane events.
Thus, in the astrological treatise entitled "*The
Knowledge of Things Unknown*," we read that
"Thunder in January signifieth the same year great
winds, plentiful of corn and cattel peradventure;
in February, many rich men shall die in great
sickness; in March, great winds, plenty of corn,
and debate amongst people; in April, be fruitful
and merry with the death of wicked men;" and so
on through the other months of the year. One can
easily understand why thunder should be counted
peculiarly ominous. The effects produced on the
mind by its mysterious noise, and on the nerves
by the electricity in the air, are apt to lead
superstitious people to expect strange events. Particular notice was taken of the weather on certain
ecclesiastical festivals, and omens were drawn from
its condition. Thus, from "*The Husbandman's
Practice*," we learn that "The wise and cunning
masters in astrology have found that man may
see and mark the weather of the holy Christmas
night, how the whole year after shall be in his
making and doing, and they shall speak on this
wise. When on the Christmas night and evening
it is very fair and clear weather, and is without
wind and without rain, then it is a token that

this year will be plenty of wine and fruit. But
if the contrariwise, foul weather and windy, so
shall it be very scant of wine and fruit. But if
the wind arise at the rising of the sun, then it
betokeneth great dearth among beasts and cattle
this year. But if the wind arise at the going
down of the same, then it signifieth death to come
among kings and other great lords." We do not
suppose that anyone nowadays attends to such
Yule-tide auguries, but there are not wanting those
who have a lingering belief in the power of
Candlemas and St. Swithin's Day to foretell the
sort of weather to be expected in the immediate
future.

Witches were believed to be able to raise the
wind at their pleasure. In a confession made at
Auldearn in Nairnshire, in the year 1662, certain
women, accused of sorcery, said, "When we raise
the wind we take a rag of cloth and wet it in
water, and we take a beetle and knock the rag
on a stone, and we say thrice over—

> 'I knock this rag upon this stane,
> To raise the wind in the devil's name.
> It shall not lie until I please again!'"

When the wind was to be allayed the rag was
dried. About 1670 an attempt was made to drain
some two thousand acres of land belonging to the
estate of Dun in Forfarshire. The Dronner's, *i.e.*,
Drainer's Dyke—remains of which are still to be
seen behind the Montrose Infirmary—was built in

connection with the scheme. But the work was destroyed by a terrible storm, caused, it was believed, by a certain Meggie Cowie—the last to be burned for witchcraft in the district. About eighty years before, a notable witch-trial in the time of James VI. had to do with the raising of a storm. A certain woman, Agnes Sampson, residing in Haddingtonshire, confessed that she belonged to a company of two hundred witches, and that they were all in the habit of sailing along the coast in sieves to meet the devil at the kirk of North Berwick. After one of these interviews the woman took a cat and christened it, and, after fixing to it parts of a dead man's body, threw the creature into the sea in presence of the other witches. The king, who was then returning from Denmark with his bride, was delayed by contrary winds, and such a tempest arose in the Firth of Forth that a vessel, containing valuable gifts for the queen on her arrival, sank between Burntisland and Leith. The Rev. T. F. Thiselton Dyer makes the suggestion in his "*Folklore of Shakespeare*," that it was probably to these contrary winds that the author of "*Macbeth*" alludes when he makes the witch say—

> "Though his bark cannot be lost,
> Yet it shall be tempest-tost."

Even down to the end of last century, and probably later, some well-educated people believed that the devil had the power of raising the wind. The phrase, the prince of the power of the air, applied to him in Scripture, was interpreted in a literal way. "*The Diary of the Rev. John Mill*," minister in Shetland from 1740 till 1803, bears witness to such a belief. In his introduction to the work, the editor, Mr. Gilbert Goudie, tells us: "He (Mill) was often heard talking aloud with his (to others) unseen foe; but those who heard him declared that he spoke in an unknown tongue, presumably Hebrew. After one of these encounters the worthy man was heard muttering, 'Well, let him do his worst; the wind aye in my face will not hurt me.' This was in response to a threat of the devil, that wherever he (Mill) went, he (Satan) should be a-blowing 'wind in his teeth,' in consequence of which Mill was unable ever after to get passage out of Shetland." On the 5th of November, 1605, a terrible storm swept over the north of Scotland and destroyed part of the cathedral at Dornoch. As is well known, the day in question was selected by Guy Fawkes for blowing up the Houses of Parliament. In his "*Cathedral of Caithness, at Dornoch*," Mr. Hugh F. Campbell tells us: "When the news of the gunpowder plot reached the north, the co-incidence of time at once impressed the imagination of a superstitious age. The storm was invested with an element of the marvellous." Mr. Campbell then quotes the following curious passage from Sir Robert Gordon, specially referring to Satan's connection with the tempest:—"The same verie night that this execrable plott should have been put in execution all the inner stone pillars of the north syd of the body of the cathedral church at Dornogh—lacking the rooff before—were blowen from the verie roots and foundation quyt and clein over the outer walls of the church: such as hath sein the same. These great winds did even then prognosticate and forshew some great treason to be at hand; and as the divell was busie then to trouble the ayre, so wes he bussie by these hiss fyrebrands to trouble the estate of Great Britane."

The notion that storms, especially when accompanied by thunder and lightning, were the work of evil spirits, came out prominently during the middle ages in connection with bells. The ringing of bells was believed to drive away the demons, and so allay the tempest. A singular superstition concerning the causation of storms was brought to light in Hungary during the autumn of 1892 in connection with the fear of cholera. At Kidzaes a patient died of what was thought to be that disease, and a *post mortem* examination was ordered by the local authorities. Strenuous opposition, however, was offered by the villagers on the ground that the act would cause such a hail-storm as would destroy their crops. Feeling ran so high that a riot was imminent, and the project had to be abandoned. Eric, the Swedish king, could control the winds through his enchantments. By turning his cap he was able to bring a breeze from whatever quarter he wished. Mr. G. L. Gomme, in his "*Ethnology in Folklore*," remarks, "At Kempoch Point, in the Firth of Clyde, is a columnar rock called the Kempoch Stane, from whence a saint was wont to dispense favourable winds to those who paid for them, and unfavourable to those who did not put confidence in his powers—a tradition which seems to have been carried on by the Innerkip witches who were tried in 1662, and some portions of which still linger among the sailors of Greenock." The stone in question consists of a block of grey mica schist six feet in height and two in diameter. It is locally known as Granny Kempoch. In former times sailors and fishermen sought to ensure good fortune on the sea by walking seven times round the stone. While making their rounds they carried in their hand a basket of sand, and at the same time uttered an eerie chant. Newly-married couples used also to walk round the stone by way of luck.

At the beginning of the present century a certain woman, Bessie Miller by name, lived in Stromness, in Orkney, and eked out her livelihood by selling winds to mariners. Her usual charge was sixpence. For this sum, as Sir W. Scott tells us, "she boiled her kettle, and gave the barque advantage of her prayers, for she disclaimed all unlawful arts. The wind, thus petitioned for, was sure to arrive, though sometimes the mariners had to wait some time for it." Her house was on the brow of the steep hill above the town, "and for exposure might have been the abode of Eolus himself." At the time of Sir Walter's visit

to Stromness, Bessie Miller was nearly a hundred
years old, and appeared "withered and dried up
like a mummy." We make her acquaintance in
the "*Pirate*," under the name of Norna of the
Fitful Head. In his "*Rambles in the Far North*,"
Mr. R. M. Fergusson tells of another wind-compelling
personage, named Mammie Scott, who also belonged
to Stromness, and practised her arts there, till within
a comparatively recent date. "Many wonderful tales
are told of her power and influence over the weather.
Her fame was widely spread as that of Bessie. A
captain called upon Mammie one day to solicit a
fair wind. He was bound for Stornoway, and
received from the reputed witch a scarlet thread
upon which were three knots. His instructions
were, that if sufficient wind did not arrive, one
of the knots was to be untied; if that proved in-
sufficient, another knot was to be untied; but he
was on no account to unloose the third knot, else
disaster would overtake his vessel. The mariner
set out upon his voyage, and, the wind being light,
untied the first knot. This brought a stronger
breeze, but still not sufficient to satisfy him. The
second knot was let down, and away the vessel
sped across the waters, round Cape Wrath. In a
short time the entrance to Stornoway harbour was
reached, when it came into the captain's head to
untie the third knot in order to see what might
occur. He was too near the end of his voyage to
suffer any damage now; and so he felt emboldened

to make the experiment. No sooner was the last
knot set free than a perfect hurricane set in from
a contrary direction, which drove the vessel right
back to Hoy Sound, from which she had set out,
where he had ample time to repent of his folly."

Within the last half-century there lived in Stonehaven an old woman, who was regarded with considerable awe by the sea-faring population. Before
a voyage it was usual to propitiate her by the gift
of a bag of coals. On one occasion, two brothers,
owners of a coasting smack, after setting sail, had
to return to port through stress of weather, the
storm being due, it was believed, to the fact that
one of the brothers had omitted to secure the woman's
good offices in the usual way. The brother who
was captain of the smack seems to have been a
firm believer in wind-charms, for it is related of
him that during a more than usually high wind
he was in the habit of throwing up his cap into
the air with the exclamation, "She maun hae something." *She*, in this case, was the wind, and not
the witch: and the cap was meant as a gift to
propitiate the storm. Dr. Charles Rogers, in his
"*Social Life in Scotland*," tells us that "the seamen
of Shetland, in tempestuous weather, throw a piece
of money into the window of a ruinous chapel dedicated to St. Ronald in the belief that the saint will
allay the vehemence of the storm." According to
the same writer, "Shetland boatmen still purchase
favourable winds from elderly women, who pretend

to rule or to modify the storms." "There are now in Lerwick," Dr. Rogers continues, "several old women who in this fashion earn a subsistence. Many of the survivors of the great storm of the 20th of July, 1881—so fatal on northern coasts—assert that their preservation was due to warnings which they received through a supernatural agency."

Human skulls have their folklore. The lifting of them from their usual resting-places has, in popular belief, been connected with certain mysterious occurrences. According to a story told by Mr. Wirt Sikes, in his "*British Goblins*," a man who removed a skull from a church to prove to his companions that he was free from superstition was overtaken by a terrible whirlwind, the result, it was thought, of his rash act. In some Highland districts it used to be reckoned unlucky to allow a corpse to remain unburied. If from any cause, human bones came to the surface, care was taken to lay them below ground again, as otherwise disastrous storms would ensue.

We have a good example of the association of wind-charms with water in the case of a certain magical stone referred to by Martin as existing in his day in the island of Fladda, near Skye. There was a chapel to St. Columba on the island, and on the altar lay the stone in question. The stone was round, of a blue colour; and was always moist. "It is an ordinary custom," Martin relates, "when any of the fishermen are detained in the isle

by contrary winds, to wash the blue stone with
water all round, expecting thereby to procure a
favourable wind, which, the credulous tenant, living
in the isle, says never fails, especially if a stranger
wash the stone." The power of the Fladda stone
was equalled by a certain well in Gigha, though
in the latter instance a dweller in the island, rather
than a stranger, had power over it. When a foreign
boat was wind-bound on the island, the master of
the craft was in the habit of giving some money to
one of the natives, to procure a favourable breeze.
This was done in the following way. A few feet
above the well was a heap of stones, forming a cover
to the spring. These were carefully removed, and
the well was cleared out with a wooden dish or
clam-shell. The water was then thrown several
times towards the point, from which the needed wind
should blow. Certain words of incantation were
used, each time the water was thrown. After the
ceremony, the stones were replaced, as the district
would otherwise have been swept by a hurricane.
Pennant mentions, in connection with his visit to
Gigha, that the superstition had then died out. In
this he was in error, for the well continued to be
occasionally consulted to a later date. Even within
recent years, the memory of the practice lingered
in the island; but there seemed some doubt, as to
the exact nature of the required ritual. Captain
T. P. White was told by a shepherd, belonging to
the island, that, if a stone was taken out of the well,

a storm would arise and prevent any person crossing over, nor would it abate till the stone was taken back to the well.

From the evidence of an Irish example, we find that springs could allay a storm, as well as produce a favourable breeze. The island of Innismurray, off the coast of Sligo, has a sacred well called Tobernacoragh. When a tempest was raging, the natives believed that by draining the water of this well into the sea, the wrath of the elements could be calmed. Mr. Gomme, in his " *Ethnology in Folklore*," when commenting on the instance, remarks, "In this case the connection between well-worship and the worship of a rain-god is certain, for it may be surmised that if the emptying of the well allayed a storm, some complementary action was practised at one time or other in order to produce rain, and in districts more subject to a want of rain than this Atlantic island, that ceremony would be accentuated at the expense of the storm-allaying ceremony at Innismurray." The Routing Well, at Monktown, in Inveresk parish, Mid-Lothian, was believed to give notice of an approaching storm by uttering sounds resembling the moaning of the wind. As a matter of fact, the noises came from certain disused coal-workings in the immediate neighbourhood, and were due to the high wind blowing through them. The sounds thus *accompanied* and did not *precede* the storm.

To procure rain, recourse was had to various

superstitious practices. Martin tells of a stone, five feet high, in the form of a cross, opposite St. Mary's Church, in North Uist. "The natives," he says, "call it the 'Water Cross,' for the ancient inhabitants had a custom of erecting this sort of cross to procure rain, and when they had got enough, they laid it flat on the ground, but this custom is now disused." Among the mountains of British Columbia, is a certain stone held in much honour by the Indians, for they believe that it will produce rain when struck. Rain-making is an important occupation among uncivilised races, and strange rites are sometimes practised to bring about the desired result. By some savages, human hair is burned for this end. Mr. J. G. Frazer, in "*The Golden Bough*," has some interesting remarks on rain-production. After enumerating certain rain-charms among heathen nations, he remarks, "Another way of constraining the rain-god is to disturb him in his haunts. This seems the reason why rain is supposed to be the consequence of troubling a sacred spring. The Dards believed that if a cowskin or anything impure is placed in certain springs storms will follow. Gervasius mentions a spring, into which, if a stone or a stick were thrown, rain would at once issue from it and drench the thrower. There was a fountain in Munster such that if it were touched or even looked at by a human being it would at once flood the whole province with rain." Curious survivals of ancient rain-charms are to be found in modern folk-customs. Thus, in connection with the

Q

rejoicings of the harvest-home in England, when the
last load of grain was being carried on the gaily
decorated hock-cart to the farm-yard, it was customary
to throw water on those taking part in the ceremony.
This apparently meaningless frolic was in reality a
rain-charm. A Cornish custom, at one time popular
at Padstow on the first of May, can be explained on
the same principle. A hobby-horse was taken to the
Traitor's Pool, a quarter of a mile from the town.
The head was dipped in the pool, and water was
sprinkled on the bystanders.

Such charms depend for their efficacy on what
is called "sympathetic magic." Mimic rain is produced
on the earth, in the hope that the same liquid will
be constrained to descend from the heavens, to bring
fresh fertility to the fields. Professor Rhys, in his
"*Celtic Heathendom*," traces the connection between
modern rain-charms and the rites of ancient paganism. He there quotes the following particulars
regarding Dulyn, in North Wales, from a description
of the place published in 1805:—"There lies in
Snowdon Mountain a lake called Dulyn, in a dismal
dingle surrounded by high and dangerous rocks; the
lake is exceedingly black, and its fish are loathsome,
having large heads and small bodies. No wild
swan or duck or any kind of bird has ever been
seen to light on it, as is their wont on every other
Snowdonian lake. In this same lake there is a
row of stepping stones extending into it; and if
any one steps on the stones and throws water so

as to wet the furthest stone of the series, which
is called the *Red Altar*, it is but a chance that you
do not get rain before night, even when it is hot
weather." The spot was, probably in pre-Christian
times, the scene of sacrifices to some local deity.
Judging from the dismal character of the neighbourhood, we may safely infer that fear entered
largely into the worship paid there to the *genius
loci*. The Fountain of Barenton, in Brittany, was
specially celebrated in connection with rain-making.
During the early middle ages, the peasantry of the
neighbourhood resorted to it in days of drought.
According to a time-honoured custom, they took
some water from the fountain and threw it on a
slab hard by; rain was the result. Professor Rhys
reminds us that this fountain "still retains its
pluvial importance; for, in seasons of drought, the
inhabitants of the surrounding parishes, we are told
go to it in procession, headed by their five great
banners and their priests ringing bells and chanting
psalms. On arriving, the rector of the canton dips
the foot of the cross in the water, and it is sure
to rain within a week's time." The Barenton
instance is specially interesting, for part of the
ceremony recalls what happened in connection with
a certain Scottish spring, viz., Tobar Faolan at
Struan, in Athole. This spring, as the name implies,
was dedicated to Fillan. In his "Holiday Notes in
Athole," in the "*Proceedings of the Society of Antiquaries of Scotland*," volume xii. (new series), Mr.

J. Mackintosh Gow says, "It is nearly one hundred
yards west from the church, at the foot of the bank,
and close to the river Garry. It is overgrown
with grass and weeds, but the water is as clear and
cool as it may have been in the days of the saint.
There is no tradition of its having been a curing
or healing well, except that, in pre-Reformation days,
when a drought prevailed and rain was much
wanted, an image of the saint, which was kept in
the church, used to be taken in procession to the
well, and, in order that rain might come, the feet
of the image were placed in the water; and this,
of course, was generally supposed to have the
desired effect." At Botriphnie, in Banffshire, six
miles from Keith, the wooden image of St. Fumac
used to be solemnly washed in his well on the
third of May. We may conclude that the ceremony
was intended as a rain-charm. It must have been
successful, on at least one occasion, for the river
Isla became flooded through the abundance of rain.
Indeed, the flooding was so great that the saint's
image was swept away by the rushing water. The
image was finally stranded at Banff, where it was
burned as a relic of superstition by order of the
parish minister about the beginning of the present
century. In Glentham Church, Lincolnshire, is a
tomb, with a figure locally called "Molly Grime."
From "*Old English Customs and Charities*," we
learn that, till 1832, the figure was washed every
Good Friday with water from Newell Well by

seven old maids of Glentham, who each received a
shilling, " in consequence of an old bequest connected
with some property in that district." Perhaps its
testator was not free from a belief in the efficacy
of rain-charms. Otherwise, the ceremony seems
meaningless. If the keeping clean of the figure was
the only object, the seven old maids should not
have limited their duties to an annual pilgrimage
from the well to the church.

CHAPTER XIV.

TREES AND SPRINGS.

Tree-worship — Ygdrasil — Personality of Plants — Tree-ancestors — "Wassailing" — Relics of Tree-worship — Connla's Well— Cutting down Trees Unlucky—Spring at Monzie—Marriage Well—Pear-Tree Well—Some Miraculous Trees—External Soul—Its Connection with Trees, &c.—Arms of Glasgow.

TREES were at one time worshipped as well as fountains. Ygdrasil, the world-tree of Scandinavian mythology, had three roots, and underneath each, was a fountain of wonderful virtues. This represents the connection between tree and well in the domain of mythology. But the same superstition was connected with ordinary trees and wells. Glancing back over the history of civilisation, we reach a period, when vegetation was endowed with personality. As plants manifested the phenomena of life and death like man and the lower animals, they had a similar kind of existence attributed to them. Among some savages to-day, the fragrance of a flower is thought to be its soul. As there was thus no hard and fast line between man and the vegetable kingdom, the one could be derived from the other; in other words, men could have trees as their ancestors. Curious survivals of such a belief lie both revealed and concealed in the language of to-day. Though we are far separated from such a phase of archaic religion, we speak of the *branches* of a family. At one time such an expression represented a literal fact, and not a mere metaphor. In like manner, we call a son, who resembles his father, "a chip of the old block." But how few when using the phrase are alive to its real force! Mr. Keary, in his "*Outlines of Primitive Belief,*" observes, "Even when the literal notion of the descent from a tree had been lost sight of, the close connection between the prosperity of the tribe and the life of its fetish was often strictly held. The village tree of the German races was originally a tribal tree with whose existence the life of the village was involved."

The picturesque ceremony known as the "Wassailing of Apple-trees," kept up till lately in Devon and Cornwall, carries our thoughts back to the time when tree-worship was a thriving cult in our land. It was celebrated on the evening before Epiphany (January 6th). The farmer, accompanied by his labourers, carried a pail of cider with roasted apples in it into the orchard. The pail was placed on the ground, and each one of the company took from it a cupful of the liquid. They then stood before the trees and repeated the following lines:—

> " Health to thee, good apple tree,
>   Well to bear pocket-fulls, hat-fulls,
>   Peck-fulls, bushel bag-fulls."

Part of the contents of the cup was then drunk, and the remainder was thrown at the tree amid shouts from the by-standers. Relics of the same cult can be traced in the superstitious regard for such trees as the rowan, the elder, &c., and in the decoration of the May-pole and the Christmas Tree. According to an ancient Irish legend, a certain spring in Erin, called Connla's Well, had growing over it nine mystical hazel trees. Year by year these trees produced their flowers and fruit simultaneously. The nuts were of a brilliant crimson colour and contained in some mysterious way the knowledge of all that was best in poetry and art. Professor O'Curry, in his "*Lectures on the Manners and Customs of the Ancient Irish*," refers to this legend, and says, " No sooner were the beautiful nuts produced on the trees than they always dropped into the well, raising by their fall a succession of shining red bubbles. Now, during this time the water was always full of salmon, and no sooner did the bubbles appear than these salmon darted to the surface and ate the nuts, after which they made their way to the river. The eating of the nuts produced brilliant crimson spots on the bellies of these salmon, and to catch and eat these salmon became an object of more than mere gastronomic interest among those who were anxious to become distinguished in the arts and in literature without being at the pains and delay of long study, for the fish was supposed to have become filled with the knowledge which

was contained in the nuts, which, it was believed,
would be transferred in full to those who had the
good fortune to catch and eat them."

In many cases it was counted unlucky to cut down
trees, since the spirits, inhabiting them, would resent
the injury. In the sixteenth century the parishioners
of Clynnog, in Caernarvonshire, refrained from
destroying the trees growing in the grounds of St.
Beyno. Even though he was their patron saint, he
was quite ready to harm anybody who took liberties
with his grove. Loch Siant Well, in Skye, was
noted for its power to cure headaches, stitches, and
other ailments, and was much frequented in consequence. Martin says, "There is a small coppice
near to the well, and there is none of the natives
dare venture to cut the least branch of it for fear of
some signal judgment to follow upon it." Martin
also tells us that the same reverence was for long
paid to the peat on the island of Lingay. This
island, he says, "is singular in respect of all the
lands of Uist, and the other islands that surround
it, for they are all composed of sand, and this, on
the contrary, is altogether moss covered with heath,
affording five peats in depth, and is very serviceable
and useful, furnishing the island Borera, &c., with
plenty of good fuel. This island was held as consecrated for several ages, insomuch that the natives
would not then presume to cut any fuel in it."

When trees beside wells had rags hung on them
as offerings, they would naturally be reverenced, as

the living altars for the reception of the gifts. But even when not used for this purpose, they were sometimes thought to have a mysterious connection with the springs they overshadowed. In the parish of Monzie, Perthshire, is a mineral well held in much esteem till about the year 1770. At that time two trees, till then the guardians of the spring, fell, and with their fall its virtue departed. On the right bank of the Clyde, about three-quarters of a mile from Carmyle village, is the once sylvan district of Kenmuir. There, at the foot of a bank, is a spring locally known as "The Marriage Well," the name being derived, it is said, from two curiously united trees beside its margin. These trees were recently cut down. In former times, it was customary for marriage parties, the day after their wedding, to visit the spring, and there pledge the bride and bridegroom in draughts of its sparkling water. On the banks of the Kelvin, close to the Glasgow Botanic Gardens, once flowed a spring styled the Pear-Tree, Pea-Tree, or Three-Tree Well, the last name being probably the original one. In former times it was a recognised trysting-place for lovers. A tragic story is told in connection with it by Mr. James Napier in his "*Notes and Reminiscences of Partick.*" A maiden, named Catherine Clark, arranged to meet her lover there by night,

> "nor did she ever dream
> But that he was what he did ever seem."

She never returned to her home. "A few days after,"

remarks Mr. Napier, "her body was found buried near a large tree which stood within a few yards of the Pea-Tree Well. This tree was afterwards known as 'Catherine Clark's Tree,' and remained for many years an object of interest to the visitors to this far-famed well, and many a sympathising lover carved his name in rude letters on its bark. But the tree was also an object of terror to those who had to pass it in dark and lonely nights, and many tales were told of people who had seen a young female form dressed in white, and stained with blood, standing at the tree foot." The tree was removed many years ago. The spring too is gone, the recent extension of the Caledonian Railway to Maryhill having forced it to quit the field.

Near the moat of Listerling, in county Kilkenny, Ireland, is a holy well dedicated to St. Mullen, who is said to have lived for a while in its neighbourhood. A fine hawthorn, overshadowing it, grew—if we can believe a local legend—from the staff of the saint, which he there stuck into the ground. This reminds one of the famous Glastonbury Thorn, produced from the staff of Joseph of Arimathea, who fixed it in the ground one Christmas Day. The staff took root at once, put forth branches, and next day was covered with milk-white blossoms. St. Servanus's staff, too, had a miraculous ending. He threw it across the Firth of Forth, and when it fell on the Fife coast, it took root and became an apple-tree. A group of thorn-bushes, near Aghaboe, in Queen's County,

Ireland, was dedicated to St. Canice. The spring, overshadowed by them, was much resorted to for the purposes of devotion. At Rearymore, in the same county, some hawthorns, growing beside St. Finyan's spring, were, and doubtless still are, religiously preserved by the natives. In the Isle of Man is Chibber Unjin, signifying The Well of the Ash. Beside it grew an ash tree, formerly decorated with votive offerings.

What has been called the *external soul* has an important place in folklore, and forms the theme of many folk-tales. Primitive man does not think of the soul as spiritual, but as material—as something that can be seen and felt. It can take different shapes. It can leave the body during sleep, and wander about in the guise of an animal, such as a mouse. Considerable space is devoted to this problem in Mr. J. G. Frazer's " *Golden Bough.*" Mr. Frazer there remarks, " There may be circumstances in which, if the life or soul remains in the man, it stands a greater chance of sustaining injury than if it were stowed away in some safe and secret place. Accordingly, in such circumstances, primitive man takes his soul out of his body and deposits it for security in some safe place, intending to replace it in his body when the danger is past; or, if he should discover some place of absolute security, he may be content to leave his soul there permanently. The advantage of this is, that so long as the soul remains unharmed in the place where he has deposited it, the man himself is immortal; nothing

can kill his body, since his life is not in it." Sometimes the soul is believed to be stowed away in a tree,
injury to the latter involving disaster to the former.
The custom of planting trees, and calling them after
certain persons may nowadays have nothing to do
with this notion; but, undoubtedly, a real connection
was at one time believed to exist between the part-
ners in the transaction. A certain oak, with mistletoe
growing on it, was mysteriously associated with the
family of Hay. The superstition is explained in the
following lines:—

> " While the mistletoe bats on Errol's oak
>   And that oak stands fast,
> The Hays shall flourish, and their good grey hawk
>   Shall not flinch before the blast.
>
> But when the root of the oak decays
>   And the mistletoe dwines on its withered breast,
> The grass shall grow on the Earl's hearthstone,
>   And the corbies craw in the falcon's nest."

At Finlarig Castle, near Killin, in Perthshire, are
several trees, believed to be linked with the lives of
certain individuals, connected by family ties with the
ruined fortress. Aubrey gives an example of this
superstition, as it existed in England in the seventeenth century. He says, " I cannot omit taking
notice of the great misfortune in the family of the
Earl of Winchelsea, who, at Eastwell, in Kent, felled
down a most curious grove of oaks near his own noble
seat, and gave the first blow with his own hands.
Shortly after, the countess died in her bed suddenly,
and his eldest son, the Lord Maidstone, was killed at

sea by a cannon bullet." In the grounds of Dalhousie Castle, about two miles from Dalkeith, on the edge of a fine spring is the famous Edgewell Oak. Sir Walter Scott, in his "*Journal*," under date May 13th, 1829, writes, "Went with the girls to dine at Dalhousie Castle, where we were very kindly received. I saw the Edgewell Tree, too fatal, says Allan Ramsay, to the family from which he was himself descended." According to a belief in the district, a branch fell from this tree, before the death of a member of the family. The original oak fell early in last century, but a new one sprang from the old root. An editorial note to the above entry in the "*Journal*" gives the following information :—" The tree is still flourishing (1889), and the belief in its sympathy with the family is not yet extinct, as an old forester, on seeing a branch fall from it on a quiet still day in July, 1874, exclaimed, 'The laird's deed, noo !' and, accordingly, news came soon after that Fox Maule, eleventh Earl of Dalhousie, had died."

The *external soul* was sometimes associated with objects other than living trees. Dr. Charles Rogers tells us that "a pear, supposed to have been enchanted by Hugh Gifford, Lord of Yester, a notable magician in the reign of Alexander III., is preserved in the family of Brown of Colston, as heirs of Gifford's estate." The prosperity of the family is believed to be linked with the preservation of the pear. Even an inanimate object would serve the purpose. The glass drinking-cup, known as the

"Luck of Edenhall," is connected with the fortunes of the Musgrave family, and great care is taken to preserve it from injury. Tradition says that a company of fairies were making merry beside a spring near the mansion-house, but that, being frightened by some intruder, they vanished, leaving the cup in question, while one of them exclaimed:—

> "If this cup should break or fall,
> Farewell the luck of Edenhall."

Some living object, however, either vegetable or animal, was the usual repository of the *external soul.* A familiar folk-tale tells of a giant whose heart was in a swan, and who could not be killed while the swan lived. Hunting was a favourite occupation among the inhabitants of the Western Isles; but on the mountain Finchra, in Rum, no deer was killed by any member of the Lachlan family, as it was believed that the life of that family was in some way linked with the life of these animals. A curious superstition is mentioned by Camden in his *"Britannia."* In a pond near the Abbey of St. Maurice, in Burgundy, were put as many fish as there were monks. When any monk was taken ill, one of the fish was seen to float half-dead on the surface of the pond. If the fish died the monk died too, the death of the former giving warning of the fate of the latter. In this case the *external soul* was thought of as stowed away in a fish. As is well known, the Arms of the City of Glasgow are a bell, a tree, a fish with a ring in its mouth, and a bird. The popular explanation of these emblems connects them with certain miracles, wrought by Kentigern, the patron saint of the burgh. May we not hold that an explanation of their symbolism is to be sought in a principle, that formed an article in the beliefs of men, long before Kentigern was born, as well as during his time and since? The bell, it is true, had, doubtless, an ecclesiastical association; but the other three symbols point, perhaps, to some superstitious notion like the above. In various folk-tales, as well as in Christian art, the soul is sometimes typified by a bird. As we have just seen, it has been associated with trees and fish. We are entitled therefore to ask whether the three symbols may not express one and the same idea under different forms. It is, of course, open to anyone to say that there were fish in the river, on whose banks Kentigern took up his abode, and quite a forest with birds singing in it around his cell, and that no further explanation of the symbolism need be sought. All these, it is true, existed within the saint's environment, but may they not have been regarded as types of the soul under the guise of objects familiar to all, and afterwards grouped together in the burgh Arms? On this hypothesis, the symbols have survived the belief that gave them birth, and serve to connect the practical life of to-day, with the vague visions and crude conjectures of the past.

CHAPTER XV.

Charm-Stones in and out of Water.

Stone-worship—Mysterious Properties of Stones—Symbolism of Gems—Gnostics—Abraxas Gems—Gems in Sarcophagi—Life-stones—Use of Amulets in Scotland—Yellow Stone in Mull—Baul Mulny—Black Stones of Iona—Stone as Medicine—Declan's Stone—Curing-stones still used for Cattle—Mary, Queen of Scots—Amulet at Abbotsford—Highland Reticence—Aberfeldy Curing-stone—Lapis Ceranius and Lapis Hecticus—Bernera—St. Ronan's Altar—Blue Stone in Fladda—Baul Muluy again—Columba's White Stone—Loch Manaar—Well near Loch Torridon—Stones besides Springs—Healing-stones at Killin—Their connection with Fillan—Mornish—Altars and Crosses—Iona—Clach-a-brath—Cross at Kilberry—Lunar Stone in Harris—Perforated Stones—Ivory—Barbeck's Bone—Adder-beads—Sprinkling Cattle—Elf-bolts—Clach-na-Bratach—Clach Dearg—Lee Penny—Lockerbie Penny—Black Penny.

WE have already seen that in early times water was an object of worship. Stones also were reverenced as the embodiments of nature-deities. "In Western Europe during the middle ages," remarks Sir J. Lubbock in his "*Origin of Civilisation,*" "we meet with several denunciations of stone-worship, proving its deep hold on the people. Thus the worship of stones was condemned by Theodoric, Archbishop of Canterbury, in the seventh century, and is among

R

the acts of heathenism forbidden by King Edgar
in the tenth, and by Cnut in the eleventh century."
Even as late as the seventeenth century, the Presbytery of Dingwall sought to suppress, among other
practices of heathen origin, that of rendering
reverence to stones, the stones in question having
been consulted as to future events. It is not
surprising therefore that stones had certain mysterious properties ascribed to them. In all ages
precious stones have been deservedly admired for
their beauty, but, in·addition, they have frequently
been esteemed for their occult qualities. "In my
youth," Mr. James Napier tells us, in his "*Folklore
in the West of Scotland*," "there was a belief in
the virtue of precious stones, which added a value
to them beyond their real value as ornaments.
. . . . Each stone had its own symbolic meaning
and its own peculiar influence for imparting good
and protecting from evil and from sickness its
fortunate possessor." By the ancient Jews, the
topaz and the amethyst were believed to guard
their wearers respectively against poison and drunk-
enness; while the diamond was prized as a
protection against Satanic influence. Concerning
the last-mentioned gem, Sir John Mandeville, writing
about 1356, says, "It makes a man stronger and
firmer against his enemies, heals him that is lunatic,
and those whom the fiend pursues and torments."
By certain sects of the Gnostics, precious stones
were much thought of as talismans. Among the

sect founded by Basilides of Egypt, the famous
Abraxas gems were used as tokens by the initiated.
The Gnostics also placed gems inscribed with mystic
mottoes in sarcophagi, to remind the dead of certain
prayers that were thought likely to aid them in
the other world. In Scandinavia, warriors were in
the habit of carrying about with them amulets called
life-stones or victory-stones. These strengthened
the hand of the wearer in fight. In our own country,
the use of amulets was not uncommon. A flat
oval-shaped pebble, measuring two and a half inches
in greatest diameter, was presented in 1864 to the
Society of Antiquaries of Scotland. It had been
worn as a charm by a Forfarshire farmer, who died
in 1854 at the age of eight-four. When in use, it
had been kept in a small bag and suspended by
a red string round the wearer's neck.

Even when stones were not used as amulets,
they were sometimes held in superstitious regard.
When in Mull, Martin was told of a yellow stone,
lying at the bottom of a certain spring in the
island, its peculiarity being that it did not get hot,
though kept over the fire for a whole day. The
same writer alludes to a certain stone in Arran,
called Baul Muluy, *i.e.*, "Molingus, his Stone Globe."
It was green in colour, and was about the size of a
goose's egg. The stone was used by the islanders,
when great oaths had to be sworn. It was also
employed to disperse an enemy. When thrown
among the front ranks, the opposing army would

retreat in confusion. In this way the Macdonalds
were said to have gained many a victory. When
not in use, the Baul Muluy was carefully kept
wrapped up in cloth. Among oath-stones, the *black
stones* of Iona were specially famous. These were
situated to the west of St. Martin's Cross, and were
called black, not from their colour—for they were
grey—but from the effects of perjury in the event
of a false oath being sworn by them. Macdonald,
Lord of the Isles, knelt on them, and, with uplifted
hands, swore that he would never recall the rights
granted by him to his vassals. Such a hold had
these oath-stones taken on the popular imagination,
that when anyone expressed himself certain about
a particular thing, he gave weight to his affirmation,
by saying that he was prepared to "swear upon
the black stones." Bishop Pocoke mentions that
the inhabitants of Iona "were in the habit of
breaking off pieces from a certain stone lying in
the church," to be used "as medicine for man or
beast in most disorders, and especially the flux."

Charm-stones were sometimes associated with early
saints. The following particulars about St. Declan's
Stone are given by Sir Arthur Mitchell in the tenth
volume of the "*Proceedings of the Society of Antiquaries of Scotland*":—"We are told in the life of
St. Declan that a small stone was sent to him from
Heaven while he was saying Mass in a church in
Italy. It came through the window and rested
on the altar. It was called Duivhin Deaglain or

Duivh-mhion Deaglain, *i.e.*, 'Declan's Black Relic.'
It performed many miracles during his life, being
famous for curing sore eyes, headaches, &c.; and is
said to have been found in his grave sometime, I
think, during last century. Its size is two and a-
fourth by one and three-fourth inches, and on one
side there is a Latin cross, incised and looped at the
top. At the bottom of the stem of this cross there is
another small Latin cross. On the other side of the
stone there is a circle, one and a-fourth inch in
diameter, and six holes or pits." Curing stones are
still used occasionally in connection with the diseases
of cattle, particularly in Highland districts; but
they have ceased to do duty in the treatment of
human ailments. Mary Queen of Scots seems to
have been a firm believer in their efficacy. In a
letter to her brother-in-law, Henry the Third of
France, written on the eve of her execution, the
Queen says, "She ventures to send him two rare
stones, valuable for the health, which she hopes will
be good, with a happy and long life, asking him to
receive them as the gift of his very affectionate
sister-in law, who is at the point of death, and in
token of true love towards him." In a case of
curiosities at Abbotsford, there is an amulet that
belonged to Sir Walter Scott's mother. It somewhat
resembles crocodile skin in colour, and has a setting
of silver. The amulet was believed to prevent
children from being bewitched.

It is nowadays difficult to ascertain the whereabouts

of curing-stones in the Highlands, owing to the
reticence of those who still have faith in their virtues.
Till lately there was one in the neighbourhood of
Aberfeldy that had been in use, it is believed, for
about three hundred years.   In shape, the charm
somewhat resembled a human heart, and consisted of
a water-worn pebble fully three inches in greatest
length.   When required for the cure of cattle, it was
rubbed over the affected part or was dipped in water,
the water being then given to the animal to drink.
Recently the family who owned it became extinct,
and the charm passed into other hands.   Martin
gives some curious information with regard to the
employment of charm-stones, among the inhabitants
of the Western Isles.   After describing a certain kind
of stone, called *lapis ceranius,* found in the island
of Skye, he remarks, "These stones are by the
natives called 'Cramp-stones,' because (as they say)
they cure the cramp in cows by washing the part
affected with water in which this stone had been
steeped for some hours."   He mentions also, that in
the same island, the stone called *lapis hecticus* was
deemed efficacious in curing consumption and other
diseases.   It was made red-hot, and then cooled in
milk or water, the liquid being drunk by the patient.
On Bernera, the islanders frequently rub their breasts
with a particular stone, by way of prevention, and
say it is a good preservative for health.   Martin
adds, "This is all the medicine they use: Providence
is very favourable to them in granting them a good

state of health, since they have no physician among them." In connection with his visit to the island of Rona, the same writer observes, "There is a chapel here dedicated to St. Ronan, fenced with a stone wall round; and they take care to keep it neat and clean, and sweep it every day. There is an altar in it, on which there lies a big plank of wood, about ten feet in length; every foot has a hole in it, and in every hole a stone, to which the natives ascribe several virtues: one of them is singular, as they say, for promoting speedy delivery to a woman in travail." The blue stone in Fladda, already referred to in connection with wind-charms, did duty as an oath-stone, and likewise as a curing-stone, its special function being to remove stitches in the side. The Baul Muluy in Arran, alluded to above, also cured stitches in the side. When the patient would not recover, the stone withdrew from the bed of its own accord.

A certain white stone, taken by Columba from the river Ness, near what is now the town of Inverness, had the singular power of becoming invisible, when the illness of the person requiring it would prove fatal. The selection of this stone was made in connection with the saint's visit to the court of Brude, king of the Picts, about the year 563. Adamnan, who tells the story, thus describes an interview between Columba and Brochan (the king's chief Druid or Magus), concerning the liberation of a female slave belonging to the latter: "The venerable

man, from motives of humanity, besought Brochan the
Druid to liberate a certain Irish female captive, a
request which Brochan harshly and obstinately
refused to grant. The saint then spoke to him as
follows :—' Know, O Brochan, know, that if you refuse
to set this captive free, as I advise you, you shall die
before I return from this province.' Having said
this in presence of Brude the king, he departed from
the royal palace, and proceeded to the river Nesa,
from which he took a white pebble, and, showing it
to his companions, said to them :—' Behold this white
pebble, by which God will effect the cure of many
diseases.' Having thus spoken, he added, ' Brochan
is punished grievously at this moment, for an angel
sent from heaven, striking him severely, has broken
in pieces the glass cup which he held in his hands,
and from which he was in the act of drinking, and he
himself is left half-dead.' " Messengers were sent by
the king to announce the illness of Brochan, and to
ask Columba to cure him. Adamnan continues :—
" Having heard these words of the messengers, Saint
Columba sent two of his companions to the king
with the pebble which he had blessed, and said to
them :—' If Brochan shall first promise to free his
captive, immerse this little stone in water, and let him
drink from it ; but if he refuse to liberate her, he will
that instant die.' The two persons sent by the saint
proceeded to the palace, and announced the words of
the holy man to the king and to Brochan, an
announcement which filled them with such fear that

he immediately liberated the captive and delivered her to the saint's messengers. The stone was then immersed in water, and, in a wonderful manner and contrary to the laws of nature, it floated on the water like a nut or an apple, nor could it be submerged. Brochan drank from the stone as it floated on the water, and instantly recovered his perfect health and soundness of body." The wonderful pebble was kept by King Brude among his treasures. On the day of the king's death, it remained true to itself, for, when its aid was sought, it could nowhere be found.

According to a tradition current in Sutherland, Loch Manaar in Strathnaver was connected with another white pebble, endowed with miraculous properties. The tradition, as narrated by the Rev. Dr. Gregor in the "*Folklore Journal*" for 1888, is as follows:—"Once upon a time, in Strathnaver, there lived a woman who was both poor and old. She was able to do many wonderful things by the power of a white stone which she possessed, and which had come to her by inheritance. One of the Gordons of Strathnaver having a thing to do, wished to have both her white stone and the power of it. When he saw that she would not lend it, or give it up, he determined to seize her, and to drown her in a loch. The man and the woman struggled there for a long time, till he took up a heavy stone with which to kill her. She plunged into the lake, throwing her magic stone before her and crying, 'May it do good to all created things save a Gordon of Strathnaver!' He stoned her to death in the water, she crying, 'Manaar! Manaar!' (Shame! Shame!). And the loch is called the Loch of Shame to this day." The loch had a more than local fame, for invalids resorted to it from Orkney in the north and Inverness in the south: its water was deemed specially efficacious on the first Monday of February, May, August, and November, (O. S.). The second and third of these dates were the most popular. The patient was kept bound and half-starved for about a day previous, and immediately after sunset on the appointed day, he was taken into the middle of the loch and there dipped. His wet clothes were then exchanged for dry ones, and his friends took him home in the full expectation of a cure. Belief in the loch's powers was acknowledged till recently, and is probably still secretly cherished in the district.

In a graveyard beside Loch Torridon, in Ross-shire, is a spring, formerly believed to work cures. From time immemorial three stones have been whirling in the well, and it was usual to carry one of these in a bucket of water to the invalid who simply touched the stone. When put back into the well, the stone began to move round and round as before. On one occasion a woman sought to cure her sick goat in the usual way, but the pebble evidently did not care to minister to any creature lower than man, for when replaced in the well, it lay motionless at the bottom ever afterwards. A certain Katherine Craigie, who was burned as a witch in Orkney in 1643, used

pebbles in connection with the magical cures wrought
by her. Her method, as described by Dr. Rogers in
his "*Social Life in Scotland*," was as follows:—"Into
water wherewith she washed the patient she placed
three small stones; these, being removed from the
vessel, were placed on three corners of the patient's
house from morning till night, when they were
deposited at the principal entrance. Next morning
the stones were cast into water with which the sick
person was anointed. The process was repeated every
day till a cure was effected."

At some wells, what the water lacked in the
matter of efficacy was supplied by certain stones
lying by their margins. These stones, in virtue of
a real or fancied resemblance to parts of the human
body—such as the eye or arm—were applied to the
members corresponding to them in shape, in the
expectation that this would conduce to a cure.
At Killin, in Perthshire, there are several stones
dedicated to Fillan, at one time much used in the
way described. These are, however, not beside a
spring, but in the mill referred to in a previous
chapter. They lie in a niche in the inner wall,
and have been there from an unknown past.
Whenever a new mill was built to replace the old
one, a niche was made in the wall for their reception.
They are some seven or eight in number. The
largest of them weighs eight lbs. ten oz. Special
interest attaches to at least two of them, on
account of certain markings on one side, consisting

of shallow rounded hollows somewhat resembling
the cup-marks which have proved such a puzzle
to archæologists.   There is reason to believe that
the stones in question were at one time used in
connection with milling operations, the hollows
being merely the sockets where the spindle of the
upper millstone revolved.   On the saint's day (the
ninth of January), it was customary till not very
long ago, for the villagers to assemble at the
mill, and place a layer of straw below the stones.
This custom has a particular interest, for we find
a counterpart to it in Scandinavia, both instances
being clearly survivals of stone-worship.   "In certain
mountain districts of Norway," Dr. Tylor tells us
in his "*Primitive Culture*," "up to the end of the
last century, the peasants used to preserve round
stones, washed them every Thursday evening (which
seems to show that they represented Thor), smeared
them with butter before the fire, laid them on the
seat of honour on fresh straw, and at certain times
of the year steeped them in ale, that they might
bring luck and comfort to the house."   The ritual
here is more elaborate than in the case of the
Killin stones; but the instances are parallel as
regards the use of straw.   Fully a couple of miles
from Killin, below Mornish, close to Loch Tay, is
the lonely nettle-covered graveyard of Cladh Davi,
and on a tombstone in its enclosure lie two
roundish stones, believed to belong to the same
series as those in the mill, and marked with

similar hollows. These stones were thought to cure
pectoral inflammation, the hollows being filled with
water, and applied to the breasts. The Rev. Dr.
Hugh MacMillan, after describing the stones in the
volume of the *Proceedings of the Society of
Antiquaries of Scotland*" for 1883-84, mentions that
"not long since, a woman, who was thus afflicted,
came a considerable distance, from the head of Glen
Lochay, to make use of this remedy."

Charm-stones were sometimes kept on the altars
of ancient churches, as in the case of St. Ronan's
Chapel, and the church in Iona already referred
to. At other times they were associated with
crosses. Sir Arthur Mitchell tells of an Irish
curing-stone in shape like a dumb-bell, preserved
in Killaghtee parish, County Donegal. "There is,"
he says, "a fragment of a stone cross on the top
of a small cairn. In a cleft or hollow of this
cross is kept a famous healing stone, in whose
virtues there is still a belief. It is frequently
removed to houses in which sickness exists, but
it is invariably brought back, and those living
near the cross can always tell where it is to be
found, if it has been so removed. Pennant, in
connection with his visit to Iona, speaks of certain
stones lying in the pedestal of a cross to the
north-west of St. Oran's Chapel. "Numbers who
visit this island," he remarks, "think it incumbent
on them to turn each of these thrice round,
according to the course of the sun. They are

called Clach-a-brath—for it is thought that the
brath, or 'end of the world,' will not arrive till
the stone on which they stand is worn through."
Pennant thought that these stones were the successors of "three noble globes of white marble,"
which, according to Sacheverel, at one time lay
in three stone basins, and were turned round in
the manner described, but were afterwards thrown
into the sea by the order of the ecclesiastical
authorities. MacCulloch says that, in his day, the
superstition connected with the Clach-a-brath had
died out in Iona. We do not think that this was
likely. Anyhow he mentions that "the boys of
the village still supply a stone for every visitor
to turn round on its bed; and thus, in the wearing of this typical globe, to contribute his share
to the final dissolution of all things." MacCulloch
alludes to the same superstition as then existing
on one of the Garveloch Isles. Sometimes hollows
were made on the pedestals of crosses, not for the
reception of stone-balls, but to supply occupation
to persons undergoing penance. A sculptured cross
at Kilberry, in Argyllshire, has a cavity of this
kind in its pedestal. In connection with his visit
to Kilberry, Captain White was told that "one of
the prescribed acts of penance in connection with
many of the ancient Irish crosses required the
individual under discipline, while kneeling before
the cross, to scoop out a cavity in the pedestal,
pestle-and-mortar fashion; and that such cavities,

where now to be seen, show in this way, varying
stages of the process."

One of the wonders of Harris, when Martin visited
the island, was a lunar stone lying in a hole in a
rock. Like the tides, it felt the moon's influence, for
it advanced and retired according to the increase or
decrease of that luminary. Perforated stones were
formerly much esteemed as amulets. If a stone, with
a hole in it, was tied to the key of a stable-door, it
would prevent the witches from stealing the horses.
Pre-historic relics of this kind were much used to
ward off malign influences from cattle, or to cure
diseases caused by the fairies. Ure, in his "*History
of Rutherglen and Kilbride*," refers to a ring of
black schistus found in a cairn in the parish of
Inchinnan. It was believed to work wonderful cures.
About a hundred years ago, a flat reddish stone,
having notches and with two holes bored through
it, was presented to the Society of Antiquaries of
Scotland. It came from Islay, and had been used
there as a charm. It belonged to the Stone Age,
and had, doubtless, served its first possessor as a
personal ornament. Ivory had magical properties
attributed to it. The famous "Barbeck's Bone"
—once the property of the Campbells of Barbeck,
in Craignish parish, Argyllshire, and now in the
National Museum of Antiquities—is a piece of ivory
seven inches long, four broad, and half an inch thick.
At one time it had a great reputation in the West
Highlands for the cure of insanity. It was counted

so valuable that, when it was lent, a deposit of one
hundred pounds sterling had to be made.

The antiquarian objects, popularly called *adder-
beads, serpent stones*, or *druidical beads*, were frequently used for the cure of cattle. The beads
were dipped in water, and the liquid was then
given to the animals to drink. These relics of a
long-forgotten past have been found from time to
time in ancient places of sepulture, and as they
usually occur singly, it has been conjectured that
they were placed there as amulets. " Many of them,"
remarks Sir Daniel Wilson in his *" Pre-historic
Annals*," " are exceedingly beautiful, and are char-
acterised by considerable ingenuity in the variations
of style. Among those in the Scottish Museum there
is one of red glass spotted with white; another of
dark brown glass streaked with yellow; others of
pale green and blue glass, plain and ribbed; and
two of curiously figured patterns, wrought with
various colours interwoven on their surface." A
fine specimen of this species of amulet was discovered
in a grave mound at Eddertoun, in Ross-shire, during
the progress of the railway operations in 1864. The
Rev. Dr. Joass, who interested himself in the antiquarian discoveries then made, thus describes the
find :—" The glass, of which this bead was composed,
was of a dark blue colour, and but partially transparent. It was ornamented by three volutes, which
sufficed to surround it. These were traced in a
yellow pigment (or enamel) as hard as the glass,

and seeming to sink slightly below the surface into
the body of the bead, as could be seen where this
was flattened, as if by grinding at the opposite ends
of its orifice." These *adderbeads* seem to have been
common in the seventeenth century. Edward Llwyd,
who visited Scotland in 1699, saw fifty different
forms of them between Wales and the Scottish
Highlands. Crystal balls, he tells us, were frequently
put into a tub of water on May Day, the contents
of the tub being sprinkled over cattle to keep them
from being bewitched.

Flint arrow-heads—the weapons of early times—
became the amulets of a later age. In folklore
they are known as elf-bolts. Popular credulity
imagined that they were used by the fairies for
the destruction of cattle. When an animal was
attacked by some sudden and mysterious disease,
it was believed to be "elf-shot" even though no
wound could be seen on its body. To cure the
cow, the usual method was to make it drink some
water in which an elf-bolt had been dipped, on the
principle of taking a hair of the dog that bit you.
Elf-arrows were at one time thought to be serviceable to man also. The custom was not unknown
of sewing one of them in some part of the dress
as a charm against the influence of the evil eye.
Occasionally one still sees them doing duty as
brooches, and in that form, if not now prized as
amulets, they are esteemed as ornaments.

Sir J. Y. Simpson, in his *"Archæological Essays,"*

s

gives some interesting particulars about two ancient
charm-stones, the property of two Highland families
for many generations. Of these, the Clach-na-
Bratach, or Stone of the Standard, belongs to
the head of the Clan Donnachie. It is described
as "a transparent, globular mass of rock crystal of
the size of a small apple. Its surface has been
artificially polished." The stone was picked up by
the then chief of the clan shortly before the battle
of Bannockburn. It was found in a clod of earth
adhering to the standard when drawn out of the
ground, and on account of its brilliancy the chief
foretold a victory. In later times it was used to
predict the fortunes of the clan. We are told that
before the battle of Sheriffmuir, in 1715, which
proved so disastrous to the cause of the Stuarts,
as well as to that of Clan Donnachie, the Clan-na-
Bratach was found to have a flaw, not seen till
then. When wanted to impart curative virtue to
water, the Clach-na-Bratach was dipped in it thrice
by the hand of the chief. The other charm-stone
alluded to is the Clach Dearg, or Stone of Ardvoirlich. It resembles the Clach-na-Bratach in appearance, though it is somewhat smaller in size. It
differs from it, moreover, in being surrounded by
four silver bands of eastern workmanship. The
charm has belonged to the family of Ardvoirlich
from an unknown past, but there is no tradition
as to its early history. As a healing agent it has
had more than a local fame. When its help was

sought certain rules had to be attended to. The person coming to Ardvoirlich was required to draw the water himself, and bring it into the house in the vessel in which the charm was to be dipped. A bottle of this water was then carried to the invalid's home. If the bearer called at any house by the way, it was requisite that the bottle should be left outside, otherwise the water would lose its power.

In the mansion-house of Lee, some three miles north of Lanark, is kept the Lee Penny, an amulet of even greater fame than the Clach-na-Bratach or the Clach Dearg. This charm—the prototype of Sir Walter Scott's "*Talisman*"—is a semi-transparent gem of a dark red colour. It is set in a silver coin, believed to be a groat of Edward the Fourth. In shape it rudely resembles a heart. This circumstance doubtless strengthened the original belief in its magical powers, if, indeed, it did not give rise to it. The tradition is, that Sir Simon Lockhart, an ancestor of the present owner of the estate, left Scotland along with Sir James Douglas, in the year 1330, to convey the heart of Robert Bruce to the Holy Land. Douglas was killed in Spain in a battle with the Moors, and Sir Simon returned to Scotland, bringing the heart with him. He had various adventures in connection with this mission. One of these was the capture of a Saracen prince, who, however, obtained his freedom for a large sum. While the money was being counted out the

amulet in question accidentally fell into the heap
of coin, and was claimed as part of the ransom.
Previous to its appearance in Scotland it had been
much esteemed as a cure for hemorrhage and
fever. After it was brought to our shores its fame
increased rather than waned. During the reign of
Charles the First it was taken to Newcastle-on-Tyne
to stay a pestilence raging there, a bond for six
thousand pounds being given as a guarantee of its
safe return. The amulet did its work so well,
that to ensure its retention in the town the bond
would have been willingly forfeited. It was
reckoned of use in the treatment of almost any
ailment, but specially in cases of hydrophobia. A
cure effected by it at the beginning of last century
is on record. Lady' Baird of Saughton Hall, near
Edinburgh, showed what were believed to be
symptoms of rabies from the bite of a dog. At
her request the Lee Penny was sent to Saughton
Hall. She drank and bathed in water in which
it had been dipped, and restoration was the result.
The amulet was also used for the cure of cattle,
and when every other remedy failed recourse was
had to the wonder-working gem. When it was
employed for therapeutic purposes, the following
was the *modus operandi:*—It was drawn once round
the vessel containing the water to be rendered
medicinal, and was then plunged thrice into the
liquid; but no words of incantation were used.
For this reason the Reformed Church, when seek-

ing to abolish certain practices of heathen origin,
sanctioned the continued use of the Lee Penny as
a charm. A complaint was made against the Laird
of Lee "anent the superstitious using of ane stane
set in silver for the curing of diseased cattell."
The complaint came before the Assembly which
met in Glasgow; but the case was dismissed on
the ground that the rite was performed "wtout
using onie words such as charmers and sorcerers
use in their unlawfull practices; and considering
that in nature there are mony things seen to work
strange effects, q.ʳ· of no human wit can give a
reason."   Nevertheless the Laird of Lee was admonished "in the useing of· the said stane to tak
heed that it be used hereafter w.ᵗ the least scandal
that possiblie may be."   Belief in the efficacy of
the amulet continued to hold its ground in the
neighbourhood of Lee till towards the middle of
the present century.   In 1839 phials of water
which had felt its magical touch were to be seen
hanging up in byres to protect the cattle from
evil influences.   Some fifteen years earlier a Yorkshire farmer carried away water from Lee to cure
some of his cattle which had been bitten by a
mad dog. Attached to the amulet is a small silver
chain which facilitated its use when its services
were required.   The charm is kept in a gold box,
presented by the Empress Maria Theresa.

Another south-country amulet, not, however, so
famous as the Lee Penny, is the piece of silver,

known as the Lockerbie Penny. It was, and still is, we suppose, used to cure madness in cattle. In his "*Folklore of the Northern Counties*," Mr. Henderson gives the following particulars about the charm:— "It is put in a cleft stick and a well is stirred round with it, after which the water is bottled off and given to any animal so affected. A few years ago, in a Northumbrian farm, a dog bit an ass, and the ass bit a cow; the penny was sent for, and a deposit of fifty pounds sterling actually left till it was restored. The dog was shot, the cuddy died, but the cow was saved through the miraculous virtue of the charm." After the death of the farmer who borrowed the Penny, several bottles of water were found stowed away in a cupboard labelled "Lockerbie Water." Mr. Henderson also mentions another Border amulet, known as the Black Penny, for long the property of a family at Hume-byers. It is larger than an ordinary penny, and is believed to be a Roman coin or medal. When brought into use it should be dipped in a well, the water of which runs towards the south. Mr. Henderson adds:—"Popular belief still upholds the virtue of this remedy; but, alas! it is lost to the world. A friend of mine informs me that half a generation back the Hume-byers Penny was borrowed by some persons residing in the neighbourhood of Morpeth and never returned."

CHAPTER XVI.

Pilgrimages to Wells.

NOWADAYS people put Murray or Black, or some
similar volume, into their portmanteau, and set off
by rail on what they call a pilgrimage. In this
case the term is a synonym for sight-seeing, usually
accomplished under fairly comfortable conditions.
In ancient times pilgrimages were, as a rule, serious
matters with a serious aim. Shakespeare says, in
" *Two Gentlemen of Verona* ":—

> " A true devoted pilgrim is not weary
> To measure kingdoms with his feeble steps.'

The object of such journeys was to benefit either
soul or body, or both. The doing of penance, or
the fulfilling of a vow, sent devotees to certain
sacred spots, sometimes in distant lands, sometimes
within our own four seas. Cuthbert's shrine at
Durham, where the saint's body was finally deposited in 1070, after its nearly two hundred years'
wanderings, was a noted resort of pilgrims in the
middle ages, and many cures were wrought at it.
Archbishop Eyre, on the authority of Reginald of
Durham, tells of a certain man of noble birth,
belonging to the south of England, who could not
find relief for his leprosy. He was told to light
three candles, and to dedicate them respectively to
St. Edmund, St. Etheldrith, and St. Cuthbert, and
to visit the shrine of the saint whose candle first
burned out. The candles were lighted, and the omen
indicated the last-mentioned saint. Accordingly, he
travelled to the north country, and, after various
religious exercises, drew near the shrine of Cuthbert,
and was cured. The shrine in question was known
even as far off as Norway. On one occasion, at
least, viz., in 1172, its miraculous aid was sought
by an invalid from that country. A young man
of Bergen, who was blind, deaf, and dumb, had
sought relief at Scandinavian shrines for six years,
but in vain. The bishop suggested that he should
try the virtue of an English shrine, and recommended
that lots should be cast, to determine whether it
was to be that of St. Edmund, St. Thomas, or St.

Cuthbert. The lot fell to St. Cuthbert. The young
man passed through Scotland to Durham, and returned home cured. The miracle, doubtless, still
further increased the sanctity of the saint's tomb.

The Cross of Crail, in Fife, had the power of
working wonderful cures; and many were the pilgrims who flocked to it. Aberdour, in the same
county, had more than a local fame. The name
of The Pilgrims' Well there tells its own tale. This
well is now filled up, but for centuries it attracted
crowds of pilgrims. In the fifteenth century the
spot was so popular that about 1475, at the suggestion of Sir John Scott, vicar of Aberdour, the Earl
of Morton granted a piece of land for the erection
of an hospital to accommodate the pilgrims. This
hospital was named after St. Martha. It is not
certain to whom the Pilgrims' Well was dedicated;
but Fillan was probably its patron, as the Rev. Wm.
Ross conjectures, in an article on the subject in the
third volume of the "*Proceedings of the Society of
Antiquaries of Scotland.*" The church of Aberdour
was dedicated to the saint in question; and the well
was near the old churchyard.

.Ninian's shrine at Whithorn was the scene of
various miracles during the middle ages. In 1425
James the First granted a safe-conduct to all
strangers, coming to Scotland to visit it; and James
the Fourth made a pilgrimage to it once a year,
and sometimes oftener. "It is likely," remarks the
Rev. Daniel Conway in an article on consecrated

springs in the south-west of Scotland, "that the spots in Wigtownshire, where Holy Wells were, marked the route pursued by pilgrims bent on doing homage to the relics of St. Ninian at Whithorn." Whithorn was not the only shrine visited by James the Fourth. He went repeatedly on pilgrimage to St. Andrews, Dunfermline, and Tain, and left offerings at the shrines of their respective saints. When on pilgrimage the king was usually accompanied by a large retinue, including a company of minstrels. He liked to have his dogs and hawks with him too, to have a little hunting by the way.

St. Kentigern's Well, in the so-called crypt of Glasgow Cathedral, has already been mentioned. In the immediate neighbourhood is the spot believed to mark the last resting place of the saint. Till the Reformation his shrine attracted crowds of pilgrims. On special occasions his relics were displayed, including his bones, his hair shirt, and his scourge, and a red liquor that flowed from his tomb. These, along with other relics belonging to the cathedral, were taken to France by Archbishop Beaton in 1560. In the ancient parish of Dundurcus, Elginshire, not far from the river Spey, once stood the Chapel of Grace, and close to it was a well of the same name. The place was a favourite resort of pilgrims. Lady Aboyne went to it once a year, a distance of over thirty miles, and walked the last two miles of the way on her bare feet. In 1638 an attempt was made to put a stop to the pilgrimages,

by destroying what then remained of the chapel.
The attempt, however, seems to have been fruitless,
for in 1775, Shaw, the historian of Moray, mentions
that to it "multitudes from the western isles do
still resort, and nothing short of violence can restrain
their superstition." In 1435, when Æneas Silvius
(afterwards Pope Pius the Second) was sailing from
the low countries to Scotland on a political mission,
he was twice overtaken by a storm, and was in
such danger that he vowed to make a pilgrimage,
should he escape drowning. At length he reached
the Haddingtonshire coast in safety, and, to fulfil
his vow, set off barefoot, over ice-covered ground, to
Whitekirk, ten miles away, where there were a
chapel and well, dedicated to the Virgin. The
journey left its mark on the pilgrim, for we are
told that he had aches in his joints ever afterwards.
St. Adrian's Chapel, in the Isle of May, in the Firth
of Forth, had a great reputation before the Reformation. The island has still its Pilgrims' Haven, and
its Pilgrims' Well close by.

Archæology bears witness to the popularity of
pilgrimages in former times. Between Moxley
Nunnery, in Yorkshire, and St. John's Well, about
a mile away, are the remains of a causeway, laid
down for the convenience of devotees. At Stenton,
in Haddingtonshire, near the road leading to Dunbar,
is the well of the Holy Rood, covered by a small
circular building with a conical roof. The well is
now filled up. Its former importance is indicated

by the fact that the pathway between it and the
old church, some two hundred yards off, had a stone
pavement, implying considerable traffic to and from
the spring.   In the quiet Banffshire parish of Inver-
aven, is a spring, at Chapelton of Kilmaichlie, near
the site of an ancient chapel.   The spring is now
almost forgotten, but its casing of stone shows that,
at one time, it was an object of interest in the
neighbourhood.

The author of "*Marmion*," when describing the
arrival, at Lindisfarne, of the bark containing St.
Hilda's holy maids from Whitby, has the following
picturesque lines :—

> "The tide did now its flood-mark gain,
> And girdled in the saint's domain :
> For, with the flow and ebb, its style
> Varies from continent to isle ;
> Dry-shod, o'er sands, twice every day,
> The pilgrims to the shrine find way ;
> Twice, every day, the waves efface
> Of staves and sandalled feet the trace."

Towards the end of the same poem, in connection
with the Lady Clare's quest of water for the dying
Marmion, we find the following reference :—

> "Where shall she turn ?—behold her mark
>   A little fountain cell,
> Where water, clear as diamond-spark,
>   In a stone basin fell !
> Above, some half-worn letters say,
> ' Drink . weary . pilgrim . drink . and . pray .
> For . the . kind . soul . of . Sybil . Grey .
>   Who . built . this . cross . and . well.'"

In England, during the middle ages, there were various attempts to regulate the custom of making pilgrimages to wells. A canon of King Edgar, of date 963, prohibited the superstitious resorting to fountains, and in 1102, one of the canons of St. Anselm permitted only such wells to be visited as were approved of by the bishop. In Scotland, vigorous efforts were made, after the Reformation, to abolish the practice. Both Church and State combined to bring about this result. In an Act of Parliament, of date 1581, allusion is made to the "pervers inclination of mannis ingyne to superstitioun through which the dregges of idolatrie yit remanis in divers pairtis of the realme be useing of pilgrimage to sum chappellis, wellis, croces, and sic other monumentis of idolatrie, as also be observing of the festual dayis of the santes sumtyme namit their patronis in setting forth of bain fyres, singing of caroles within and about kirkes at certane seasones of the yeir." In 1629 the practice was sternly forbidden by an edict from the Privy Council. In connection with this edict, Dalyell remarks, "It seems not to have been enough that congregations were interdicted from the pulpit preceding the wonted period of resort, or that individuals, humbled on their knees, in public acknowledgment of their offence, were rebuked or fined for disobedience. Now, it was declared that, for the purpose of restraining the superstitious resort, 'in pilgrimages to chappellis and wellis, which is so frequent and common in

this kingdome, to the great offence of God, scandall
of the kirk, and disgrace of his Majesteis government;
that commissioners cause diligent search at all such
pairts and places where this idolatrous superstitioun
is used, and to take and apprehend all suche persons
of whatsomever rank and qualitie whom they sall
deprehend going in pilgrimage to chappellis and
wellis, or whome they sall know thameselffes to be
guiltie of that cryme, and to commit thame to waird,
until measures should be adopted for their trial and
punishment.'" Prior to the date of the above edict
the Privy Council had not been idle, crowds of people
were in the habit of making a pilgrimage on May
Day to Christ's Well, in Menteith, where they
performed certain superstitious rites. Accordingly,
in 1624, a Commission was issued to a number of
gentlemen belonging to the district instructing them
to station themselves beside the well, to apprehend
the pilgrims and to remove them to the Castle of
Doune. Even such measures did not cause the
practice to cease.

In 1628 several persons were accused before the
kirk-session of Falkirk of going in pilgrimage to
the well in question, and being found guilty, were
ordered to appear in church three appointed Sundays,
clad in the garb of penitents. The same year the
following warning was issued by the aforesaid kirk-
session :—" It is statute and ordained that if any
person or persons be found superstitiously and
idolatrously, after this, to have passed in pilgrimage

to Christ's Well, on the Sundays of May to seek
their health, they shall repent *in sacco* and linen
three several Sabbaths, and pay twenty lib. (Scots)
toties quoties for ilk fault; and if they cannot pay
it the baillies shall be recommended to put them in
ward, and to be fed on bread and water for aught
days."

Scottish ecclesiastical records, indeed, bear ample
testimony to the zeal displayed by the Church in
putting a stop to such visits. In his "*Domestic
Annals of Scotland,*" Chambers gives the following
picture of what was done by the kirk-session of
Perth. The example shows the lines usually followed
in connection with such prosecutions:—"At Huntingtower there was a well, the water of which was
believed to have sanative qualities when used under
certain circumstances. In May, 1618, two women
of humble rank were before the kirk-session of
Perth, 'who, being asked if they were at the well
in the bank of Huntingtower the last Sabbath, if
they drank thereof, and what they left at it,
answered, that they drank thereof, and that each
of them left a prin (pin) thereat, which was found
to be a point of idolatrie in putting the well in
God's room.' They were each fined six shillings,
and compelled to make public avowal of their
repentance." In the parish of Nigg, Kincardineshire,
is St. Fittack's or St. Fiacre's Well, situated close
to the sea. It is within easy reach of Aberdeen
across the Dee. Many a visit was paid to it by

the inhabitants of that burgh, from motives of superstition. The Aberdeen kirk-session, however, did its duty in the matter, and repeatedly forbade such visits. In 1630, " Margrat Davidson, spous to Andro Adam, was adjudget in ane unlaw of fyve poundis to be payed to the collector for directing hir nowriss with hir bairne to Sanct Fiackres Well, and weshing the bairne tharin for recovirie of hir health ; and the said Margrat and hir nowriss were ordainit to acknowledge thair offence before the Session for thair fault, and for leaveing ane offering in the well." The saint, to whom the well was dedicated, is believed to have migrated from Scotland to France early in the seventh century, and to have been held in much esteem there. From Butler's " *Lives of the Saints* " we get the curious information that " the name *fiacre* was first given to hackney coaches, because hired carriages were first made use of for the convenience of pilgrims who went from Paris to visit the shrine of this saint." A·well at Airth, in Stirlingshire, was for long a centre of attraction. What was done there may be learned from some entries in the local kirk-session records quoted in Hone's " *Every-Day Book* " :—" Feb. 3, 1757. Session convenit. Compeared Bessie Thomson, who declairit schoe went to the well at Airth, and that schoe left money thairat and after the can was fillat with water, they keepit it from touching the ground till they cam hom." " February 24th.—Compeired Robert Fuird, who declared he went to the well of

Airth and spoke nothing als he went, and that
Margrat Walker went with him, and schoe said ye
belief about the well, and left money and ane napkin
at the well, and all was done at her injunction."
" March 21.—Compeired Robert Ffuird who declairit
yat Margrat Walker went to ye well of Airth to
fetch water to Robert Cowie, and when schoe com
thair schoe laid down money in God's name, and
ane napkin in Robert Cowie's name." The session
ordered the delinquents to be admonished.

Years went on, and modes of thought gradually
changed. Church and State alike began to respect
the liberty of the subject. Though visits continued
to be paid to holy wells, they ceased to be reckoned
as offences. People might still resort to the spots,
so familiar to their ancestors, and so much revered
by them; but they no longer found themselves shut
up in prison, or made to do penance before the whole
congregation. Old customs continued to hold sway,
though less stress was laid on the superstitions, lying
behind them. Thus it came to pass, that pilgrimages
to holy wells became more and more an excuse for
mirthful meetings among friends. This was specially
true of Craigie Well, in the parish of Avoch, in the
Black Isle of Cromarty. The time for visiting the
spring was early in the morning of the first Sunday
in May. The well was situated near Munlochy Bay,
a few yards above high-water-mark, and gets its
name from the crags around. A correspondent of
Chambers's " Book of Days " thus describes what he

T

saw and heard:—"I arrived about an hour before sunrise, but long before, crowds of lads and lasses from all quarters were fast pouring in. Some, indeed, were there at daybreak who had journeyed more than seven miles. Before the sun made his appearance, the whole scene looked more like a fair than anything else. Acquaintances shook hands in true Highland style, brother met brother, and sister met sister, while laughter and all kinds of country news and gossip were so freely indulged in, that a person could hardly hear what he himself said." Amid all the stir and bustle the spring itself was not neglected, for everyone took care to have a drink. Some used dishes, while others, on hands and knees, sucked up the water with the mouth. These latter were now and again ducked over head and ears by their acquaintances, who much enjoyed the frolic. No one went away without leaving a thread, or patch of cloth on a large briar bush near the spring. Besides St. Fittack's Well, there is another in Nigg parish called Downy Well. It used to be resorted to in May, by persons who drank the water, and then crossed by a narrow neck of land, called The Brig of a'e Hair, to Downy Hill— a green headland in the sea—where they amused themselves by carving their names in the turf.

Brand, in his *Popular Antiquities*," gives the following particulars about a custom that still prevailed in Cumberland, when he wrote about forty years ago:—" In some parts of the North of England it has been a custom from time immemorial for the lads and lasses of the neighbouring villages to collect together at springs or rivers, on some Sunday in May, to drink sugar and water, where the lasses gave the treat: this is called "Sugar and Water Sunday." They afterwards adjourn to the public-house, and the lads return the compliment in cakes, ale, punch, &c. A vast concourse of both sexes assemble for the above purpose at the Giant's Cave, near Eden Hall in Cumberland, on the third Sunday in May."

We do not know whether sacred dramas were ever performed beside Scottish springs; but Stow informs us that the parish clerks of London made an annual pilgrimage to Clark's Well, near the Metropolis, "to play some large history of Holy Scripture." He also mentions that a Miracle Play, lasting eight days, was performed at Skinner's Well in the time of Henry the Fourth. South of the Tweed, springs were often the scenes of festivity. Thus, to take only one example, we find that pilgrims to St. Margaret's Well, at Wereham in Norfolk, were in the habit, in pre-Reformation days, of regaling themselves with cakes and ale, and indulging in music and dancing. What occurred in Ireland down to the beginning of the present century may be gathered from a passage in Mason's "*Statistical Account of Ireland*" reprinted in the "*Folklore Journal*" for 1888. After referring to religious assemblies at Holy Wells the writer remarks:—"At these places are always erected booths or tents as in Fairs for selling whisky, beer, and ale,

at which pipers and fiddlers do not fail to attend,
and the remainder of the day and night (after
their religious performances are over and the priest
withdrawn) is spent in singing, dancing, and drinking to excess. . . . Such places are frequently
chosen for scenes of pitched battles, fought with
cudgels by parties not only of parishes but of
counties, set in formal array against each other
to revenge some real or supposed injury."   In
Roman Catholic districts of Ireland, what are called
patrons, *i.e.*, gatherings in honour of the patron
saints of the place, are still popular.   From an
article on " *Connemara Folklore*," by G. H. Kinahan,
in the " *Folklore Journal* " for 1884, we learn that
a consecrated spring at Cashla Bay has, beside it, a
large conical mound of sea-shells.   These are the
remains of the shell-fish forming the food of the
pilgrims during the continuance of the patron, and
cooked by them on the top of the mound.   Last
century, in Ireland, the custom of carrying the
water of famous wells to distant parts, and there
selling it, was not unknown.   A correspondent of
the " *Gentleman's Magazine* " mentions that about
1750 this was done in connection with a miraculous
spring near Sligo; and that, some years earlier, the
water of Lough Finn was sold in the district, where
he lived, at sixpence, eightpence, and tenpence per
quart, according to the different success of sale the
carriers had on the road.   A thatched cottage stood
close to the site of St. Margaret's Well at Restalrig,

and was inhabited by a man who carried the water of the spring to Leith for sale.

Mr. William Andrews, in his "*Old Time Punishments*," tells of booths having been set up beside a Lincolnshire gibbet in 1814, to supply provisions for the crowds who came to see a murderer hanging in chains there. Less gruesome were the fairs at one time held in the neighbourhood of springs, though even they had certain unpleasant concomitants, which led in the end to their discontinuance. In the united parish of Dunkeld and Dowally is Sancta Crux Well, at Crueshill. Till towards the middle of the present century, it was such a popular resort, that tents were set up and refreshments sold to the pilgrims. Alcohol was so freely partaken of that drunken brawls often ensued, and right-minded people felt that the gathering would be more honoured in the breach than in the observance. St. Fillan's Fair, at Struan, took place on the first Friday after New Year's Day (O.S.). It was held on a spot close to the church, and not far from St. Fillan's Well. It is now discontinued, but its stance is still known as Croft-an-taggart, *i.e.*, The Priest's Croft. The Well Market, now held at Tomintoul, in Kirkmichael parish, Banffshire, but formerly beside Fergan Well, has already been referred to. Writing in April, 1892, a correspondent, who has resided in the parish for nearly half-a-century, mentions the following particulars concerning the spring:—"The healing virtue of its

water is still believed in, especially on the first
Sunday of May, when parties still gather and watch
the arrival of Sunday morning with special care,
many of them remaining there the whole night
and part of the Sabbath. Whoever first washes
in the water or drinks of it is cured of any disease
or sore with which they may be troubled." Our
correspondent adds :—" The annual market of the
district was held at Fergan Well, and the foundations
of the tents or booths where goods were sold are still
visible: and very probably there was a kind of
mountain dew partaken of stronger than the water
that now flows from Fergan Well." ·We shall have
something more to say about fairs in the next
chapter.

Though modern enlightenment has not entirely
abolished the practice of resorting to consecrated
springs, it has, as a rule, produced a desire for
secrecy on the part of the pilgrims. When supersti-
tous motives are absent, and springs are visited
merely from curiosity or love of frolic, there is no
sense of shame, and hence no need for concealment.
But when the pilgrims regard the practice as a
magical rite, they usually prefer to keep the rest
of the world in the dark as to their doings. Sir
Arthur Mitchell truly remarks in his "*Past in the
Present*"—"It is well enough understood that the
business is not a Christian one, and that the engaging
in it is not a thing which it would be easy to justify.
There is a consciousness that it has not been gone

about as an empty, meaningless ceremony, but that it has involved an acknowledgment of a supernatural power controlling human affairs and influenced by certain rites and offerings—a power different from that which is acknowledged by Christians. Hence it happens that there is a difficulty in getting people to confess to these visits, and, of course, a greater difficulty still in getting them to speak, freely and frankly, about the feelings and beliefs which led to them."

CHAPTER XVII.

Sun-Worship and Well-Worship.

Fairs—Their Connection with Holy Days—Nature-festivals—Modes of Marking Time—Ecclesiastical Year and Natural Year—Christmas—Fire-festivals—Hallow E'en and Mid-summer Fires—Beltane—Its Connection with Sun-worship—Sun-charms—Carrying Fire—Clavie at Burghead—Fiery-circle—Traces of Sun-worship in Folk-customs—In Architecture—Turning Sunways—Widdershins—When Wells were Visited—May—Influence of Pagan Rites—Folklore of May Day—Sundays in May—Sunday Wells—Sunday, why Chosen—Lammas—Festival of St. Peter ad Vincula—Gule of August—Sun and Well-worship—Time of Day for Using Wells—Fonts of the Cross—Walking Sunways round Wells—Doing the Reverse—Witch's Well—South-running Water.

In his *"Scottish Markets and Fairs"* Sir J. D. Marwick observes:—"Simple home needs, such as plain food and clothing, articles of husbandry, and other indispensable appliances of life gave rise to markets held at frequent fixed times, at suitable centres. But as society grew and artificial needs sprung up, these could only be met by trade; and trade on anything beyond a very limited scale was only then practicable at fairs. Wherever large numbers of persons were drawn together, at fixed times, for purposes of business or religion or pleasure,

an inducement was offered to the merchant or pedlar,
as well as to the craftsman, to attend, and to
provide by the diversity and quality of his wares
for the requirements of the persons there congre-
gated." In the last chapter allusion was made to
such gatherings in connection with springs. We
shall now look at the dates when they were held,
in order to trace their connection with nature-
festivals. Fairs, as distinguished from markets, were
of comparatively rare occurrence at any given place.
In the majority of instances, they can be traced
back to some gathering held in connection with
what were originally holy days, and afterwards
holidays. Such holy days commemorated a local
saint, the fame of whose sanctity was confined to
more or less narrow limits, or one whom Christendom
at large delighted to honour; or, again, a leading
event in sacred or legendary history deemed worthy
of a place in the ecclesiastical year. A few dates
when fairs are, or were held at various Scottish
centres may be selected from Sir J. Marwick's list.
At Abercorn they were held on Michaelmas and
St. Serf's Day; at Aberdeen, on Whitsunday, Holy
Trinity, Michaelmas, and St. Nicholas's Day; at
Charlestown of Aboyne, on Candlemas, Michaelmas,
and Hallowmas; at Annan, on Ascension-day and
Michaelmas; at Ayr, on Mid-summer and Michaelmas;
at Biggar, on Candlemas and Mid-summer; at Clack-
mannan, on St. Bartholomew's Day; at Cromdale,
on St. Luke's Day, St. Peter's Day, Michaelmas,

and St. George's Day; at Culross, on St. Serf's Day,
Martinmas, and St. Matthew's Day; at Dalmellington,
on Fastern's E'en and Hallow E'en; at Dalmeny, on
St. John the Baptist's Day and St. Luke's Day; at
Doune, on Martinmas, Yule, Candlemas, Whitsunday,
Lammas, and Michaelmas; at Dumbarton, on Patrick-
mas, Mid-summer, and Lammas; at Fraserburgh, on
St. John the Baptist's Day and Michaelmas; at Fyvie,
on Fastern's Eve, St. Peter's Day, and St. Magdalene's
Day; at Hamilton, on St. Lawrence's Day and Martinmas; at Inveraray, on Michaelmas and St. Brandane's
Day; at Stranraer, on St. Barnabas' Day and Lammas.
Among the fairs at Auchinblae were; Pasch Market
in April, and one called May Day to be held on
the 22nd of that month.   This series might be
indefinitely enlarged; but as it stands it shows
that the leading nature-festivals, such as Yule,
Easter, Whitsuntide, Mid-summer, Michaelmas, and
Hallowmas have a prominent place among the
dates selected. An examination of Sir J. Marwick's
list further shows that the dates of fairs were
often fixed, not with reference to any particular
holy day, but to some day of a particular month,
such as the second Tuesday, or the third Thursday.
Many of these occur in May. In ancient documents
—in Acts of Parliaments, for instance—dates were
commonly fixed by a reference to holy days.   In
Presbyterian Scotland such a method of marking
time is not now in fashion, though some relics of the
practice survive.   We are still familiar with Whit-

sunday and Martinmas as term-days, but how few
now ever think of them as ecclesiastical festivals!

The meaning of customs associated with the
various holy days has come to be duly recognised
by the student of ecclesiastical antiquities. While
the Christian year was being evolved in the course
of centuries, certain festivals were introduced, as
one might say, arbitrarily, *i.e.*, without being linked
to any pre-Christian usages. From the point of
view of Church clebrations, they have not the same
significance as those others that received, as their
heritage, certain rights in vogue before the spread
of Christianity. In other words, the leading pagan
festivals had a new meaning put into them, and,
when adopted by the Church, were exalted to a
position of honour. In .virtue of this, the ecclesiastical year was correlated to the natural year, with
its varying seasons and its archaic festivals. There
is no doubt that in early times the Church sought
to win nations from paganism by admitting as
many of the old customs as were deemed harmless.
We have seen how this was effected in the case of
fountains, as shown by Columba's exorcism of the
demons inhabiting springs. The same principle prevailed all round. The old Saturnalia of the Romans,
for instance, became the rejoicings of Christmas.
To the distinctively Christian aspects of the festival
we do not, of course, allude, but to the customs still
in vogue at the Yule season; and these are nothing
more than a revised edition of the old pagan rites.

Among other Aryan peoples the winter solstice was
was also commemorated by similar merry-makings.
Church festivals, such as Candlemas, Easter, St.
John's Day, St. Peter's Day, Michaelmas, Hallowmas,
Christmas, &c., absorbed many distinctive features
of the old pagan fire-festivals, held in connection
with the changes of the seasons. The kindling of
fires out of doors, on special occasions, is familiar
to all of us. They may be called modern folk-
customs; but their origin is ancient enough to give
them special significance. Even to the present time,
twinkling spots of light may be seen along the shores
of Loch Tay on Hallow E'en, though the mid-summer
fires do not now blaze on our Scottish hills, as they
continue to do in Scandinavia and elsewhere. Among
the Bavarian Highlands these mid-summer fires are
popularly known as *Sonnenwendfeuer*, *i.e.*, solstice-
fires. That they are so called and not St. John's
fires (though lighted in connection with his festival)
is significant. In Brittany a belief prevailed that
if a girl danced nine times round one of the St.
John's fires before midnight she would be married
within the year.

The most important fire-festival in Scotland was
that of Beltane at the beginning of May. It was
celebrated generally throughout our land. To the
south of the Forth several sites are known to have
been specially associated with Beltane fires. In
Lanarkshire two such sites were, the hills of Tinto
and Dechmont. Tinto, indeed, means the hill of

fire. It was used for beacon-fires as well as for those connected with nature-festivals, and was well adapted for the purpose, being 2335 feet above the sea, and 1655 feet above the Clyde at its base. Though not nearly so high, Dechmont hill commands a splendid view over the neighbouring country. Early in the present century a quantity of charcoal was discovered near its summit hidden beneath a stratum of fine loam. The country people around expressed no surprise at the discovery, as they were familiar with the tradition that the spot had been used for the kindling of Beltane fires. In Peeblesshire, too, the Beltane festival long held its ground. In the fifteenth century the town of Peebles was the scene of joyous May Day gatherings. From far and near, holiday-makers, dressed in their best, came together to join in the Beltane amusements. Who has not heard of the poem, *"Peblis to the Play,"* attributed to King James the First? The play consisted of a round of rural festivities—archery and horse-racing being the chief recreations. Pennant gives a minute account of Beltane rites as practised about 1772. "On the first of May the herdsmen of every village hold their Bel-tein, a rural sacrifice. They cut a square trench on the ground, leaving the turf in the middle; on that they make a fire of wood, on which they dress a large caudle of eggs, butter, oat-meal, and milk, and bring, besides the ingredients of the caudle, plenty of beer and whisky; for each

of the company must contribute something. The
rites begin with spilling some of the caudle on the
ground by way of libation; on that, every one
takes a cake of oatmeal, upon which are raised
nine square knobs, each dedicated to some particular
being, the supposed preserver of their flocks and
herds, or to some particular animal, the real destroyer
of them; each person then turns his face to the
fire, breaks off a knob, and flinging it over his
shoulders, says, 'This I give to thee, preserve thou
my horses; this to thee, preserve thou my sheep';
and so on. After that they use the same ceremony
to the noxious animals, 'This I give to thee, O
fox! spare thou my lambs; this to thee, O hooded
crow! this to thee, O eagle!' When the ceremony
is over they dine on the caudle; and after the
feast is finished, what is left is hid by two persons
deputed for that purpose; but on the next Sunday
they reassemble and finish the reliques of the first
entertainment."

An examination of the dates when fire-festivals
were held shows that they had a distinct connection
with the sun's annual cycle. When several leading
Church festivals fell to be observed about the same
time of the year, they had often some features in
common. Thus the pagan mid-summer festival
had as its lineal successor, not only St. John's
Day (24th June), but St. Vitus's Day and St.
Peter's Day, respectively the fifteenth and the
twenty-ninth of the same month. The kindling

of fires was a feature of all three. Mediæval fire-festivals were thus the gleanings of rites derived from archaic sun-worship.

The question arises, what connection was there between the custom and the cult? Mr. J. G. Frazer, in his "*Golden Bough*," has collected a variety of facts which go to show that the lighting of these fires was primarily intended to ensure the shining of the sun in the heavens. Mr. Frazer thus sums up the evidence: "The best general explanation of these European fire-festivals seems to be the one given by Mannhardt, namely, that they are sun-charms or magical ceremonies intended to ensure a proper supply of sunshine for men, animals, and plants. Savages resort to charms for making sunshine, and we need not wonder that primitive man in Europe has done the same. Indeed, considering the cold and cloudy climate of Europe during a considerable part of the year, it is natural that sun-charms should have played a much more prominent part among the superstitious practices of European peoples than among those of savages who live nearer the equator. This view of the festivals in question is supported by various considerations drawn partly from the rites themselves, partly from the influence which they are believed to exert upon the weather and on vegetation." After alluding to certain sun-charms, Mr. Frazer continues, "In these the magic force is supposed to take effect through mimicry or sympathy; by imitating the desired result you actually produce it; by counterfeiting the sun's progress through the heavens you really help the luminary to pursue his celestial journey with punctuality and despatch. . . . The influence which these bonfires are supposed to exert on the weather and on vegetation goes to show that they are sun-charms, since the effects ascribed to them are identical with those of sunshine. Thus, in Sweden, the warmth or cold of the coming season is inferred from the direction in which the flames of the bonfire are blown; if they blow to the south it will be warm, if to the north, cold. No doubt at present the direction of the flames is regarded merely as an augury of the weather, not as a mode of influencing it. But we may be pretty sure that this is one of the cases in which magic has dwindled into divination." Hence a good supply of light and heat is not only foretold, but guaranteed.

The view that these fires were reckoned mock-suns is confirmed by the custom, at one time common, of carrying lighted brands round the fields to ensure their fertility. Blazing torches were thus carried in Pennant's time in the middle of June. Martin refers to the carrying of fire in the Hebrides. "There was an antient custom in the Island of Lewis to make a fiery circle about the houses, corn, cattle, &c., belonging to each particular family. An instance of this round was performed in the village Shadir, in Lewis, about sixteen years ago (*i.e.*, *circa* 1680), but it proved fatal to the practiser, called MacCallum; for, after he had carefully performed this round, that very night following he and his family were sadly surprised, and all his houses, corn, cattle, &c., were consumed with fire. This superstitious custom is quite abolished now, for there has not been above this one instance of it in forty years past." Till a later date in Lewis, fire continued to be carried round children before they were baptised, and round mothers before they were churched, to prevent evil spirits from doing harm.

Burghead, in Elginshire, is still the scene of an annual fire-festival, celebrated on the last day of the year (O.S.). It is locally known as *the burning of the clavie.* On the afternoon of the day in question, careful preparations are made for the ceremony. A tar barrel is sawn across, and of it the clavie is made. A pole of firwood is stuck through the barrel, and held in its place by a large nail driven in by a stone, no hammer being used. The clavie is then filled with tar and pieces of wood. After dark these combustibles are kindled, according to ancient practice, by a burning peat from a neighbouring cottage. The clavie is then lifted by one of the men and carried through the village amid the applause of the inhabitants. Notwithstanding the risk from the burning tar, the possession of the clavie, while on its pilgrimage, is eagerly coveted. In former times, a stumble on the

U

part of the bearer was counted unlucky for himself
personally, and for the village as a whole.   After
being borne about for some time, the still blazing
clavie is placed on an adjacent mound called the
Doorie, where a stone column was built some years
ago for its accommodation.   A hole in the top of
the column receives the pole.   There the clavie is
allowed to burn for about half-an-hour, when it is
thrown down the slope of the mound.   The burning fragments are eagerly snatched up and carried
away by the spectators.   These fragments were
formerly kept as charms to ensure good fortune to
their possessors.   In the seventeenth and eighteenth
centuries the Church discountenanced the burning
of the clavie as idolatrous and sinful, and certain
penalties were threatened against all who took part
in it.   The antiquity of the custom may be inferred
from the fact, that two hundred years ago it was
called old.   At that time lights were carried round
the boats in the harbour, and certain other ceremonies were performed, all pointing to a pagan
origin.   Formerly the custom was in vogue, not
only at Burghead, but at most of the fishing villages
along the Morayshire coast.   The object in every
case was the same, viz., the blessing of the boats
to ensure a good fishing season.

A singular survival of sun-worship is to be found
in the use of a fiery circle as a curative agent.   In the
volume of the "*Proceedings of the Society of Antiquaries of Scotland*" for 1889-90, the Rev. Dr. Stewart

of Nether Lochaber recounts a recent instance of its use in the Highlands. A dwining child, a year and a half old, was pronounced by a "wise woman" of the district to be suffering from the effects of an "evil eye." The rite, called in Gaelic, *Beannachd-na-Cuairte*, *i.e.*, "Blessing of the Circle," was accordingly resorted to. A straw rope was wound round the greater part of an iron hoop, and, oil being applied, the whole was set on fire. The hoop was then held vertically, and through the blazing circle the child was passed and repassed eighteen times to correspond to the months of its life. The blazing hoop was then extinguished in a neighbouring burn. The result was in every way to the satisfaction of the child's relatives. In the same article Dr. Stewart gives an account, sent to him by a friend, of a similar superstition common in Wigtownshire till about half-a-century ago. In this case, the healing influence came through the channel of the iron tire of a new cart wheel. After fire had been applied to it to make it fit the wheel, the tire was passed over the head of the patient, who was thus placed in the middle of a glowing circle.

So much for the traces of sun-worship in rites connected with fire. There are traces of it also in certain folk-customs, at one time common, and not yet extinct. Highlanders were formerly in the habit of taking off their bonnets to the rising sun. Akin to this is the feeling underlying the Venetian expedition to the Lido, annually repeated in July, when thousands cross to

that island at dawn, and utter a loud shout when the
sun rises above the horizon.   In cases where sun-
worship is a national cult we naturally expect it to
have a marked influence on the sacred customs and
architecture of its votaries.   One example will suffice.
In his "*Pre-historic Man*," Sir Daniel Wilson thus
describes the great annual festival of the Peruvians,
held at the summer solstice:—"For three days previous, a general fast prevailed; the fire on the great
altar of the sun went out, and in all the dwellings of
the land no hearth was kindled.   As the dawn of the
fourth day approached, the Inca, surrounded by his
nobles, who came from all parts of the country to
join in the solemn celebration, assembled in the great
square of the capital to greet the rising sun.   The
temple of the national deity presented its eastern
portal to the earliest rays, emblazoned with his golden
image, thickly set with precious stones, and as the
first beams of the morning were reflected back from
this magnificent emblem of the god of day, songs
of triumph mingled with the jubilant shout of his
worshippers.   Then, after various rites of adoration,
preparations were made for rekindling the sacred fire.
The rays of the sun, collected into a focus by a con-
cave mirror of polished metal, were made to inflame
a heap of dried cotton; and a llama was sacrificed as
a burnt offering to the sun."   Even after sun-worship
has ceased to be a national cult, we find it continuing
to regulate the position of buildings, devoted to a
totally different worship.   In this way what is com-

monly styled the "orientation" of Christian churches
can be accounted for. Indeed, so much had the sun
to do with churches, that when one was built in
honour of a particular saint, it was made to face the
point of the horizon, where the sun rose on the
festival of the saint in question.

In our own land much stress used to be laid
on the necessity. of turning according to the
course of the sun, *i.e.*, from left to right. To do
so tended to bring prosperity to whatever was
being undertaken at the time. Martin often refers
to such a turn under the title of *Dessil*, a word
of Gaelic origin, in connection with which, it is
interesting to note that in Gaelic *Deas* signifies
both south and to the right. Martin mentions
certain stones, round which the inhabitants of the
Western Isles made what he calls "a religious
turn." In the island of Eigg, he tells us:—"There
is a heap of stones called *Martin Dessil*, *i.e.*, a
place consecrated to the saint of that name, about
which the natives oblige themselves to make a tour
round sunways." It was also customary when anyone wished well to another to walk round him
thrice sunways. The following are some of Martin's own experiences in the matter of the Dessil:—
"Some are very careful, when they set out to sea,
that the boat be first rowed about sunways; and
if this be neglected they are afraid their voyage
may prove unfortunate. I had this ceremony paid
me (when in the island of Ila) by a poor woman

after I had given her an alms. I desired her to
let alone that compliment, for I did not care for
it; but she insisted to make these three ordinary
turns, and pray'd that God and MacCharmaig, the
patron saint of that island, might bless and prosper
me in all my designs and affairs. I attempted
twice to go from Ila to Collonsay, and at both
times they row'd about the boat sunways, tho' I
forbid them to do it; and by a contrary wind
the boat and those in it were forced back. I
took boat again a third time from Jura to Collonsay, and at the same time forbid them to row
about their boat, which they obey'd, and then we
landed safely at Collonsay without any ill adven-
ture, which some of the crew did not believe
possible for want of the round." This superstition
lingered long after Martin's time, and probably still
directs the course of many a fishing-boat when
being put to sea. In connection with events of
moment—such as baptisms, bridals, and burials—
the necessity for turning sunways was felt to be
specially binding; but even in matters of no particular importance the rule was held to apply. If
movement sunways was lucky, movement in a contrary direction was the reverse. Such a movement
was, and still is, known as *Widdershins* or *Wither-
shins*, the Shetland form being *Witherwise*. To
go Widdershins was to go against the sun, and
was hence regarded as a violation of the established
order of things. In his "*Darker Superstitions*"

Dalyell remarks:—"The moving widderschynnes, as if withdrawing from the deified orb of day, inferred a guilty retreat, and was associated with the premeditated evil of sorcery."

We have thus glanced at the relations of springs to fairs, of fairs to Church festivals, of Church festivals to nature festivals, and of these to sun-worship. We shall now gather together the threads of the argument, and indicate some of the chief points of connection between well-worship and sun-worship. To do this, we must inquire when springs were mainly visited. When a well was under the patronage of a saint, the festival day of that saint was in some cases the day selected. It would be natural to regard this as the rule. But, as a matter of fact, pilgrimages were commonly made on days other than the festival of the patron saint. As may be remembered, the Holy Pool in Strathfillan was mainly resorted to on the first day of the quarter (O.S.); and St. Fillan's Spring at Comrie on 1st May and 1st August. As may be also remembered, the waters of Loch Manaar, in Sutherland, were thought to possess special virtue on the first Monday of February, May, August, and November (O.S.), the second and third of these dates being specially popular. What the practice was at Mochrum Loch, in Wigtownshire, is clear from Symson's account in his "*Description of Galloway*." "This loch," he says, "is very famous in many writers, who report that it never freezeth in the greatest

frosts. . . . Whether it had any virtue of old
I know not, but sure I am it hath it not now.
However, I deny not but the water thereof may
be medicinal, having received several credible in-
formations that several persons, both old and young,
have been cured of continued diseases by washing
therein.   Yet still I cannot approve of their washing three times therein, which they say they must
do, neither the frequenting there of the first Sunday
of February, May, August, and November, although
many foolish people affirm that, not only the water
of this loch, but also many other springs and wells,
have more virtue on those days than any other."
Close to the Welltrees meadow in Sanquhar parish,
once flowed a spring dedicated to St. Bridget.   In
his history of the parish, Mr. James Brown tells
us that, according to the testimony of the old
people, it was customary for the maidens of Sanquhar to resort on May Day to St. Bride's Well,
where each presented nine smooth white stones as
an offering to the saint.   Till about the beginning
of the present century, a well at Sigget, in Aberdeenshire, was regularly visited on Pasch Sunday,
and the usual offerings were left by the pilgrims.
There is, or was a belief at Chapel-en-le-Frith,
in Derbyshire, that on Easter Eve a mermaid
appears in a certain pool; and at Rostherne, in
Cheshire, that another mermaid comes out of the
lake there on Easter Day and rings a bell.   Mr.
Moore mentions that in the Isle of Man Ascension

Day and the first Sunday of August were the
principal days for visiting consecrated springs. As
previously stated, part of the May Day rites at
Tullie-Beltane, in Perthshire, consisted in drinking
water from a spring, and in walking nine times
round it. St. Anthony's Well, near Edinburgh, is
not yet forgotten on May Day by people who like
to keep up old customs. There is no doubt that
of all the months of the year May was the one,
when Scottish springs were most visited. The
same rule held elsewhere. In his "*Romances of
the West of England*," Mr. Hunt has the following:—
"The practice of bathing rickety children on the
first three Wednesdays in May is still far from
uncommon in the outlying districts of Cornwall.
The parents will walk many miles for the purpose
of dipping the little sufferers in some well from
which the healing virtue has not entirely departed.
Among these holy wells, Cubert is far famed. To
this well the peasantry still resort, firm in the faith
that there, at this special season, some mysterious
virtue is communicated to its waters. On these
occasions, only a few years since, the crowd assembled
was so large that it assumed the character of a
fair." A spring at Glastonbury, in Somerset, on
account of a miraculous cure, believed to have been
wrought by its water, became specially popular
about the middle of last century. In 1751, as
many as ten thousand persons are said to have
visited it during the month of May.

The popularity of May did not depend on the
better weather following the bleakness of winter
and spring. At least, if it did so, it was only in a
subordinate degree. To find the main reason, we
have to look to the continued influence of ancient
pagan rites. As we have seen, May in Scotland
was ushered in by the Beltane Festival. We have
also seen that its manifestly heathen customs survived
till a late period in the midst of a Christian
civilisation. On the hypothesis of a pagan origin
alone, can certain May Day customs and beliefs be
satisfactorily explained. Some Beltane rites still
survive in the Highlands, though fires are no longer
kindled. In the neighbourhood of Kingussie,
Inverness-shire, bannocks and hard-boiled eggs
continue to be rolled down the hills on the first
of May (O.S.). Till quite lately, these bannocks
were used for purposes of divination. They were
marked on one side with a cross—the sign of life;
and on the other with a circle—the sign of death.
Each bannock was rolled down thrice, and its
owner's fate was decided by the sign that was on
the upper surface oftenest when the bannock rested
at the foot of the hill. The time was counted
specially suited for love-charms. On May Day, in
the north of England, a gold ring was dropped
into a syllabub composed of various ingredients.
Whoever got hold of the ring with a ladle would
be the first among the company to be married.
The prophetic powers of May Day are still believed

in, in some parts of the north of Ireland. If a maiden places a certain plant below her pillow overnight, she will have a vision of her coming husband.

On May Day, the supernatural world was revealed, and witches and other uncanny creatures were abroad. In connection with his visit to Scotland, Pennant says:—"In some parts of the country is a rural sacrifice, different from that before mentioned. A cross is cut on some sticks, which is dipped in pottage, and the Thursday before Easter one of each placed over the sheep-cot, the stable, or the cow-house. On the first of May they are carried to the hill, where the rites are celebrated, all decked with wild flowers, and after the feast is over, replaced over the spots they were taken from." The cross in this case, was, doubtless, made from the wood of the rowan or mountain ash. In the Isle of Man, it was customary, at one time, to gather primroses on May Eve, and strew them before the door of every house to keep away witches. Aubrey tells us:—"'Tis commonly said in Germany that the witches do meet in the night before the first day of May upon an high mountain called the Blocksberg, where they, together with the devils, do dance and feast, and the common people do, the night before the said day, fetch a certain thorn and stick it at their house door, believing the witches can then do them no harm." In our own country, too, hawthorn branches were formerly used on May Day as a

charm against witches. The hawthorn had likewise another mystic property attributed to it. The
dew on its branches on the first of May had the
power of giving beauty to the maiden who washed
her face with it. May-dew from the grass was
equally efficacious, except when gathered from within
a fairy ring, as the fairies would in that case
counteract the influence of the charm. A curative
power was also ascribed to May-dew. Till quite
lately there was a belief in some parts of England
that a weakly child would be made strong by being
drawn over dewy grass on the morning in question.
To effect a complete cure, the treatment had to be
repeated on the two following mornings. Dew from
the grave of the last person buried in the parish
churchyard was counted specially remedial if applied
to the affected part before sunrise on May-morning.

The May-sun also got the credit of working
cures. In his "*Nether Lochaber*" the Rev. Dr.
Stewart tells us that "it was an article of belief
in the hygiene code of the old highlanders that
the invalid suffering under any form of internal
ailment, upon whom the sun of May once fairly
shed its light, was pretty sure of a renewed lease of
life until at least the next autumnal equinox." The
old English custom, known as "going a-Maying,"
when old and young flocked into the woods early
on May-morning to gather flowers and green boughs,
was handed on from a time when the worship of
trees was an article of religious faith.

Another old custom in England, viz., the blowing of horns at an early hour on the first of May, had probably its origin in pre-Christian times. It still survives in Oxfordshire and Cornwall. From Hone's "*Every-Day Book*" we learn that till the third decade of the present century, and doubtless later, the poorer classes in Edinburgh poured forth at daybreak from street and lane to assemble on Arthur's Seat to see the sun rise on May-morning. Bagpipes and other musical instruments enlivened the scene, nor were refreshments forgotten. About six o'clock a crowd of citizens of the wealthier class made their appearance, while the majority of the first-comers returned to the town. At nine o'clock the hill was practically deserted. Two centuries earlier an attempt was made by the kirk-session of Perth to put a stop to an annual gathering on May Day at a cave in the face of Kinnoul hill adjoining the town. This cave was called the Dragon Hole, and was the scene of ancient rites of a superstitious nature. Other illustrations might be selected from the Folklore of May Day, but those given above show that the season was held in much superstitious regard. Accordingly, we need not be surprised that well-worship took its place among the rites of May Day, and of May Month also, since the whole of May was deemed a charmed time.

The Sundays of May—particularly the first—were very frequently chosen for visits to conse-

crated springs. The Chapel Wells in Kirkmaiden
parish have already been referred to in connection
with Co' Sunday. The White Loch of Merton, and
St. Anthony's Spring at Maybole, and others that
might be named were principally resorted to on the
first Sunday of May. Indeed, wells occasionally got
their name from the fact of their being visited on
Sundays. Thus Tobordmony, near Cushendall, in
County Antrim, signifies in Irish the Sunday Well.
There is a farm in Athole called Pit-alt-donich or
Balandonich. The name is derived by Mr. J.
Mackintosh Gow from the Gaelic Pit-alt-didon-ich,
and is interpreted by him as meaning "the hamlet
of the Sunday burn." There is a spring on the farm,
formerly much frequented on the first Sunday of
May (O.S.). In the Isle of Man is a spring called
Chibber Lansh, consisting of three pools. In former
times it had a considerable reputation for the cure
of sore eyes; but it was thought to exert its
power on Sundays alone. Pilgrims frequently spent
Saturday night beside springs in order to begin
the required ritual on the following morning. The
question why Sunday was specially selected is one
of interest. Its choice may have been due in part
to the fact, mentioned by Dalyell, that, in ruder
society, the precise course of time requires some
specific mark, and in part, to the notion underlying
the popular saying, "the better the day, the better
the deed." But there was undoubtedly another
factor in the selection of the day. We have seen

that the chief Church festivals borrowed certain
rites from other festivals earlier in the field.   In
like manner, Sunday was the heir of usages quite
unconnected with it in origin; or, to change the
metaphor, it was a magnet attracting to itself various stray particles of paganism that remained after
the break up of the old Nature-worship.   Students
of English history in the seventeenth century cannot fail to remember, how strenuously the Puritans
sought to put down Sunday amusements, and how
even the edicts of James the First and Charles the
First permitted only certain games to be played on
Sunday, certain others being declared inconsistent
with the aim of that Christian festival.

Bourne, in his " *Popular Antiquities*," published in
1725, remarks :—" In the southern parts of this nation
the most of country villages are wont to observe
some Sunday in a more particular manner than
the other common Sundays of the year, viz., the
Sunday after the Day of Dedication, *i.e.*, the Sunday
after the Day of the Saint to whom their church
was dedicated.   Then the inhabitants deck themselves in their gaudiest clothes, and have open
doors and splendid entertainments for the reception
and treating of their relations and friends who visit
them on that occasion from each neighbouring town.
The morning is spent for the most part at church,
the remaining part of the day in eating and drinking,
and so is also a day or two afterwards, together
with all sorts of rural pastimes and exercises, such

as dancing on the green, wrestling, cudgelling, &c.
Agreeable to this, we are told that formerly, on
the Sunday after the Encœnia, or Feast of the
Dedication of the Church, it was usual for a great
number of the inhabitants of the village, both grown
and young, to meet together at break of day, and
to cry, 'Holy Wakes, Holy Wakes,' and after Matens
go to feasting and sporting, which they continued
for two or three days."

Quoting from the "*Presbyterie Buik of Aberdein,*
19th June, 1607, in M.S." Dalyell observes:—"In
the North of Scotland, young men conducted themselves 'pro phanelie on the Sabboathes in drinking,
playing at futteball, dancing, and passing fra
paroche to paroche—and sum passes tò St. Phitallis
Well to the offence of God and ewill of mony.'"
In connection with this, a remark from Dr. J. A.
Hessey's Bampton Lecture on Sunday may be
quoted.   When comparing it with the Holy days
instituted in mediæval times, he says, the former
perhaps "was even worse observed than the other
days, for in spite of the Church, men had a vague
impression that it was one of specially allowed
intermission of ordinary employments.   This they
interpreted to mean of more special permission
of dissipation than the other days noted in the
kalendar."   After describing the island of Valay,
near North Uist, where there were Chapels to St.
Ulton and St. Mary, Martin says, "Below the
Chapel there is a flat thin stone call'd Brownie's

Stone upon which the antient inhabitants offer'd
a cow's milk every Sunday." That this offering of
milk, though made on Sundays, was a pagan and
not a Christian rite, can hardly be disputed. At
some places, *e.g.*, at Glasgow, Crail, and Seton,
Sunday was at one time the weekly market day, but
by an Act of James the Sixth, in 1579, the holding
of markets on Sunday was prohibited throughout
the realm. The Sundays in May were certainly the
most popular for visits to springs, but these occurring
about the time of the other leading nature-festivals
were also in fashion. Sun-worship, as we have
seen, was the back-ground of all such festivals.
We need not wonder, therefore, that consecrated
springs were frequented on a day whose very name
suggested a reminiscence of a solar pagan cult.

We have discussed Beltane, let us now look at one
other leading nature-festival, viz., Lammas, on the
first day of August, to discover what light it throws
on our subject. The Church dedicated the opening
day of August to St. Peter ad Vincula. A curious
mediæval legend arose to connect this dedication with
another name for the festival, viz., the *Gule of August*.
At the heart of this legend was the Latin word *Gula*,
signifying the throat. The daughter of Quirinus, a
Roman tribune, had some disease of the throat which
was miraculously cured through kissing St. Peter's
chains, and so the day of the chains was designated
the *Gule of August*. As a matter of fact, the word is
derived from the Cymric Gwyl, a feast or holiday,

X

and we have confirmation of the etymology in the circumstance, that in Celtic lands the time was devoted to games, and other recreations. In Ireland a celebrated fair, called Lugnasadh, was held at Tailtin (now Teltown), in Meath, for several days before and after the first of August, and there was another at Cruachan, now Rath Croghan, in Roscommon. A third was held at Carman, now Wexford. Its celebration was deemed so important that, as Professor Rhys tells us, in his "*Celtic Heathendom*," "among the blessings promised to the men of Leinster from holding it were, plenty of corn, fruit, and milk, abundance of fish in their lakes and rivers, domestic prosperity, and immunity from the yoke of any other province. On the other hand, the evils to follow from the neglect of this institution were to be failure and early greyness on them and their kings." In legendary accounts of Carman, the place has certain funereal associations. "If we go into the story of the fair of Carman," Professor Rhys observes, "we are left in no doubt as to the character of the mythic beings whose power had been brought to an end at the time dedicated to that fair; they may be said to have represented the blighting chills and fogs that assert their baneful influence on the farmer's crops. To overcome these and other hurtful forces of the same kind, the prolonged presence of the sun-god was essential, in order to bring the corn to maturity."

That the Gule of August was a Nature-festival may

be further inferred from the fact that among many Anglo-Saxon peoples it was called *Hláf-mœsse,* *i.e.,* Loaf-mass, eventually shortened into Lammas. Our English ancestors offered on that day bread made from the early grain, as the first-fruits of the harvest. In Scotland, the Lammas rites were handed down from an unknown past and survived till the middle of last century. They were closely connected with country life, and were taken part in, mainly by those who had to do with the tending of cattle. The herds of Mid-Lothian held Lammas in special favour. For some weeks prior to that date they busied themselves in building what were called Lammas towers, composed of stones and sods. These towers were about seven or eight feet high, sometimes more. On the day of the festival they were surmounted by a flag formed of a table-napkin decked with ribbons. During the building of the towers attempts were sometimes made by rival parties to throw them down, and accordingly they had to be kept constantly watched. On Lenie hill and Clermiston hill two such towers used to be built, about two miles apart, but within sight of each other. These were the respective trysting-places of herds belonging to different portions of Cramond and Corstorphine parishes. On Lammas morning the herds met at their respective towers, and, after a breakfast of bread and cheese, marched to meet each other, blowing horns, and having a piper at their head. Colours were carried aloft by each party, and the demand to lower them was the signal for a contest,

which sometimes ended in rather a curious manner.
Games for small prizes closed the day's proceedings.

At one time temporary structures formed of sods and
sticks, and known as Lammas houses, were built in
South Wales in connection with the festival. Inside
these a fire was kindled for the roasting of apples.
Anyone, by paying a penny, could enter and have
an apple. Professor Rhys speaks of other Lammas
rites in the Principality. "Gwyl Awst," he observes,
"is now a day for fairs in certain parts of Wales, and
it is remembered, in central and southern Cardigan-
shire, as one on which the shepherds used, till comparatively lately, to have a sort of pic-nic on the
hills. One farmer's wife would lend a big kettle for
making in it a plentiful supply of good soup or
broth, while, according to another account, everybody
present had to put his share of fuel on the fire with
his own hands. But, in Brecknockshire, the first of
August seems to have given way sometime before
Catholicism had lost its sway in Wales, to the first
holiday or feast in August; that is to say, the first
Sunday in that month. For then crowds of people,
early in the morning, make their way up the mountains called the Beacons, both from the side of
Caermarthenshire and Glamorgan; their destination
used to be the neighbourhood of the Little Van Lake,
out of whose waters they expected, in the course of
the day, to see the Lady of the Lake make her mo-
mentary appearance." Professor Rhys bears further
witness to the connection of Lammas rites with our

present subject when he says, "A similar shifting from
the first of August to the first Sunday in that month,
has, I imagine, taken place in the Isle of Man. For,
though the solstice used to be, in consequence probably
of Scandinavian influence, the day of institutional
significance in the Manx summer, inquiries I have
made in different parts of the island, go to show that
middle-aged people, now living, remember that, when
they were children, their parents used to ascend the
mountains very early on the first Sunday in August
(O.S.), and that in some districts at least they were
wont to bring home bottles full of water from wells
noted for their healing virtues." Another proof that
the ceremonies of Lammas-tide had some link with
those of archaic Water-worship is to be found in the
circumstance mentioned by Dalyell, that, "in Ireland
the inhabitants held it an inviolable custom to drive
their cattle into some pool or river on the first
Sunday of August as essential to the life of the
animals during the year." This was regularly done
till towards the end of the seventeenth century. It
may be remembered that in Scotland, during the
same century, horses were washed in the sea at
Lammas, doubtless with the same end in view.

We shall now glance at some traces of Sun-worship
in the rites of Well-worship. In countries where the
worship of the sun had an acknowledged place in
the popular religion, the temples to that luminary
were found associated with fountains. In his "*Holy
Land and the Bible*," the Rev. J. Cunningham Geikie

remarks, "The old name of Bethshemish, which
means the house of the sun, is now changed to Ain
Thenis—the fountain of the sun—living water being
found in the valley below. Both point to the Phil-
istine Sun-worship, and both names are fitting, for
every sun-house or temple needed, like all other
ancient sanctuaries, a fountain near it to supply
water for ablutions and libations." When evidence
of this kind fails us, we have another kind within
reach, viz., that derived from the employment of
fire to symbolise the sun on the principle already
explained. At St. Bede's Well, near Jarrow, in
Durham, it used to be customary to kindle a bonfire
on Mid-summer Eve. In connection with the same
festival a bonfire was lighted at Toddel-Well, near
Kirkhampton in Cumberland, and the lads and lasses,
who were present, were in the habit of leaping
through the flames. In a cave at Wemyss, in Fife,
is a well, to which young people at one time carried
blazing torches on the first Monday of January (O.S.).
The time of day when consecrated springs were made
use of has a bearing on the point under review. The
water was thought to have a peculiar efficacy either
just after sunset or just before sunrise. The moment
when the sun was first seen above the horizon was also
reckoned particularly favourable. To the same class of
superstitions belongs the Scandinavian belief, referred
to by Mr. Lloyd in his "*Peasant Life in Sweden,*" that
the water of certain sacred springs, known as Fonts
of the Cross, was turned into wine at sunrise.

The survival of rites of archaic Sun-worship in the practice of making a turn sun-ways has been already referred to.

In conclusion, we shall glance at the bearings of the practice on the question of Well-worship. To make a visit to a spring effectual, when a cure was wanted, the invalid had to pace round it from left to right, in recognition of the fact that the sun moved in the same direction. The sun, being the source of vitality, why should not an imitation of its daily motion tend to produce the same result? When speaking of Loch Siant Well, in Skye, Martin says:—" Several of the common people oblige themselves by a vow to come to this well, and make the ordinary tour about it call'd Dessil. They move thrice round the well, proceeding sunways from east to west, and so on. This is done after drinking of the water. Sometimes it was done elsewhere before drinking of the water." The importance of this motion comes clearly into view in the case of St. Andrew's Well, at Shadar, in Lewis, referred to in a previous chapter. When the wooden dish, floating on the surface of the water, turned round sun-ways, the omen was a sign that the patient concerned would recover, but a turning in the opposite direction foreboded ill." In reference to Chapel Uny Well, in Cornwall, Mr. Hunt says:—" On the first three Wednesdays in May, children suffering from mesenteric diseases are dipped three times in this well, against the sun, and dragged three times around the well on the grass in the same direction."

Mr. Lloyd tells us that, in Sweden, a remedy for whooping-cough is to drink water, "that drops from a mill-wheel, which revolves *ansols*, that is, in a contrary direction to the course of the sun." These two examples, however, are exceptions to the rule. They may, perhaps, be explained on the principle that what is in itself evil, because contrary to nature, brings good when converted into a charm. To walk round a well *widdershins* was to commit an act of sorcery. Mr. J. G. Barbour, in his "*Unique Traditions of the West and South of Scotland,*" recounts the trial and fate of a lonely old woman, who lived in the Kirkcudbrightshire parish of Iron-gray, early in the seventeenth century. She was accused of witchcraft, and, when convicted of the crime, met her death by being rolled down hill inside a blazing tar barrel. Various were the charges brought against her, one of them being that, at certain hours she walked round the spring near her cottage wuddershins. Mr. Barbour adds, "The well, from which she drew the water for her domestic use, and where the young rustic belles washed their faces, still retains the name of the Witch's Well." Faith in the benefit of turning sun-ways and faith in the efficacy of south-running water belong to the same class of superstitions. Both have a direct reference to the sun's course. The water of a stream flowing to meet the sun, when its mid-day beams are casting their sweet influences upon the earth, must absorb and retain a power to bless and heal. So, at least,

men thought, nor were they slow to take advantage
of the virtue that mingled with the water. Bodily
ailments were cured by washing in it, and it was
used as one of the many remedies to remove the evil
effects of witchcraft. In this, as in the other rites
previously alluded to, we see the influence of a cult
that did not pass away, when the sun ceased to be
worshipped as a divinity. In other words, Well-
worship cannot be adequately understood if we leave
out of account archaic Sun-worship, and its modern
survivals.

CHAPTER XVIII.

WISHING-WELLS.

To bring about the accomplishment of a cherished
desire by means of certain rites has been a favourite
mode of divination. By this method it was thought
that destiny could be coerced, and the wish made
the father of its own fulfilment. The means were
various; but, underlying them all, was the notion that
the doing of something, in the present, guaranteed
the happening of something in the future. A mere
wish was not sufficient. A particular spot, hallowed
by old associations, had to be visited, and a time-
honoured ceremony observed. But the ritual might
be of the simplest. It was perchance to some rustic
gate that the village maiden stole in the gathering
gloaming, and there, with beating heart, breathed
the wish that was to bring a new happiness into
her life. Love charms, indeed, form an important

group of wishing superstitions. To this class belong
Hallow E'en rites, such as eating an apple before a
mirror, and sowing hemp seed. These rites gave
the maiden a vision of her destined husband. In
the one case, she saw his face in the glass, and in
the other, she saw him in the attitude of pulling
hemp. The dumb-cake divination, on the Eves of
St. Mark and St. John, also belongs to the same
class of charms. Not more than three must take
part in the mystical ceremony. Concerning the
cake, an English rule says:—

> " Two make it,
> Two bake it,
> Two break it,

and the third must put it under each of their
pillows, but not a word must be spoken all the
time." Fasting on St. Agnes's Eve was requisite
on the part of any maiden, who sought on that
festival to have a vision of her bridegroom to be.
According to an old Galloway custom, a maiden
pulled a handful of grass when she first saw the new
moon. While she pulled she repeated the rhyme—

> " New moon, new moon, tell me if you can,
> Gif I have a hair like the hair o' my gudeman."

The grass was then taken into the house, and
carefully examined. If a hair was found amongst
the grass, it would correspond in colour with the
hair of the coming husband. In connection with
all such charms, it is certainly true what an old
song says that " love hath eyes."

Her Majesty the Queen visited Innis · Maree in September, 1877. When describing her visit, Mr. Dixon, in his "*Gairloch*," says:—"She fixed her offering in the wishing tree, a pleasantry which most visitors to the island repeat, it being common report that a wish silently formed, when any metal article is attached to the tree, will certainly be realised. It is said that if anyone removes any offering that has been fixed on the tree, some misfortune, probably the taking fire of the house of the desecrator, is sure to follow." On a hill near Abbotsbury, in Dorset, stands St. Catherine's Chapel. In its south doorway are wishing holes. The knee is placed in one of the holes, and the hands in the two above; and in this posture the visitor performs the wishing ceremony. Half-way down the cliff near Stackpole Head, in Pembrokeshire, is an ancient structure of rude masonry styled St. Govan's Chapel, at one time the retreat of some recluse. Professor Cosmo Innes, in the third volume of the "*Proceedings of the Society of Antiquaries of Scotland*," gives an account of a visit to the spot, and adds:—"The curious part of St. Govan's abode is his bed, or rather his coffin, for it is a vertical interstice between two immense slabs of rock, into which a body of common size can be forced with some difficulty, the prisoner remaining upright. The rock is polished by the number of visitors fitting themselves into the saint's bed of penance, and the natives make you feel in the inner surface the indentures caused by

the ribs of the saint!" The polishing is mainly
due to the fact that the space has for long been
used for wishing purposes. Those who desire to
test the efficacy of the spell must turn themselves
round within the hollow and think of nothing else
during the process, except what they are wishing for—
a rather difficult test under the circumstances! Close
to the chapel is St. Govan's Well, under a covering
of stone-work. The spring had formerly a great
reputation as a health resort. Beside the remains
of the once splendid monastic buildings at Walsingham, in Norfolk, are wishing wells consisting of two
small circular basins of stone. In pre-Reformation
times they were much resorted to for the cure of
disease. Being close to St. Mary's Chapel, they
were appropriately dedicated to the Virgin, to whom
the gift of healing was ascribed. Since then they
have been popular as wishing wells. The necessary
ritual is thus described by Brand in his "*Popular
Antiquities*":—"The votary, with a due qualification
of faith and pious awe, must apply the right knee,
bare, to a stone placed for that purpose between the
wells. He must then plunge to the wrist each hand,
bare also, into the water of the wells which are near
enough to admit of this immersion. A wish must
then be formed, but not uttered with the lips, either
at the time or afterwards, even in confidential com-
munication to the dearest friend. The hands are
then to be withdrawn, and as much of the water as
can be contained in the hollow of each is to be

swallowed.   Formerly the object of desire was most
probably expressed in a prayer to the Virgin.   It is
now only a silent wish, which will certainly be accomplished within twelve months, if the efficacy of the
solemn rite be not frustrated by the incredulity or
some other fault of the votary."

Pennant tells of a cistern connected with St. John's
Well, near Moxley Nunnery, at one time much used
for bathing.   Near these, and below the surface of
the water, was a piece of rock called the Wishing
Stone.   Anyone who kissed this stone with firm
belief in the efficacy of the charm would have his
desire granted.   In this case the power of securing
the fulfilment of wishes went hand in hand with the
power of curing diseases.   Generally speaking, however, as in the case of Walsingham just mentioned,
the former power supersedes the latter.   In other
words, *healing* wells are transformed into *wishing*
wells.   When such is the case, they are, as far as
folklore in concerned, in the last stage of their history.
In the wood, clothing the steep hill of Weem, in Perthshire, is St. David's Well, said to be named after a
former laird who turned hermit.   The spring has
a considerable local fame, and many have been the
wishes silently breathed over its water.   Part of an
ancient stone cross lies at its margin, and on it the
visitor kneels while framing his or her wish.   Visitors
to wishing wells commonly drop into the water a
coin, pin, or pebble, thus keeping up, usually without
being aware of the fact, the custom of offering a gift to

the *genius loci*. The Rev. Dr. Gregor thus describes what was dropped into the Bride's Well, in the neighbourhood of Corgarff, Aberdeenshire:—"This well was at one time the favourite resort of all brides for miles around. On the evening before the marriage, the bride, accompanied by her maidens, went 'atween the sun an' the sky' to it. The maidens bathed her feet and the upper part of her body with water drawn from it. This bathing ensured a family. The bride put into the well a few crumbs of bread and cheese, to keep her children from ever being in want."

Desires of any kind may be cherished at wishing-wells, but there is no doubt that matters matrimonial usually give direction to the thoughts. According to a Yorkshire belief, whoever drops five white pebbles into the Ouse, near the county town, when the minster clock strikes one on May morning, will see on the surface of the water whatever he or she wishes. Near Dale Abbey, in Derbyshire, is a certain holy well. To get full advantage of its help, one has to go between the hours of twelve and three on Good Friday, drink the water thrice, and wish. There is no doubt about the meaning of the following lines from the Bard of Dimbovitza, a collection of Roumanian Folk-Songs:—

> "There, where on Sundays I go alone,
> To the old, old well with the milk-white stone,
> Where by the fence, in a nook forgot,
> Rises a Spring in the daisied grass,
> That makes whoso drinks of it love—alas!
> My heart's best belovèd, he drinks it not."

In Sir Walter Scott's "*Pirate*" one of the characters
expresses the wish that providence would soon send
a wreck to gladden the hearts of the Shetlanders.
At the other extremity of Britain, viz., in the Scilly
Isles, the same hope was at one time cherished. St.
Warna, who had to do with wrecks, was the patron
saint of St. Agnes, one of the islands of the group.
She had her holy well, and there the natives
anciently dropped in a crooked pin and invoked
the saint to send them a rich wreck.

It would be useless to attempt to give a list of
Scottish wishing-wells; but the following may be
mentioned.   There is one in West Kilbride parish,
Ayrshire, close to a cave at Hunterston.   There is
another at Ardmore, in Dumbartonshire.   At Rait,
in Perthshire, is St. Peter's Wishing-well.   In the
united parishes of Kilcalmonell and Kilberry, in
Argyllshire, is the ancient ecclesiastical site of
Kilanaish.   "Near the burial-ground," Captain White
tells us, "is its holy well, where it is proper to
wish the usual three wishes, which, on my last
visit to the place, our party, including one lady,
devoutly did."   The same writer gives the following particulars about another Argyllshire spring:—
"Near the Abbey of Saddell, Kintyre, is a fine
spring of the class known throughout Scotland as
Wishing-wells, which has always borne the name
of Holy-well.   It had the usual virtues and wishing
powers ascribed to it.   A pretty little pillar with
cross cut upon it which has been mistaken for one

of ancient date is scooped out into a small basin to
catch the drip of the water. It was erected by a
Bishop Brown, when residing at Saddell, in the
beginning of the present century, to replace another
one that had formerly stood there. Beside it, flows
a stream called Alt-nam-Manach (the Monk's Burn),
and this, with the spring, no doubt formed the
water supply of the monastery."

St. Anthony's Well, beside St. Anthony's ruined
Chapel, near Edinburgh, is probably the best known
of Scottish wishing-wells. Its sanative virtues have
already been alluded to, but it is nowadays more
noted for its power of securing the fulfilment of
wishes than the recovery of health. A pleasant
picture of the romantic spot is given by Sir Daniel
Wilson in his " *Memorials of Edinburgh in the
Olden Time*":—" The ancient Hermitage and Chapel
of St. Anthony, underneath the overhanging crags
of Arthur's Seat, are believed to have formed a
dependency of the preceptory at Leith, and to
have been placed there, to catch the seaman's eye
as he entered the Firth, or departed on some long
and perilous voyage; when his vows and offerings
would be most freely made to the patron saint, and
the hermit who ministered at his altar. No record,
however, now remains to add to the tradition of its
dedication to St. Anthony; but the silver stream,
celebrated in the plaintive old song, 'O waly, waly
up yon bank,' still wells clearly forth at the foot
of the rock, filling the little basin of St. Anthony's

Y

Well, and rippling pleasantly through the long
grass into the lower valley." The song in question
gives expression to the grief of Lady Barbara
Erskine, wife of James, Marquis of Douglas, in
the time of Charles II., in connection with her
desertion by her husband—

1. "O waly, waly up the bank
    And waly, waly down the brae,
   And waly, waly yon burnside,
    Where I and my love wont to gae !
   I lean'd my back unto an aik,
    I thoucht it was a trusty tree ;
   But first it bow'd, and syne it brak :
    Sae my true love did lichtly me.

2. O waly, waly, but love be bonnie,
    A little time while it is new ;
   But when it's auld, it waxes cauld,
    And fades away like morning dew.
   O wherefore should I busk my heid,
    Or wherefore should I kame my hair ?
   For my true love has me forsook,
    And says he'll never love me mair.

3. Now Arthur's Seat shall be my bed,
    The sheets shall ne'er be pressed by me.
   St. Anton's Well shall be my drink
    Since my true love has forsaken me.
   Martinmas wind, when wilt thou blaw,
    And shake the green leaves aff the tree ?
   O gentle death ! when wilt thou come ?
    For of my life I am wearie !

4. 'Tis not the frost that freezes fell
    Nor blawing snaw's inclemencie ;
   'Tis not sic cauld that makes me cry,
    But my love's heart's grown cauld to me.

When we came in by Glasgow toun
We were a comely sicht to see ;
My love was clad in the black velvet,
And I mysel in cramasie.

5. But had I wist, before I kissed,
That love had been sae ill to win,
I'd lock'd my heart in a case of gold,
And pinn'd it wi' a siller pin.
Oh ! oh ! if my young babe were born,
And set upon the nurse's knee.
And I mysel were dead and gane,
And the green grass growing over me !"

Fortunately, the associations of St. Anthony's Well have not all been so sad. as the above. Many a hopeful moment has been passed beside its margin. A little girl from Aberdeenshire, when on a visit to friends in Edinburgh, made trial of the sacred spring. She was cautioned not to tell anyone what her wish was, else the charm would have no effect. On her return home, however, her eagerness to know whether the wish had, in the meantime, been fulfilled, quite overcame her ability to keep the secret. Her first words were, " Has the pony come ? " St. Anthony must have been in good humour with the child, for he provided the pony, thus evidently condoning the breach of silence in deference to her youth. Surely there must be something in wishing-wells, after all, besides water.

CHAPTER XIX.

MEANING OF MARVELS.

MR. J. M. BARRIE is a true interpreter of the youthful mind when he says, in the "*Little Minister,*" "Children like to peer into wells to see what the world is like at the other side." Grown-up people are also alive to the mystery of a spring. "Look into its depth," observes Mr. E. H. Barker in his "*Wayfaring in France,*" "until the eye, getting reconciled to the darkness, catches the gleam of the still water far below the ferns that hang from the gaping places in the mossy wall, and you will find yourself spellbound by the great enchantress, Nature, while understanding nothing of the mysterious influence." In days of less enlightenment "the weight of all this unintelligible world" was even more felt than now, and the minds of men were ever on the outlook for the marvellous. What is to us a source of not unpleasing mystery was then a cause of dread. We marvel and make poetry. Our far-off ancestors trembled and sought refuge in magical rites. We still speak of the charms of nature, but the phrase has to us an altered meaning. When we remember how little science there was at one time, we need not be surprised that the phenomena of the outer world were misinterpreted, and hence gave rise to fallacies. This was markedly so in the case of springs. While quenching thirst—a natural function to perform—they became endowed with virtues of an exceptional character, and were esteemed as the givers of health. Even amid the darkness of those distant days we can detect a glimmering of light, for such ideas were not wholly false. Erroneous ideas seldom are. Springs have indeed a health-giving power. Whether or not we accept the full-blown doctrines of modern hydropathy, we must allow that cold water is an excellent tonic. As an acute writer has remarked, "Cold braces the nerves and muscles, and, by strengthening the glands, promotes secretion and circulation, the two grand ministers of health." Allusion has been made to the mineral waters of Peterhead. The secret of their power is well described by Cordiner in his "*Antiquities and Scenery of the North of*

Scotland," where he says:—" A mineral well in the
summer months gives great gaiety to the place ;
its salutary virtues have been long, I believe,
justly celebrated. The salt-water baths adjoining
are much frequented in nervous disorders : their
effect in strengthening the constitution is often
surprising. Owing to the open peninsulated situation, the air of this place is esteemed peculiarly pure
and heathful ; even the fogs rising from the sea are
thought to be medicinal ; the town is therefore much
enlivened by the concourse of company who frequent
it on these accounts. Without derogating anything
from the merits of the baths and mineral, one may
reasonably conclude that the custom of walking
several hours before breakfast, and meeting the
morning breezes from the sea along these cool and
refreshing shores, the probability of meeting with
choice of companions as an inducement to these
early rambles, the perpetual cheerfulness indulged
by society entirely disengaged from business and
care, and their various inventions to chase away
languor, probably contribute no less to the health
of the company than the peculiar virtues of the
healing spring."

Truth can commonly be found underlying superstition. The power, possessed by certain aspects of
external nature to soothe the troubles of the mind, is
one of the commonplaces of modern poetry. This
thought, when rendered into folklore, becomes the
idea that certain spots are " places of safety from

supernatural visitants." Such was the belief connected with Our Lady's Well, at Threshfield, near
Linton, in Craven, Yorkshire. Whoever took refuge
there was free from the power of magical spells. When
sailing among the sea-lochs of Lewis, MacCulloch had
an experience which he thus describes in his " *Western
Islands*":—" On one occasion the water was like a
mirror, but black as jet, from its depth and from the
shadow of the high cliffs which overhung it. The
tide, flowing with the rapidity of a torrent, glided
past without a ripple to indicate its movement, while
the sail aloft was filled by a breeze that did not reach
the surface. There was a death-like silence while the
boat shot along under the dark rocks like an arrow ;
to a poetical imagination it might have appeared
under a supernatural influence : like the bark of
Dante, angel-borne." If such were the reflections of
an educated man like MacCulloch, what must have
been the thoughts of our ignorant forefathers when
confronted by the ever-recurring marvels of the outer
world ! Nature is still misinterpreted by credulous
people through a lack of knowledge of her laws. A
good example of this, bearing, not, however, on water,
but on tree-worship, is given by Dr. J. Fergusson, in
his " *Tree and Serpent Worship*." A god was said to
have appeared in a certain date-palm in a village a
few miles from Tessore, and the tree was promptly
adorned by the Brahmins with garlands and offerings.
Dr. Fergusson observes :—" On my inquiring how the
god manifested his presence, I was informed that,

soon after the sun rose in the morning, the tree raised
its head to welcome him, and bowed it down again
when he departed. As this was a miracle easily tested,
I returned at noon and found it was so. After a
little study and investigation, the mystery did not
seem difficult of explanation. The tree had originally grown across the principal pathway through the
village, but at last hung so low that, in order to
enable people to pass under it, it had been turned
aside and fastened parallel to the road. In the operation the bundle of fibres which composed the root
had become twisted like the strands of a rope. When
the morning sun struck on the upper surface of them,
they contracted in drying, and hence a tendency to
untwist, which raised the head of the tree. With the
evening dews they relaxed, and the head of the tree
declined."

In the chapter on "Some Wonderful Wells," we
glanced at the mysterious origin of certain springs.
In ancient times, no less than in the present, strange
sights must have been witnessed. *We* have not a
monopoly of thunderstorms, earthquakes, landslips, or
deluges of rain. The same phenomena prevailed in
early times. The difference is, that we have science
to keep them in their proper place. During the heavy
rains of January 1892, a spring near the house of
Rurach, at Kintail, in Ross-shire, suddenly burst its
bounds and became a raging torrent. Usually the
surplus water from the spring flowed away in the
form of a trickling stream, but on the occasion in

question it rushed on with such force and volume
that it scooped out a channel twenty feet deep
and forty feet broad. The event not unnaturally
caused a good deal of wonder in the neighbourhood. Had it happened several centuries earlier,
some malignant water-spirit would doubtless have
been reckoned the active agent. During the operations connected with the formation of the railway
tunnel through Moncrieff Hill, close to Perth, the
water of a certain spring in the neighbourhood
suddenly failed. It happened that a clergyman,
whose manse stood not far from the spring, sent, when
in the extremity of illness, for a draught of its water.
It was his last draught. He died immediately after;
and at the same time, the spring dried up. The co-
incidence did not pass without remark in the district,
but whether or not it gave rise to a superstition we
do not know. In the dark ages it certainly would
have done so. In the annals of hagiology, the early
saints were associated in a special way with water.
They had, for instance, the power of allaying storms.
St. Nicholas, the patron saint of sailors, exercised this
power more than once. Adamnan records the same
miracle in connection with Columba, abbot of Iona;
and Cainneck, abbot of Aghaboe. According to a
Shropshire legend, Milburga, when followed by a
certain prince, was saved from her unwelcome pur-
suer by the river Corve rising in flood after she had
crossed.

The superstition that water, under certain circumstances, assumed the hue of blood, as in the case of St. Tredwell's Loch in Orkney, &c., claims special attention.   We call this belief a superstition, inasmuch as a special miracle was thought to be involved in the matter; but we nowadays know, that such appearances show themselves without any miracle at all, except the constant miracle without which there would be no natural law.   Modern bacteriology has proved the existence of a certain microscopic plant, technically styled *Hæmatococcus Pluvialis* and popularly known in Germany as *Blutalge*.   In "*Notes and Queries*" for 12th March, 1892, Dr. G. H. F. Nuttall of Baltimore, observes :—"In Central Europe it has been found in pools formed by the rain in rocky hollows and stone troughs, &c.   *Hæmatococcus* often becomes intimately mixed with the pollen of conifers and minute particles of plants which are known to be carried hundreds of miles by occasional currents of air.   The rain drops in the heavens condense about such minute particles, and in falling, carry them down to the earth's surface, where, under proper conditions, these little plants multiply with enormous rapidity."   Dr. Nuttall adds, "Besides the *Hæmatococcus Pluvialis*, we have a Bacterium which has often deceived people into the belief that they were dealing with *bona-fide* blood.   This Bacterium is easily cultivated in the laboratory.   It is one of the so-called chromogenic or colour-producing Bacteria, and bears the name *Bacillus Prodigiosus*, on account of its exceedingly rapid growth.   This very

minute plant has undoubtedly been the cause of
terror among superstitious people.   The organism
will only produce its colour in the presence of oxygen,
and, as a consequence, red spots appear only on the
surface of the moist nutrient medium on which it
may fall."   Undoubtedly some such explanation
would account for certain red spots, alluded to by
Mr. Hunt, which appeared from time to time on the
stones in the churchyard of the Cornish parish of
St. Denis.   According to the belief of the district,
the spots were marks of blood, and their appearance
foretold the occurrence of some untoward event in
English history.

We have spoken of the guardian spirits of lochs
and springs.   That such spirits should have been
thought to exist is not suprising.   Since water is
one of the necessaries of life for man and beast,
animals had to frequent pools and rivers.   What
more natural than that, in days of ignorance, these
animals should have been regarded as in some
mysterious way connected with the spots they frequented.   In the same way, fish darting about in
the water would be considered its indwelling spirits.
It may not seem to us at all needful, that lochs and
springs should have guardian spirits at all.   But
man, in a certain stage of development, thinks of
nature, organic and inorganic alike, as having a
life akin to his own, with powers superior to his
own.   From a belief in guardian spirits to a belief
in the necessity of offering gifts to them is an easy

transition. A present is sometimes an expression of good-will, sometimes of a desire to obtain benefits to the giver. Offerings at lochs and springs were undoubtedly of the latter class, and were intended either to avert evil or to procure good.

In ancient times in India, when a dragon presided over a spring, the people of the district were in the habit of invoking his aid, when they wanted rain or fine weather. Certain ceremonies were necessary to procure the boon. " The chief character-istic of the serpents throughout the East in all ages," remarks Dr. Fergusson, " seems to have been their power over the wind and the rain, which they exert for either good or evil as their disposition prompts." As we have seen, certain wells in our own land could control the weather. This was so, even when the guardian spirit of the spring assumed no definite shape. The rites required to obtain the desired object were nothing less than an acknowledg-ment of the spirit's existence. The origin of the connection between weather and wells can only be guessed at. It appears that the splashing of a spring when an object was thrown into it, or the sprinkling of the water over the neighbouring ground, was thought to cause rain, through what may be called a dramatic representation of a shower. Why this should have been so, cannot be determined with certainty. Probably accidental acts of the kind described were followed, in some instances, by a fall of rain, and the belief may have sprung up

that between the two there existed the relation of
cause and effect. There was thus a confusion
between what logicians call the *post hoc* and the
propter hoc. The same explanation may perhaps
account for the belief that a favourable breeze could
be obtained, as in the case of the Gigha Well, by
the performance of certain definite rites.

Few circumstances in life have more power to
arrest attention than coincidences. Two events occur
about the same time, and we exclaim, " What a
singular coincidence!" that is, if we are not of a
superstitious temperament. If we are, we talk
mysteriously about omens and such like direful
topics. To some minds, an omen has a peculiar
fascination. It lifts them above the level of their
ordinary daily life. The postman rings the bell,
and letters are handed in. A message boy is seen
at the door, and a parcel is delivered. These, and
many more such, are incidents of frequent occurrence.
They are reckoned commonplace. We know all
about them. But let anything unusual happen,
anything that stirs the sense of awe within us, we,
at least some of us, instantly conclude that there is
magic in the matter. An unprepossessing old woman
takes a look at a child when passing. The child
ceases to thrive. There are whispers about " the evil
eye." Yes, there is no doubt about it. The child
must have been bewitched. Is it not probable that
the prophetic power ascribed to wells may be
accounted for on this principle ? Certain appearances

were observed, and certain events followed. Water gushed freely from a spring, when drawn for the use of an invalid. The invalid recovered. Of course he did, for the omen was favourable. As in private, so in public matters. Pools of water were observed to have something peculiar about them. Some crisis in the history of our nation soon succeeded. What sensible person could fail to discern a connection between the two sets of circumstances? So men, even some wise ones, have argued.

Wishing-wells, from their very nature, have a special claim on popular credulity. When a desire is eagerly cherished, we leave no stone unturned to bring about its fulfilment. There is something, be it what it may, that we eagerly covet. How are we to get it? In the stir and pressure of our day's work, we do not see any avenue leading to the fulfilment of our wish. In the quiet morning or evening, when the birds are singing overhead, we go alone to some woodland well, and there, by the margin, gather our thoughts together. One particular thought lies close to our heart, and on it we fix our attention. In the still moments, while we listen to the bubbling spring, our mind lights on a clew, and our thoughts follow it into the future. We brace ourselves up for following it in reality. We see how our design may be accomplished. We take the road that has been revealed to our inward eye, and finally reach the goal of our desire. How does this come about? We may have stooped over the spring, and with certain accompanying rites, have breathed our wish. We return to our daily work with the desire still lying close to our heart. Days, or weeks, or months pass, and at last, behold, what we were so anxious for, is ours! The charm has been successful. Of course it has. But what of the impulse towards definite action that came to us, when we were free from the touch of our ordinary troubles, and quiet-voiced Nature was our teacher and our own soul our prophet? At any rate, we went to the wishing well, and the boon we sought we can now call our own. The question remains, are all desires granted, either through visits to wishing-wells or in any other way? The experiences of life give a definite answer in the negative. How then are believers in the power of wishing-wells to account for such failures? The rites were duly attended to, yet there was no result. Why was the charm not effectual? Any sincere answer to the question ought to be an acknowledgment of ignorance.

In thus attempting to explain the philosophy of wishing-wells, we do not imply that the subjective element is the secret of success in every case. We are merely pointing out that it may be so in some cases. In other cases, according to the principle mentioned above, an explanation will be supplied by the theory of coincidences. When trees and springs were alike reckoned divinities, it was natural enough to conclude, that any tree, overshadowing a spring, was somehow mysteriously connected with it. Belief in such mysterious relations continued, as we have seen, even after tree-worship ceased as a popular cult. Certain superstitions, still in vogue in the west, are undoubtedly relics of tree-worship. In India and some other Eastern lands, the cult still flourishes vigorously. A writer in the "*Cornhill Magazine*" for November, 1872, remarks:—"The contrast between the acknowledged hatred of trees as a rule by the Bygas (an important tribe in Central India), and their deep veneration for certain others in particular, is very curious. I have seen the hillsides swept clear of forests for miles, with but here and there a solitary tree left standing. These remain now the objects of the deepest veneration; so far from being injured, they are carefully preserved, and receive offerings of food, clothes, and flowers, from the passing Bygas, who firmly believe that tree to be the home of a spirit."

We need not linger over the consideration of charm-stones in their connection with wells. In some instances, like that of the Lee Penny, they gave efficacy to water as a healing agent; but in others, as in the case of the Loch Torridon Spring, water gave efficacy to them. Indeed, they acted and reacted on each other in such a way that, in some instances, it is difficult to determine whether the talisman brought healing virtue to the water, or *vice versa*. To find the solution of the problem, we should have to carry our thoughts back to the remote days when stones and wells had a life of their own, and were thus qualified to act independently.

One can understand why holy wells retained their popularity. Even though they did not always effect a cure, people continued to believe in them and to seek their aid. Consecrated springs might throw cold water (metaphorically) on many a cherished hope; but, for all that, they remained, as of old, objects of reverence. The secret of their power lay in their appeal to the imagination. Understanding might say, it is absurd to expect that my ailment can be removed in this way; but imagination protested that there are more things in heaven and earth than are dreamed of in my philosophy. The rites to be gone through—the choice of the fitting season, the keeping of silence, the leaving of a gift—all conduced to throw a halo of romance around the practice. There was thus an appeal to the unknown and. mysterious, that gave to well-worship a strange charm. It stirred up any latent poetry in a man's nature, and linked him to something beyond himself. Springs have a double charm. They are interesting for their own sake, and for the sake of the folklore that has gathered round them. They are "like roses, beautiful in themselves, that add to their own perfection the exquisite loveliness of a mossy dell." In conclusion, take away what is distinctively mediæval in well-worship, and paganism is left. We find this paganism entering like a wedge into the substance of a Christian civilisation. It may have changed its

z

colour, but it is paganism notwithstanding. Well-worship has a definite value as a survival. It serves to unite our own age of science with one in the far past, when laws of nature, as we understand them, were unknown. As a cult it has forsaken the busy haunts of men, but lingers still in quiet places, especially among the mountains. Superstitions die hard. The epitaph of this one has still to be written. Those who are waiting for its last breath need not be surprised if they have to wait yet a while.

INDEX.

2 A